Sym-bol-o-gy
THE PSYCHOLOGICAL COVERT WAR ON HIP HOP

Book 2

BY: PROFESSOR GRIFF

AKOKO NAN   DENKYEM   FIHANKRA   NKYINKYIM   NYAME NTI

SANKOFA

NSOROMMA

FUNTUNFUNEFU-
DENKYEMFUNEFU

DWENNIMMEN

AKOMA NTOSO

NYAME BIRIBI WO SORO

GYE NYAME

EBAN

BI NKA BI

ADINKRAHENE

NYAME NTI

NKYINKYIM

FIHANKRA   DENKYEM   AKOKO NAN

About the Author

Professor Griff is a cultural entertainment analyst, internationally renowned educator, writer, producer, musician, Rock and Roll Hall of Fame recording artist, lecturer and co-founding member of the pioneering and revolutionary hip hop group Public Enemy. Author of the popular music business guide: Musick Bizness R.I.P. (Resource Information Publication), Griff stands as a highly acclaimed, seasoned entertainment industry veteran and sought-after resource on all aspects of the music business. An activist within both the conscious and hip hop communities; Griff currently stands as a permanent fixture on the international lecture circuit with his riveting and powerful discourse/book, The Psychological Covert War on Hip Hop.

An energetic and passionate educator, Griff skillfully customizes this extensively documented lecture to suit the needs of all audiences. Armed with an exemplary life of service and an impressive over twenty-year musical career, Griff captivates audiences with his universal call for social responsibility within both the hip hop community and larger culture. As perhaps a testament to his firm commitment to raise the level of consciousness of today's entire hip hop generation.

Griff effortlessly draws upon his own extensive entertainment industry experience and a vast reservoir of historical scholarship and research to deliver this poignant message. Reared in Long Island, New York and a current resident of Atlanta, Georgia; Griff maintains a coveted role as Minister of Information for Public Enemy and is currently celebrating an unprecedented sixty world tours and 20th Year Anniversary, with the group. A well-rounded music enthusiast.

Griff is also a member of the hip hop/metal band 7th Octave, and has created an empowering youth hip hop curriculum entitled Kidhoppaz, designed to fuse education and entertainment into a positive, effective instructional module. Musically, Griff has recorded nine albums with his group Public Enemy. However, he has long distinguished himself as a talented and acclaimed solo artist as well. Namely, while signed to Luke Records Griff wrote, produced and recorded three powerful and thought-provoking albums entitled: Pawns in the Game (1990), Kaoz II Wiz-7-Dome (1991) and Disturb N Tha Peace (1992). Also, in 1998, Griff released Blood of the Profit on Lethal Records. With his group Confrontation Camp Griff recorded the album Objects in the Mirror May be Closer than they Appear (2000) and The Word Became Flesh (2001); with his group 7th Octave he recorded the album The Seventh Degree (2004). Griff has appeared in the following films: Turntables and The Chip Factor, in addition he spearheaded the production of the informative documentary entitled Turn off Channel Zero.

Griff holds a Bachelor of Science degree in Education, is a licensed personal security defense instructor, and an accomplished martial artist. Griff is an avid lecturer, known for his innate ability to impart life-changing ideas, concepts and techniques for the spiritual/personal growth and development of all who attend his lectures. Griff is uniquely equipped to meet the needs of an international wide-ranging audience.

Remaining true to his title as Minister of Information, Professor Griff has continued his vigilance by providing information for the masses. Most recently, he has published the Atlanta Musick Bizness Resource Information Publication (R.I.P.) providing invaluable industry information for those interested in breaking into the business of MuSick. Griff's current projects include: 7th Octave - God Damage Album; The Psychological Covert War on Hip-Hop (book & lecture); A Warriors Tapestry, Accapella Revolution, Analytixz and Who Stole the Soul. Griff hosts his own weekly internet radio show "Sirius Mindz RnTV."

Concept for Cover Design By: Professor Griff
Graphic Artistry By: Sefu (Jamaul Phillip Smith)
for focsi yabjaya

Back Cover Photo By: Carolyn Grady

The first edition printed December 2016

Published by Heirz to the Shah
ISBN# 978-0-9991069-0-7

All Rights Reserved Copyright Pending   2016
By: Kavon Shah pka Professor Griff

Write to:
Kavon Shah
P.O.Box 11902
Atlanta, Ga 30355

Administration: "Jan"
Anjanette L. McGhee for JM Consulting
sales@jmconsultingbiz.com and www.LikeMindzLikeMine.com

*Thanxz for your patience, sacrifice and hard work.

"WE OWN YOUR ENEMIES"

qoute from the hidden hand.......

Dedication

This is dedicated to all those that are dedicated. ~Phil Valentine

In Loving memory of

My Silent Libation

Muhammad Ali, Dr. Ben, Dr. John H. Clarke, Dr. Francis Cress Welsing, Delbert Blair, Maurice White, Kashif, Prince, Phife Dawg, Nicholas Caldwell, Dr. Sebi, Bernie Worwel, Colonial Abrams, Von Harper, Fidel Castro, Tommy Ford, Larry Bingo, Steve Cokely, Vanity, Natalie Cole

All of whom passed on while I was writing this book

Acknowledgements

Thanxz to "Jan" Anjanette L. McGhee for JM Consulting for your hard work to make this book happen. Mwalimu K. Bomani Baruti, Yaa Baruti, Kamau and Mawiyah Kambon, Professor Small, Ashra Kwesi, Merira Kwesi, Booker T. Coleman, Dr. Suzar, Queen Afua, Dr. Phil Valentine, Dr. Lialia Afrika, Dr. Melanie Stevenson, Professor Jefferies, Pastor Ray Hagins, The Public Enemy Family.

Salute to the Soul-Jahz

The honorable Louis Farrakhan, Black Dot, Khalid El-Hakim, Darren Muhammad, Jahi Muhammad and The (NOI), John Tre, Charles "B Sun" Williams, Kim Bolton, Wise Intellegent, Wise Intelligent, Tahir RBG, Lance "Free" Elliot (Heru), King Simon, Red Pill and Blue Pill, Irritated Genie, Sara Suten Seti, Sadiki Bakari, Acheria Bell, Eric Toure Muhammad, Ernie "The Ernsta" Grant, Jibril Hough and family, Rick Mathis, Khari Wynn (7th Octave), Bro Rich (UGR), Saa Neter, DJ (Black Power Awards) Charles, Princess and family at the Healthful Essence Cafe, Ralph and crew at Westend Print Shop, Emperor and DJ Cut in the Lou, To the GODs 5% Nation, True Islam, Wakil Allah, Sutec, Ahnk, my brother and soulJah Shane, Brandon, Dean Ryan, Tyson Gravity, Black and Nobel, Natee at Everyone's Place, Carl Nelson, Ava Muhammad, my sister Martone, Bro Polight, Queen Neith, Momma Akosua and my Philly family.

To The Fam

The Griffin's, Simpson's, Moore's and the Warner's, Taqiyyah K. Shah, Bed X LaJoi Shah, Rasheem Khaliqq, Khalil Amir, Nailah Miasia, Isa Shah, Randy Glaude, Jasmine Gossey, "Jade" Juanna Williams, Lanisha Moore-Munoz, Ronald Holt, my Millennium Family, Isabel Beyoso, Shawn Carter and family, Lori "Hidyah" Alexander, Aisha Ra, Carl T. Simpson.

To "Sole" Tonya Johnston, you have given so much in 27 years of your spirit that this small amount of space in this book won't allow me to express. Thank you for your healing spirit. If this lifetime will allow me to return your kindness I would need your lifetime and mine.#9 To De'jan Nicole, Cypress Soleil, Story Asaundra, and Dream Sarae give thanxz for allowing me to be me, (JoJo).

Introduction

A picture is worth a thousand words

"One Look Is Worth A Thousand Words," appears in a 1913 newspaper advertisement for the Piqua Auto Supply House of Piqua, Ohio, but ironically uses only words, not images, to invite prospective customers to see its products in their store."A picture is worth a thousand words" is an English idiom. It refers to the notion that a complex idea can be conveyed with just a single still image.

As we enter into a new era and a new age of enlightenment we are reminded that we can no longer accept what is the norm from a mind that is not normal. This reprobate mind that is hell bent on destroying all that is, puts us in direct conflict with ourselves. In "The White Psychology of White Supremacy" by Alton H. Maddox, Jr. ("Attorney-at-War") he says *"The object of warfare is to convince a people to surrender without any semblance of bloodshed. An enemy of white supremacy must be convinced to surrender without firing a weapon. Plea bargaining may be an alternative. Over ninety-five percent of all defendants surrender to a one-sided plea deal. A <u>master</u> never bargains with a "slave."* **In the book of (Hosea 4:6 KJVA) it reads: "My people are destroyed for lack of knowledge: because thou hast rejected knowledge, I will also reject thee, that thou shalt be no priest to me: seeing thou hast forgotten the law of thy God, I will also forget thy children".** "A picture is worth a thousand words" But in the language of your oppressor your words become meaningless if your mind is still in bondage. "When your god and your savior looks like your master and enslaver, you become the principal agent in your destruction." Dr. Yosef Ben Jochannan.

"We are fast approaching the stage of the ultimate inversion: the stage where the government is free to do anything it pleases, while the citizens may act only by permission; which is the stage of the darkest periods of human history, the stage of rule by brute force." -- Ayn Rand, The Nature of Government. The bible teaches us,

Thou shalt not make unto thee any graven image, *or any likeness of any thing that is in heaven above, or that is in the earth beneath,* Dresden James said "When a well-packaged web of lies has been sold gradually to the masses over generations, the truth will seem utterly preposterous and its speaker a raving lunatic." with that I present to you "Symbology". A reference book of subliminal seductive manipulation of consciousness in cultural retrograde.

How to read this Book

*"**Ask the reader not to read this book, become the answer to it.**"*
In my attempt to write this book, my first mind spoke in abstract symbol formations that left me with the awesome task of translating this body of work into a readable book. *It didn't work.* I began to approach it from an artist view point and it hit me, *Paint the words instead of writing them. H*ave the reader decode the images while they dig deep into the unfamiliar terminology. Put different everyday images on each page never having two pages relate to one another. If it only makes sense to the non-reader, then I will be successful in opening up the individual. That doorway will lead them out of the box that negative vibrations and frequencies have put them in. We are affected by colors, shapes and sounds, all of which are manipulated by a handful of people bent on destroying and controlling the entire population. (ie) useless eaters and or sheepole.

Explain to the detractors and the critics nothing. Inject it into a society where the masses are void of decoders that can lift the veil and pull up the skirt of the arch-devils and there workers of iniquity and reveal the hidden hand. If I can help to decode any of the signs and symbols that have our consciousness in a choke hold, then I have done my job. If I can unlock anyone's mind, as those before have unlocked mine, Dr. Ben, Ashra Kwesi, Steve Cokely, Thanxz to Jordan Maxwell, Michael Tsarion, David Icke, Mark Dice and Mark Passio and Alex Jones then I owe them and the ancestors a debt I can never repay.

At this point I can say I am not teaching anyone anything that the creator hasn't deposited in them at birth. I would like to think I'm that spark that set that process in motion or help in its continuum. My only desire is to lead you not to me, but back to yourself as validation to and of your consciousness.

If you feel you have wasted your money buying this book, I would say I would buy it back, but someone has need of it. Hold on to it and teach it in the way you would have written it. *"**Lets not condemn it, let's continue it.**"* Some have asked, is this book a sum total of random thoughts or a scrap book of random conversations, I said both and neither. It's a research book, it's a reference book, it's what you see, but don't see all around you. Just because you don't see it does not make it less or more real. Put aside what you thought this book would, could or should be and experience it. Steven Biko said: "The most potent weapon in the hands of the oppressor, is the mind of the oppressed."

Sym·bol·o·gy
Table of Contents

1st Degree

Symbols of Hate

"Racism (White Supremacy) is the local and global power system and dynamic, structured and maintained by persons who classify themselves as white, whether consciously or subconsciously determined, which consists of patterns of perception, logic, symbol formation, thought, speech, action and emotional response, as conducted simultaneously in all areas of people activity (economics, education, entertainment, labor, law, politics, religion, sex and war), for the ultimate purpose of white genetic survival and to prevent white genetic annihilation on planet Earth - a planet upon which the vast majority of people are classified as nonwhite (black, brown, red and yellow) by white skinned people, and all of the nonwhite people are genetically dominant (in terms of skin coloration) compared to the genetic recessive white skin people".

Francis Cress Welsing, MD

Dr. Frances Cress Welsing (born March 18, 1935 in Chicago)

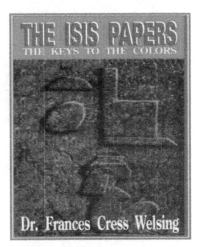

The Isis Papers: The Keys to the Colors

Dr. Frances Cress Welsing **(born March 18, 1935 in Chicago)** is an African American psychiatrist practicing in Washington, D.C.. She is noted for her "Cress Theory of Color Confrontation", which explores the practice of white supremacy. She is the author of The Isis Papers; The Keys to the Colors (1991). Queen Mother, Researcher, Author. Dr. Welsing has followed the path of a warrior in a racist and sexist society.

Objects and their racial analogies

According to Welsing, various cultural practices express white people's sense of their own inferiority:

"On both St. Valentine's Day and Mother's Day, the white male gives gifts of chocolate candy with nuts.... If his sweetheart ingests "chocolate with nuts", the white male can fantasize that he is genetically equal to the Black male.... Is it not also curious that when white males are young and vigorous, they attempt to master the large brown balls (American Football), but as they become older and wiser, they psychologically resign themselves to their inability to master the large brown balls? Their focus then shifts masochistically to hitting the tiny white golf balls in disgust and resignation — in full final realization of white genetic recessiveness."

Welsing further contended that white male sexism is rooted in envy, "because Black is always genetically dominant to White":

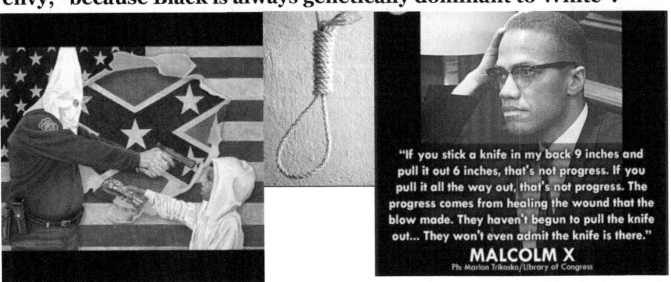

10

Attribution of Symbols: Frances Cress Welsing

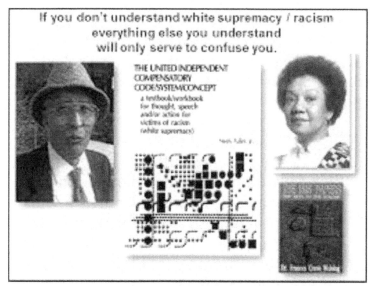

If you don't understand white supremacy / racism everything else you understand will only serve to confuse you.

THE UNITED INDEPENDENT COMPENSATORY CODE/SYSTEM/CONCEPT
a textbook/workbook for thought, speech and/or action for victims of racism (white supremacy)

She has taken stands on issues that others were afraid to deal with. She has debated and beaten top European scholars that have taken stances contrary to the lives of Afrikan people. Her actions prove that she loves Black without question!

http://www.melanindvds.com/drfrancescresswelsing.html

"No sir. I am a disciplined scientist. I refuse to impart my opinion on an area that I did not study.

My "Penis Envy" research focused on how White male racism against Black men was based upon their psychology of inferiority when they compare themselves to the physique and perceived sexual stamina of the Black male. They know that Black man's genetic seed has the power to eradicate their race so he must be destroyed or controlled by oppression.

I did no research on BLACK PEOPLE'S desire for "Little White Men Cast In Gold Statues" which they are seen kissing with joy after the secret majority White awards panel validates the artistic products of Black people.

I prefer to defer to 'Africana Studies' professors and other "Soft Science" Humanities Professors as they are valuable opinion givers for outlets like MSNBC and 'The Huffington Post.

I will say that one day some young Black scientist will follow in my footsteps and evaluate how A PANEL OF WHITE PEOPLE - such as a "Grand Jury", "Supreme Court" or "Academy Of Motion Pictures Arts And Sciences" has so much POWER to make Black people who have been indoctrinated to value AMERICAN SOCIAL TRINKETS above those that they claim are 'Authentic African' and how much damage this does to the ability of Black people to appraise themselves as EQUAL HUMAN BEINGS on their own merits - without White Establishment Affirmation.

"We are the only people who teach our enemy."
Balogun O. Abeegunde

And allow our enemy to educate our children.

Why do white people love dogs so much? For example, the dog rather than God proverbially is considered Western man's best friend. This is contrary to the beliefs of skin-pigmented peoples regarding their relationship to God. This Western concept of the dog as man's best friend is linked to the mythology of the founding of Rome. According to this mythology, Rome was founded by two orphans, Romulus and Remus, who were suckled by a wolf. Both the wolf and the dog are canines.) These two presumably white infants are said to have founded the state that began Western Civilization and culture. When this is decoded, Romulus and Remus are the symbolic representatives of the early albinos who were abandoned by their Black mothers in Africa as genetic mutant defectives and in the process of their northward migration for survival, were "left to the dogs" – suckled by wolves. This decoding explains the worship and love of the dog (canine) in Western civilization...... And, is this love and worship of the dog reflected in the mirror-image of the words "God" and "dog" – even at this "advanced" stage in the expression and evolution of Western civilization and culture? (page 27-28) **https://satanforce.wordpress.com/2016/01/13/frances-cress-welsing-was-crazy-get-over-it/**

The Fear of white genetic annihilation

Black children like <u>Darrin Manning</u> had their balls taken for less: On January 7th, 2014 Darrin Manning, a 16 year old Black boy, was castrated by a female police officer that found him suspicious. Mr. Manning was a child, a straight "A" student, he was searched, patted down, and then his testicles were squeezed by this woman of the state so hard that they ruptured as indicated by an <u>audible popping</u>.

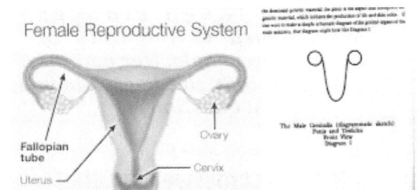

The system of Racism (White Supremacy) utilizes deceit and violence (inclusive of chemical warfare, biological warfare and psychological warfare), indeed Any Means Necessary, to achieve its ultimate goal objective of white genetic survival and to prevent white genetic annihilation on Planet Earth.

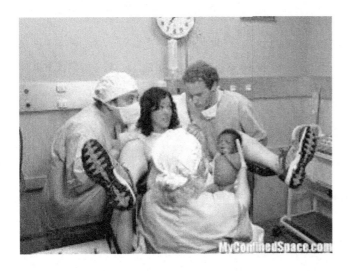

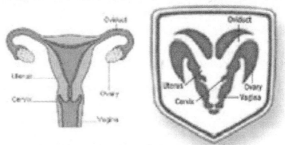

In the existing system of Racism (White Supremacy) when the term is undefined and poorly understood there is general confusion and chaos on the part of the victims of that system (local, national and global). It then becomes impossible for the victims of racism (White Supremacy) to effectively counter the global system of Racism (White Supremacy).

The African enslavement, imperialism, colonialism, neo-colonialism, fascism, etc., are all dimensions and aspects of Racism (White Supremacy).

Creation of first human couple

Darwinism is partly based on Racism. The Caucasoid falsely portrayed as the front runner of the rest of mankind lined with apes on the evolutionary chart as seen in this iconic illustration has for over a century inspired racial bias, Eugenics, Greed, Genocides and cunning scientific ventures (genetic manipulations) in quest to sustain & promote the deceitful theory which in turn is threatening Mankind, Animalia and even plant species as a whole. There is no valid proof that the bones purported to be those of Homo Habilis are not those of a baby Gorilla skeleton or a Chimp buried and naturally preserved under rock for 2.33 million years. New skills in art also allow a combination of Ape & Human remains to be mixed to purport chain links. Every prehistoric ape skeleton unearthed has been purported to be that of an ancient human which is misleading.

We need to remember that around that time a Khoi-San & Twa and Giant humans were already roaming Earth. All the Hominid evolution assertion are nothing but a THEORY and a fantasy that is been articulately presented and repeated enough times and validated in books & museums to a point it's now almost taken as a fact by many. Earth has seen advanced civilizations prior to this modern one. If Darwinism was not inscribed on rock and papyrus by ancients, it never was because its invalid and nothing but a theory and a ploy.

There are lots of proof that NOTHING this civilization has achieved so far that was not originally designed, blue printed or attempted by the ancients. Man as a result of creationism was inscribed on rocks. Man was created 4 million years ago contrary to the religious and scientific narrative. The above pictorial illustration is a subtle but powerful supremacist iconography of the zeitgeist that is largely contributed to modern Earth's imbalances. Proponents of evolution theory are masters of deception and will use great length in artistic skill and manipulation to forge evidence to mislead and sustain a grand deceit for an agenda.

https://gakondomedia.wordpress.com/2012/12/03/creation-of-first-ntu-adam-and-eve-between-lake-victoria-and-lake-tanganyika/

Be Mindful of terms like "I'll be a monkeys uncle" or "Dog is mans best friend"

Adinkra Symbols

King Kofi Adinkra was a famous Ashanti king. These symbols are everywhere in a village: on stools, pottery, paintings, and especially on cloth. The symbols stand for proverbs that remind everyone of responsibility, harmony with nature, family values, and how to live a good life.

 The King Symbol stands for **greatness and royalty.**

 "The king sees all" symbolizes **watchfulness, protectiveness and power.**

 "I have heard and kept it" symbolizes **wisdom, knowledge and learning.**

 "My star will shine one day" stands for **hope, trust, and expectation.**

 Good Luck: "Sanctify like a cat that hates filth" means **good fortune.**

 "Have Courage" stands for **valor, courage, and determination**.

 "Spider Web" or Ananse Ntotan stands for the **creativity and wisdom** of Ananse the spider.

 Two Good Friends: "The deer is always seen in pairs so one will help the other" stands for **friendship.**

 This symbol means **peace, harmony, and serenity.**

Cinematic Racist Symbology
How a Classic Movie Fueled US Racism

A scene from "The Birth of a Nation," D.W. Griffith's 1915, silent movie classic, depicting the "renegade Negro," Gus, played by white actor Walter Long in blackface, in the hands of the Klan. (Photo credit: Museum of Modern Art, Film Stills Archive.)

Nate Parker's "The Birth of a Nation," a retelling of the 1831 slave rebellion led by Nat Turner, could not be more timely. The rise of Donald Trump and the more blatant expression of racist attitudes that his candidacy has emboldened; the outcry over police brutality and the formation of Black Lives Matter; the battles over hate speech, "safe spaces" and historical curriculum on campus; the debate about how to reform a criminal justice system that some believe is the continuation of Jim Crow by other means (see Ava DuVernay's "13th" for more): these ongoing narratives all come back to the right to live an autonomous American life, and the duty to resist those who would oppose that right.

One is the symbol of the largest association of genocide in history, where people who thought differently were repressed by threats and psychological abuse. For many years millions of people, including Jews, homosexuals, the sick, etc, etc were massacred... and the other is the symbol of Nazism.

Symbols of Hate

The Tuskegee Institute records the lynching of 4,742 blacks between 1882 and 1968. This is probably a small percentage of these murders, which were seldom reported, and led to the creation of the NAACP in 1909. Through all this terror and carnage, someone - many times a professional photographer - carried a camera and took pictures of the events. These lynching photographs were often made into postcards and sold as souvenirs to the crowds in attendance. Historians have also detailed the carnival atmosphere and the social ritual of a lynching, which was often announced in advance and drew thousands of people from the surrounding area. Most disturbing is the sight of the white people, looking straight at the camera as if they had nothing to be ashamed of, often smiling.

These images are some of photography's most brutal, surviving to this day so that we may now look back upon the carnage and perhaps know our history and ourselves better. The almost one hundred images reproduced here are a testament to the camera's ability to make us remember what we often choose to forget.

Burning Cross. The image of the burning cross is one of the most potent hate symbols in the United States, popularized as a terror image by the Ku Klux Klan

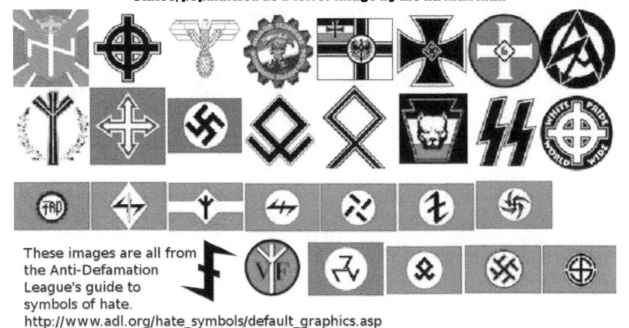

These images are all from the Anti-Defamation League's guide to symbols of hate.
http://www.adl.org/hate_symbols/default_graphics.asp

Slave patrols (called
patrollers, pattyrollers or
paddy...

The 6-pointed star or Hexagram is a Masonic Symbol. It's non-masonic use was propagated during the 19th century by Freemasons into new congregation construction in Industrial Britain and then it's farflung empire. The Menorah, not the Hexagram is the true symbol of God's covenent with the Jewish people. There is absolutely no proof that the Hexagram was ever used by, or associated with, King David or the Temple he planned and prepared for which was erected after his death by his son, King Solomon. Baigent, Lincoln, & Leigh, 'Holy Blood Holy Grail', Dell Books 1983 http://www.freemasonrywatch.org/sixpointedstar.html

Six-Pointed Star: Its Origin and Usage by O. J. Graham The first mention of the star was in **Amos 5:26** regarding the trek from Egypt to Canaan. Then in 922 B.C., when Solomon married the daughter of Pharoah and went into magic and witchcraft and built an altar to Ashtoroth and Moloch. The book traces the six pointed star from Egypt to Solomon, to Arab Magic and Witchcraft, to Druid use(references are documented).

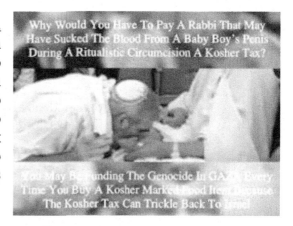

The book traces the star through **Freemasonry** usage to Mayer Amschel Bauer, who, in the 17th century, changed his name to depict the red six-pointed star (or shield) which he had hung on his door in Germany, and thus began the family of "Red Shield" or Rothschild. The research carried on through this family, to their court of arms, to **Cabala**, to **Astrology**,

to Hitler and his putting a yellow six-pointed star on all Jews during the holocaust, to the Zionist symbol, and finally to the flag of the State of Israel and beyond.

Because this symbol is comprised of a six within a six within a six (6 points, 6 triangles, 6 sides of the hexagon in the middle) the research also included a look at the 666 prophecies in the Book of Daniel etc., regarding the "wilful King" (anti-Christ) and the "mark of the beast". The Scriptural significance of the number seven and a Biblical description of the real Messiah and the seven-branched Candlestick (Menorah) which God gave to the children of Israel as an everlasting covenant (which is also mentioned in the New Testament) is covered. All the sources are written at the bottom of each page making it easy for readers to see and check for themselves.

17

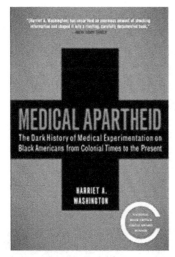

From the era of slavery to the present day, the first full history of black America's shocking mistreatment as unwilling and unwitting experimental subjects at the hands of the medical establishment.

Medical Apartheid is the first and only comprehensive history of medical experimentation on African Americans. Starting with the earliest encounters between black Americans and Western medical researchers and the racist pseudoscience that resulted, it details the ways both slaves and freed men were used in hospitals for experiments conducted without their knowledge—a tradition that continues today within some black populations. It reveals how blacks have historically been prey to grave-robbing as well as unauthorized autopsies and dissections. Moving into the twentieth century, it shows how the pseudoscience of eugenics and social Darwinism was used to justify experimental exploitation and shoddy medical treatment of blacks, and the view that they were biologically inferior, oversexed, and unfit for adult responsibilities. Shocking new details about the government's notorious Tuskegee experiment are revealed, as are similar, less-well-known medical atrocities conducted by the government, the armed forces, prisons, and private institutions.

J. Marion Sims is called "the Father of Gynecology"

intense look at the us' medical experimentations on black americans from slavery until now. Black History Books, Dark History, History Esp, Harriet Washington, Washington Spring, African American Sites History, Medical Apartheid, Medical Racism, Medical Sociology

The product of years of prodigious research into medical journals and experimental reports long undisturbed, *Medical Apartheid* reveals the hidden underbelly of scientific research and makes possible, for the first time, an understanding of the roots of the African American health deficit. At last, it provides the fullest possible context for comprehending the behavioral fallout that has caused black Americans to view researchers—and indeed the whole medical establishment—with such deep distrust. No one concerned with issues of public health and racial justice can afford not to read *Medical Apartheid*, a masterful book that will stir up both controversy and long-needed debate.

Planned Parenthood

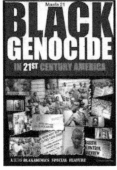

Planned Parenthood is the largest abortion provider in America. 78% of their clinics are in minority communities. Blacks make up 12% of the population, but 35% of the abortions in America. Are we being targeted? Isn't that genocide? We are the only minority in America that is on the decline in population. If the current trend continues, by 2038 the black vote will be insignificant. Did you know that the founder of Planned Parenthood, Margaret Sanger, was a devout racist who created the Negro Project designed to sterilize unknowing black women and others she deemed as undesirables of society? The founder of Planned Parenthood said, "Colored people are like human weeds and are to be exterminated." Is her vision being fulfilled today?

Hitler's Black Victims:

Drawing on interviews with the black survivors of Nazi concentration camps and archival research in North America, Europe, and Africa, this book documents and analyzes the meaning of Nazism's racial policies towards people of African descent, specifically those born in Germany, England, France, the United States, and Africa, and the impact of that legacy on contemporary race relations in Germany, and more generally, in Europe. The book also specifically addresses the concerns of those surviving Afro-Germans who were victims of Nazism but have not generally been included in or benefited from the compensation agreements that have been developed in recent years.

A picture dated 1939 shows German Nazi Chancellor and dictator Adolf Hitler, center, consulting a geographical survey map with his general staff including Heinrich Himmler, left, and Martin Bormann, right, at an identified place during World War II.

Sterilization: An Assault on Families

It was the Nazi fear of "racial pollution" that led to the most common trauma suffered by black Germans: the breakup of families. "Mixed" couples were harassed into separating. When others applied for marriage licenses, or when a woman was known to be pregnant or had a baby, the black partner became a target for involuntary sterilization.

In a secret action in 1937, some 400 of the Rhineland children were forcibly sterilized. Other black Germans went into hiding or fled the country to escape sterilization, while news of friends and relatives who had not escaped intensified the fear that dominated people's lives.

The black German community was new in 1933; in most families the first generation born in Germany was just coming of age. In that respect it was similar to the communities in France and Britain that were forming around families founded by men from the colonies.

Nazi propaganda photo depicts friendship between an "Aryan" and a black woman. The caption states: "The result! A loss of racial pride." Germany, prewar.— US Holocaust Memorial Museum
https://www.ushmm.org/wlc/en/article.php?ModuleId=10005479

19

The symbol of the Swastika and its 12,000-year-old history

(Read the article on one page)

The swastika is a symbol used by of one of the most hated men on Earth, a symbol that represents the slaughter of millions of people and one of the most destructive wars on Earth. But Adolf Hitler was not the first to use this symbol. In fact, it was used as a powerful symbol thousands of years before him, across many cultures and continents.

For the Hindus and Buddhists in India and other Asian countries, the swastika was an important symbol for many thousands of years and, to this day, the symbol can still be seen in abundance - on temples, buses, taxis, and on the cover of books. It was also used in Ancient Greece and can be found in the remains of the ancient city of Troy, which existed 4,000 years ago. The ancient Druids and the Celts also used the symbol, reflected in many artefacts that have been discovered. It was used by Nordic tribes and even early Christians used the Swastika as one of their symbols, including the Teutonic Knights, a German medieval military order, which became a purely religious Catholic Order. But why is this symbol so important and why did Adolf Hitler decide to use it?

The word 'swastika' is a Sanskrit word ('svasktika') meaning 'It is', 'Well Being', 'Good Existence, and 'Good Luck'. However, it is also known by different names in different countries - like 'Wan' in China, 'Manji' in Japan, 'Fylfot' in England, 'Hakenkreuz' in Germany and 'Tetraskelion' or 'Tetragammadion' in Greece.

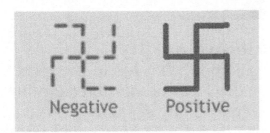

Negative — Positive

HATE ON DISPLAY

Buddhist Swastika

2553 years ago to present, 6th century BC

Religion based on understanding suffering and how to end suffering.

What Buddhist Believe
http://www.buddhanet.net/
pdf_file/whatbelieve.pdf

Nazi Hakenkreuz

Feb. 24, 1920 thru May 23, 1945

Dictatorship bent on fascism and discrimination

Used by White Supremacists.

A Sanskrit scholar **P. R. Sarkar** in 1979 said that the deeper meaning of the word is 'Permanent Victory'. He also said that as any symbol it can have positive and negative meaning depending on how it is drawn. So in Hinduism, the right-hand swastika is a symbol of the God Vishnu and the Sun, while the left-hand swastika is a symbol of Kali and Magic. The double meaning of symbols is common in ancient traditions, like for example the symbol of the pentagram (five pointed star), which is viewed as negative when pointing downwards, and positive when pointing upwards.

"Did you know?"

'Hakenkreuz' is the German word for "Swastika".

The word swastika is derived from the Sanskrit, meaning any lucky or auspicious object, and in particular a mark made on persons and things to denote good luck. It is composed of su- meaning "good, well" and asti "to be" svasti thus means "well-being." The suffix -ka either forms a diminutive or intensifies the verbal meaning, and svastika might thus be translated literally as "that which is associated with well-being," corresponding to "lucky charm" or "thing that is auspicious."

http://www.ancient-origins.net/myths-legends/symbol-swastika-and-its-12000-year-old-history-001312

Then where would you guess these come from? An educated guess would be India. But no, they are all from Africa. That's right Sub-Saharan, "Black" A-F-R-I-C-A. They are gold dust weights used by the Ashanti, to be more precise.

Hindu — Maltese — Greek — Jewish — Jain — Balinese

Lapland — Islamic — Japanese — Tibetan — Hopi — Aztec

https://selfuni.wordpress.com/2014/12/11/afrikan-swastika/

20

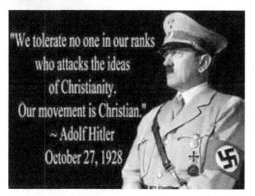

Swastika or Sun Wheel an ancient religious symbol used long before Hitler came to power. It was used in Buddhist inscriptions, Celtic monuments and Greek coins.

See The symbol of the Swastika and its 12,000-year-old history for more.

"We tolerate no one in our ranks who attacks the ideas of Christianity. Our movement is Christian."
~ Adolf Hitler
October 27, 1928

Some have suggested that his father, Alois, born to an unwed woman named Maria Schickelgruber, was the illegitimate child of Leopold Frankenberger, a young Jewish man whose family employed her as a maid. (She subsequently married Johann Georg Hiedler—later spelled "Hitler"—whose surname her son adopted.)

The International Jew began as a four-volume set of pamphlets, published by Henry Ford in the 1920s,

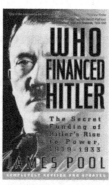

The International Jew — Henry Ford

The Transfer Agreement — EDWIN BLACK

WHO FINANCED HITLER — The Secret Funding of Hitler's Rise to Power, 1919-1933 — JAMES POOL

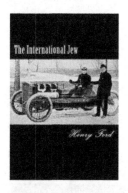

Margaret Sanger founded Planned Parenthood on October 16, 1916 in order to eliminate what she thought were "inferior races like Orientals, Jews and Blacks." She referred to them as "human weeds."

Her father was the "village atheist". She died an alcoholic and drug addict. Passport Magazine July 1968 p. 8

The Real Planned Parenthood: Leading the Culture of Death

MYTH VS. REALITY: PLANNED PARENTHOOD AND BLACK GENOCIDE

Black Lives Don't Matter: Planned Parenthood's Dirty Little Secret

Canadian Genocide A Government System of Residential Schools, 1840s - 1996, Were Killing Fields of Native Children - Victims Tell of Torture, Sexual Abuse and Mass Graves

Aboriginal children torn from their families and culture, imprisoned 10 months of the year in schools, and forbidden to speak their native language, suffered severe mental and physical punishment often described as "killing the Indian in the child".

Genocide in its cruelest form, healthy native children forced into schools and dorms infected with highly contagious tuberculosis, painfully died by the tens of thousands, treatment withheld. Untold numbers brutally murdered, their deaths never reported to their families. Sadistic Priests and nuns who ran schools of 50% death rate never charged for their horrible crimes, while government controlled media ignores the released info of 28 mass graves across Canada. Where is the mainstream media in all this?
hiddenfromhistory1@gmail.com   itccs.org   HiddenNoLonger.com

MARGARET SANGER
FOUNDER PLANNED PARENTHOOD

"Colored people are like human weeds and are to be exterminated"

Two reports in the past five years show that Planned Parenthood abortion clinics are placed at inordinately high levels in black and Latino neighborhoods, leading African-American pro-life campaigners to conclude that the abortion giant is deliberately targeting dark-skinned babies.

Transmuting The Symbols Of Fear Into Love | Symbolism is the Language of the Mysteries

Symbolism is a powerful tool for building knowledge and exploring ourselves, because it allows us to receive deep intuitive meanings, generated from the unconscious all seeing mind.

As Manly states, "it is the language of the mysteries" because a mystery is unknown, that part of us which is conditioned and molded by way of experience itself. The 7th Principle of Natural Law is Gender, within the mind this manifests as our masculine principle of conscious attention or focus while the feminine principle of the unconscious: the hidden, grounded or unactualized totality of our experience. The process of looking at symbols is used in many spiritual traditions because it creates a focal point for that which is unseen deep within, allowing it blossom into a bonafide experience, producing sensations, intuitions and feelings. This data reveals our past choices and programing (both good and bad), how we have chosen to understand our experiences. It is a process of divination, *knowing thyself*, the first step towards self empowerment and mastery.

http://sitsshow.blogspot.com/2015/05/transmuting-symbols-of-fear-into-love.html

By Manly P. Hall - Symbolism is the language of the Mysteries; in fact it is the language not only of mysticism and philosophy but of all Nature, for every law and power active in universal procedure is manifested to the limited sense perceptions of man through the medium of symbol.

Negative Images 'Brainwash' African Americans

Ad man **Tom Burrell** calls out negative images of African Americans in the media for perpetuating the myth of black inferiority. In **Brainwashed** ...

Brainwashed: Challenging the Myth of Black Inferiority

by Tom Burrell

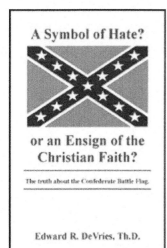

http://arresteddevelopmentmusic.com/qa-with-tom-burrell-br.../
http://www.hayhouse.com/authorbio/tom-burrell end article section

23

http://www.ferris.edu/jimcrow/antiblack.htm

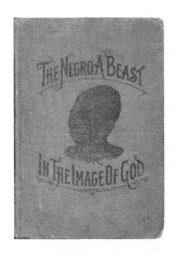

In the United States, all racial groups have been caricatured, but none as often or in as many ways as black Americans. Blacks have been portrayed in popular culture as pitiable exotics, cannibalistic savages, hypersexual deviants, childlike buffoons, obedient servants, self-loathing victims, and menaces to society.

These anti-black depictions routinely took form in material objects, such as ashtrays, drinking glasses, banks, games, fishing lures, detergent boxes, and other everyday items. This case holds objects that illustrate some of the major anti-black caricatures.

Pickaninnies, Golliwog ,Tom, Coon, JezebelTragic Mulatto, Sapphire

Benetton's Advertising Campaigns: 30 Years of Provoking the World

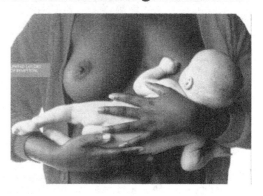

THE MYTH OF CARING: MAMMY

'The marked difference in the construction of this character, however, is the notion that, unlike other Black Americans who had been explicitly forced into subservient roles, Mammy was constructed under the fabricated notion that she gladly and willingly made herself available to tend to white households.'

Multiracial Campaign "United Colors of Benetton" – (Throughout the 80s)

In the middle 1980s, world-renowned photographer Olivero Toscani created for Benetton the first of his multiracial campaigns with the "United Colors of Benetton" slogan. This was the first series of Benetton's shocking advertisements and the one that established "United Colors of Benetton" as the company's main slogan for the following decades.

Everything has a History

If your discussion of **BLACK MEN** and their **HYPERMASCULINITY** problem doesn't include an analysis of the effects of **WHITE SUPREMACY** and historic emasculation and degradation at the hands of **WHITE MEN** on their psyche, your assessments will never lead to the **BLACK UNITY** or **BLACK LOVE** necessary between Black men and women to heal our communities.

http://rebloggy.com/post/education-us-history-black-history-blackface-black-men-african-american-history/130217324039

A Documentary by Eugene Adams. ... "SAMBO" The Black GOD & Africans In Asia (Part 1 Of 8 ...

"The Afrikan woman saw the Afrikan man as the personification of God on earth and the Afrikan man saw the Afrikan woman as the personification of Goddess on earth"
~ mama Merira Kwesi

The Doll Test for Racial Self-Hate:

In the 1940s, psychologists Kenneth and Mamie Clark designed and conducted a series of experiments known colloquially as "the **doll tests**" to **study** the psychological effects of segregation on African-American children. Drs. Clark used four **dolls**, identical except for color, to **test** children's racial perceptions.

The doll test was created based on a black female psychologist's Howard University master's thesis. In the 1940s, psychologists Kenneth Bancroft Clark and his wife, Mamie Phipps Clark, designed it to study the effects of segregation on black children, in an experiment based on Maime's Howard University master's thesis.

The landmark 1954 civil rights case *Brown v. Board of Education* is credited with shutting down "separate but equal" education for African-American kids and paving the way for school integration. Its other legacy? The tradition of questioning small children about black and white dolls in order to measure their sentiments about race.

The "doll test," introduced as social science evidence in the lower-court cases that were rolled into *Brown,* and cited by the Supreme Court in support of its conclusion that segregation harmed the psyches of black children, got a national spotlight and secured its place in civil rights history. Sixty years later, the tool to measure kids' attitudes about what color has to do with being "pretty" or "good" (or "ugly" or "bad") is still widely used shorthand for the argument that anti-black racism is internalized—and *early.*

*The **Clarks used** diaper-clad dolls, identical except for color. They showed them to black children between the ages of 3 and 7. When asked which they preferred and which was "nice" and "pretty," versus "ugly" and "bad," the majority of the kids attributed positive characteristics to the white doll.*

http://www.theroot.com/articles/culture/2014/05/ the_brown_decision_s_doll_test_11_facts/

"In many ways, African Americans have romanticized and institutionalized low expectations. Often our goal is not to be "the best" but to be "the best black"—as in "best black business" or "best black doctor" or "best black college." Inherent in these labels is a subliminal acceptance that our "best" is somehow naturally inferior or somehow different from the white 'best.'"
Tom Burrell

Multimodality and Advertising (then)

Visual statements narrate identity in order for the viewers to understand multimodality, grasp the connections between language and image, and in turn, comprehend the connections between language, image, and identity (Humphreys, 2011). What is multimodality? Well, multimodality points to the truth value of credibility that we supply to the narratives and images that comprise our world, or particular contexts (Humphreys, 2011).

In the introduction of Gunther Kress and Theo van Leeuwen's,

Reading Images: The Grammar of Visual Design, the theorists explain that "like linguistic structures, visual structures point to particular interpretations of experience and forms of social interaction" (2).

https://valmoncada.wordpress.com/2011/04/09/multimodality-in-advertising/

Multimodality and Advertising (now)

People in advertising seem to be super obsessed with black- white references, and will stop at nothing to portray White as superior in their ads, or to show some form of racial stereotype.

"IT'S TIME WE STOP WORRYING, AND GET ANGRY YOU KNOW? BUT NOT ANGRY AND PICK UP A GUN, BUT ANGRY AND OPEN OUR MINDS"
@FlyDreaddy_NattyRasta — #2Pac

Nigger Milk

Free black people grew, ate, and sold watermelons, and in doing so made the fruit a symbol of their freedom.

But the stereotype that African Americans are excessively fond of watermelon emerged for a specific historical reason and served a specific political purpose. The trope came into full force when slaves won their emancipation during the Civil War. Free black people grew, ate, and sold watermelons, and in doing so made the fruit a symbol of their freedom. Southern whites, threatened by blacks' newfound freedom, responded by making the fruit a symbol of black people's perceived uncleanliness, laziness, childishness, and unwanted public presence.

This racist trope then exploded in American popular culture, becoming so pervasive that its historical origin became obscure. Few Americans in 1900 would've guessed the stereotype was less than half a century old.

Before its subversion in the Jim Crow era, the fruit symbolized black self-sufficiency.

"New race consciousness moves us beyond labeling. It introduces a new game board. It's no longer about changing white folk's minds – it's about changing our collective mindset.

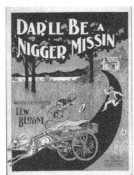

It's about people dedicated to destroying the myth of black inferiority with a powerful new media campaign." **Tom Burrell**

In George Orwell's dystopian novel *1984*, the all-powerful Party enforces political correctness by rewriting the past. Political deviations are rendered impossible by erasing true records of past events, eradicating cultural roots and traditions.

Today the world's media acts as Orwell's 'Ministry of Truth'.

One small but telling example is the worldwide publicity today for a poll to determine the public's favourite Agatha Christie novel. The winner – as reported today by practically every English-language news site in the world – was *And Then There Were None*, which the BBC is now dramatizing as a three-part series.

Not a single news site reported that this was not the book's original title: it was first published in England in 1939 as *Ten Little Niggers*. It was only American sensitivity that led to alternative titles for U.S. editions – first as *Ten Little Indians*, then once this was deemed offensive to 'Native Americans' changed again to *And Then There Were None* – but the book was not retitled in England until 1985.

Such is the progress of political correctness: in the space of just thirty years we have adopted the liberal tyranny that not only forbids such a title as *Ten Little Niggers*, but insists that today's audience shouldn't even know of its existence.

"Displaying Blackness" and the shaping of racist archetypes

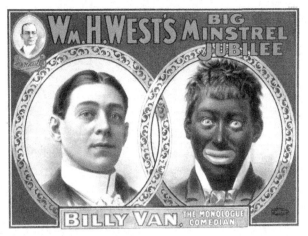

Stereotypes embodied in the stock characters of blackface minstrels not only played a significant role in cementing and proliferating racist images, attitudes, and perceptions worldwide, but also in popularizing black culture.[7] In some quarters, the caricatures that were the legacy of blackface persist to the present day and are a cause of ongoing controversy.

Another view is that "blackface is a form of cross-dressing in which one puts on the insignias of a sex, class, or race that stands in opposition to one's own."

By the mid-20th century, changing attitudes about race and racism effectively ended the prominence of blackface makeup used in performance in the U.S. and elsewhere. It remains in relatively limited use as a theatrical device and is more commonly used today as social commentary or satire. Perhaps the most enduring effect of blackface is the precedent it established in the introduction of African-American culture to an international audience, albeit through a distorted lens.[9][10] Blackface's groundbreaking appropriation,[9][10][11] exploitation, and assimilation[9] of African-

American culture—as well as the inter-ethnic artistic collaborations that stemmed from it—were but a prologue to the lucrative packaging, marketing, and dissemination of African-American cultural expression and its myriad derivative forms in today's world popular culture.

American actor John McCullough as Othello, 1878
There is no consensus about a single moment that constitutes the origin of blackface. John Strausbaugh places it as part of a tradition of "displaying Blackness for the enjoyment and edification of white viewers" that dates back at least to 1441, when captive West Africans were displayed in Portugal.[14] Whites routinely portrayed the black characters in the Elizabethan and Jacobean theater (see English Renaissance theatre), most famously in *Othello* (1604)

"Our history of feeling inferior fuels the propensity for African Americans to buy name brands we perceive to be the best knowing that we have been considered "less than" ...spawned a reflexive need to demonstrate that we are equally (if not more) worthy." **Tom Burrell**

This ad was used to sell California fig bitters. "Black Mammy" as she was called had her work cut on for her in numerous advertisements like this one.

Ethnic Notions (Documentary Film 1986)

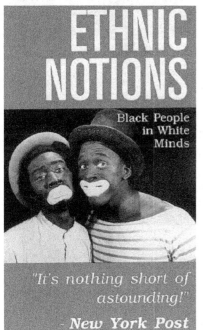

Ethnic Notions is Marlon Riggs' Emmy-winning documentary that takes viewers on a disturbing voyage through American history, tracing for the first time the deep-rooted stereotypes which have fueled anti-black prejudice. Through these images we can begin to understand the evolution of racial consciousness in America. Loyal Toms, carefree Sambos, faithful Mammies, grinning Coons, savage Brutes, and wide-eyed Pickaninnies roll across the screen in cartoons, feature films, popular songs, minstrel shows, advertisements, folklore, household artifacts, even children's rhymes. These dehumanizing caricatures permeated popular culture from the 1820s to the Civil Rights period and implanted themselves deep in the American psyche. Narration by Esther Rolle and commentary by respected scholars shed light on the origins and devastating consequences of this 150 yearlong parade of bigotry. Ethnic Notions situates each stereotype historically in white society's shifting needs to justify racist oppression from slavery to the present day. The insidious images exacted a devastating toll on black Americans and continue to undermine race relations.

31

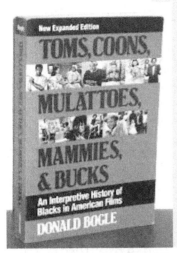

Toms, Coons, Mulattos, Mammies and Bucks

In the book he divides the portrayals of African-Americans on film into the five stereotypes of the title that range from the overtly racist to the more subtly demeaning.

He traces the history of these images from the blatantly disparaging *The Birth of a Nation* in 1915 to the "Blaxploitation" films that were a box office phenomenon around the time of the book's publication.

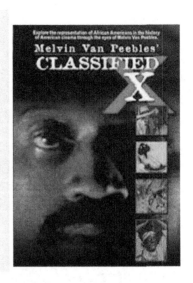

A history of the racially stereotyped portrayal of African Americans in cinema. Written and narrated by Melvin Van

Countering Negative Images of Blacks in the Media

Lincoln Theodore Monroe Andrew Perry (May 30, 1902 – November 19, 1985), better known by the stage name Stepin Fetchit, was an American comedian

Billie "Buckwheat" Thomas (The Little Rascals) beautiful pic but oh so wrong

A Ladies' Man Everyone Fights Over

These days life is looking a lot brighter.

His reality series, "Flavor of Love," a ghetto-fabulous spoof of the dating series "The Bachelor," has been a colossal hit for VH1. The show's first-season finale in March drew nearly six million viewers, making it the highest-rated show in the cable channel's history. More than three million people tuned in to watch the second-season premiere early August.

Whether you enjoyed it, or saw it as buffoonery at its finest, "Flavor of Love" was a phenomenon that swept America. From Flav's contest on who could cook the best fried chicken, to the loogey heard round the world, people where watching

"Flavor of Love" in droves, giving the network some of the highest ratings that they ever saw. With the success of the show, it lead to spin offs, and making some of its contestants household names.

"Flavor Flav" Roast

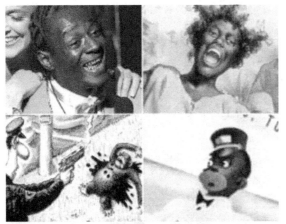

We must realize that we are not talking about ancient history, either. We have slave narratives that were written in the 1930s. The tragedy and horror of chattel slavery happened only a few generations ago. And the inferiority that was drummed into us through the media – through propaganda – has passed down from generation to generation just like a favorite family recipe.

This sickness must be addressed.

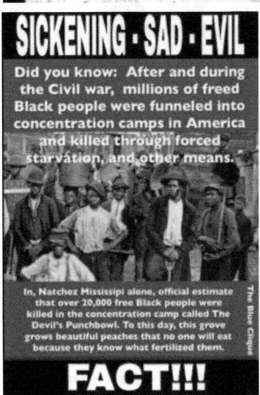

SICKENING · SAD · EVIL

Did you know: After and during the Civil war, millions of freed Black people were funneled into concentration camps in America and killed through forced starvation, and other means.

In, Natchez Mississipi alone, official estimate that over 20,000 free Black people were killed in the concentration camp called The Devil's Punchbowl. To this day, this grove grows beautiful peaches that no one will eat because they know what fertilized them.

FACT!!!

BLACK PEOPLE HAVE BEEN STEREOTYPED AS LAZY

EVER SINCE THEY STOPPED WORKING FOR FREE

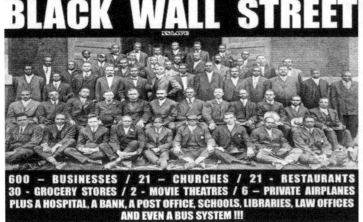

BLACK WALL STREET

600 – BUSINESSES / 21 – CHURCHES / 21 - RESTAURANTS
30 - GROCERY STORES / 2 - MOVIE THEATRES / 6 – PRIVATE AIRPLANES
PLUS A HOSPITAL, A BANK, A POST OFFICE, SCHOOLS, LIBRARIES, LAW OFFICES
AND EVEN A BUS SYSTEM !!!

THANKSGIVING IS A SPECIAL TIME TO REMEMBER ALL THE THINGS WE HAVE

AND FORGET ABOUT THE GENOCIDE THAT WAS COMMITTED TO GET IT.

Ni**Ery: When Will The Buffoonery & Coonery End?

Global Hip Hop Battles, is committed to raising people's consciousness,

If you do some research, you might notice some of the same things I've seen in this ghetto-fied hood drama: Pimps, hoes, thugs, gangsters, emasculated black men, and all kinds of other kinds of stereotypical coonery that many of us have grown tired of seeing portrayed on-screen.

Lee Daniels is apparently the man responsible for this televised monstrosity, and I wonder if a day will ever come that the majority of us will refuse to support directors who pimp their people to help bigots like Rupert Murdoch get rich from modern day minstrel shows.

Dr. Joyce Watkins: Here's why I won't support the coonery of "Empire"

"The denial of racism is for the preservation of white genetic survival."

"Mental health experts are in general agreement that persistent exposure to humiliation, brutality, and abuse, physical or emotional, can program people to humiliate, brutalize, and abuse others. Apart from the indigenous people of this country, no other ethnic group has been subjected to the centuries of abuse that Africans and their descendants have experienced."

~ Dr. Frances Cress Welsing

"In early America literature, posters, and later, film, Black males were caricatured as slow, slope-shouldered, slouchy, and sleepy. It's interesting to note that these images reveal an emphasis on looseness: loose head hanging from a horizontal neck; loose lips hanging from a downcast face; loose empty hands hanging from long, limp, simian-like arms; loose, tattered clothing, and loose shoes (if any); and loose, lazy, slurry speech."

~Tom Burrell

What does 88 mean in white supremacy?

14: This stands for the "14 words" or the battle-cry philosophy that all white supremacists live by. The 14-word phrase is, "We must secure the existence of our people and a future for white children." **88:** The eighth letter of the alphabet is H. The number 88 also means "HH," which is short for "Heil Hitler."

It is thus not surprising that white supremacists occasionally attempt to display 88 as a hand sign. It is not a very common white supremacist hand sign, probably because it involves some dexterity and effort.

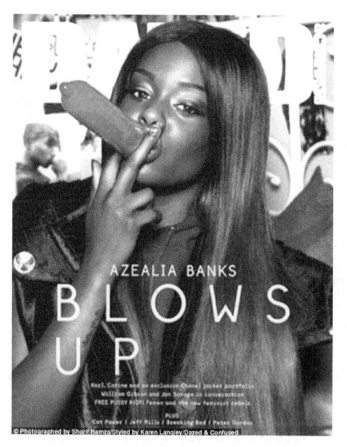

AZEALIA BANKS
BLOWS UP

© Photographed by Sharif Hamza/Styled by Karen Langley/Dazed & Confused

"Somewhere along the line producers of hip-hop came to realize that the real money, the real avenues to fortune and fame, came via music about sex, drugs, and violence; how they "made it" on the carcasses of those who trespassed on their turf—either in the streets or in the industry. Along the line, powerful forces realized there was gold in black music divisions." **Tom Burrell**

So does the majority really rule? Or does one sheep Dog control the herd?

There are many women who are just as uncomfortable about sexist images in the media of advertising, as there are people offended by messages about stereotypical images. So here's another myth is advertising: "sex sells." My question is, do they mean "sex" as in gender, or "sex" as in copulation?

50 Scent
(for men)

About 95% of the ads we see in print and on television are sexual. Either making sexual references, or issuing sexual imagery and language. Key words, key images, key situations are used to target the male and female mind. Males and females respond to different colors, sounds and words. A Man responds differently to seeing a Women in a red dress, than to a Woman in a white dress. A Woman responds differently to a Man in a dark suit, than a Man in a light suit. These responses are all linked to the sub-conscious.

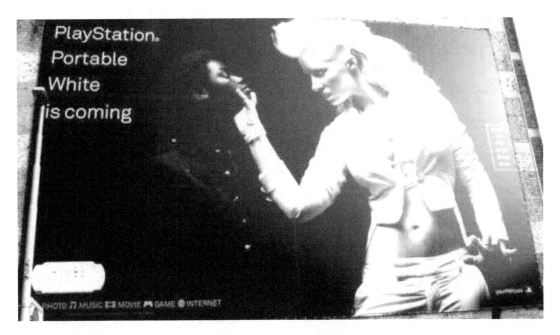

Black children use television to learn "new facts and information about life" and to learn how people "behave, talk, dress and look." The scary reality is that Black children perceive media-fed behaviours as true reflections of life."

~Tom Burrell

Decoding Racism in Advertising

American Apparel is a fashion company that claims to represent the everyday woman. To the right, we have an American Apparel blackface image that appeared in a magazine. Just like the Duncan sister's advertisement, this image draws on specific character traits that define that woman. Similar to Topsy's appearance, the colour saturation is very bright in this ad. We can also see that there is both racial and sexual grammar depicted in the advertisement. Clearly, racist imagery continues to be incorporated in advertisements today.

Got that Skin Disease that Uncle Ruckus

"The investigative team cited research based on a study of advertisements published in two popular Black magazines with majority Black female readerships. They discovered that nearly 50 percent of the ads in the publications were devoted to alcoholic beverages. Contrast those figure with the meager two percent of alcoholic ads found in whyte-oriented women's journals" **~Tom Burrell**

PETA used this image of a feral-looking black man in a cage in two different campaigns, just in case we didn't get the idea.

Volumes have been written on PETA's use of sexist and racist media strategies in order to get a quick headline. Its most recent gimmick, an ad that implies that drinking milk causes autism in children, exploits fear and misinformation about disability.

Actually, the ad isn't even a new one: It's from 2008, when PETA displayed it on a billboard in Newark, New Jersey. It came down within a week because it drew so much fire. Either PETA doesn't learn from experience, or it just doesn't care (I'm betting on the latter), because last month it dusted the ad off and gave it another run.

Beyonce Got that Skin Disease like Uncle Ruckus

L'Oréal Has a Bad History: Back in 2007, a branch of L'Oréal--Garnier--was found guilty of racial discrimination for purposely not hiring non-white women to promote its shampoo. Then in 2008 the company came under scrutiny for lightening Beyoncé's skin in this ad, which they vehemently denied doing.

HOW RACIST IS THE BEAUTY INDUSTRY?

http://blackamericantoday.blogspot.com/2013/01/
beyonce-got-that-skin-disease-that.html

Sammy Sosa. I heard your explanation and it's still not making any sense.

Light Is Right?? 15 Black Celebrities Accused Of Bleaching Their Dark Skin For Beauty

Some people can argue that Black celebrities are have been pressured to **bleach their beautiful Black skin because they think a lighter complexion** will secure them better treatment in Hollywood for television, magazines, and better endorsements.
However, we can all agree that these celebs have gotten a little lighter over the years and it ain't a filter. Do you think certain Black celebs have been busted of bleaching?

https://bossip.com/1008294/light-is-right-15-black-celebrities-accused-of-bleaching-their-dark-skin-for-beauty/

remember,.. it could always be worse....

A Newspaper Actually Used a Headline Calling
Obama The N-Word In The White House
politicususa.com/2014/07/06/new…

Obama uses N-word, says we are 'not cured' of racism

http://www.cnn.com/2015/06/22/politics/
barack-obama-n-word-race-relations-marc-
maron-interview/

Washington (CNN) President Barack Obama used the n-word during an interview released Monday to make a point that there's still plenty of room for America to combat racism.
"Racism, we are not cured of it. And it's not just a matter of it not being polite to say nigger in public," Obama said in an interview for the podcast "WTF with Marc Maron."
"That's not the measure of whether racism still exists or not. It's not just a matter of overt discrimination. Societies don't, overnight, completely erase everything that happened 200 to 300 years prior."

Post-Racial? Racist Headlines, Cartoons And Ads About President Obama

According to Liberals, if You Call Obama "Barry" You're a Stinkin' Racist

Police Department Caught Using Mug Shots For Target Practice

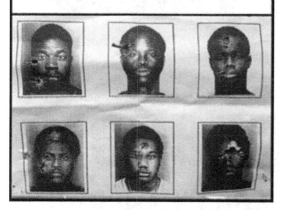

Florida police department caught using African American mug shots for target practice

Miami Beach, Florida – The North Miami Beach Police have caused nationwide controversy this week, after it was discovered that they were using mug shots from people in the community for target practice. To make matters even worse, the department has been entirely unapologetic in the matter, saying that the officers involved did not break any policies.

The disturbing practice was uncovered last month when the Florida Army National Guard's 13th Army Band went to a local shooting range for their annual weapons qualifications training.

When the soldiers arrived at the shooting range they were horrified to see that North Miami Beach Police snipers were using mug shots from their department for target practice. Even more disturbing was the fact that Sgt. Valerie Deant, one of the soldiers on the firing range that day, actually recognized one of the people in the mug shots. She quickly recognized her brother's 15-year-old mug shot that was taken after a drag racing arrest. *"I was like why is my brother being used for target practice?"* Deant asked.

Read more at http://thefreethoughtproject.com/police-department-caught-mug-shots-target-practice/#l1uS1JWhiMsBE5JU.99

Target practice with Trayvon Martin

As a result of last year's Trayvon Martin shooting, a company offered for sale a target of a faceless, silhouette wearing a hoodie with its hands in its pockets, one of which was holding two objects. These objects in the hand were non-threatening and the target was something I viewed as a no-shoot situation. While others have used it as a novelty, I used it as a tool for scenario-based firearms training. Although the targets haven't been used, I did possess those targets for training reasons.

Sign of the Times
&
Sign Language
ECONOMICS/BANKING AND FINANCE

Sign Language /Sign of The Time

"Will you never believe in me unless you see miraculous signs, Where disagreement arises among believers is their purpose, as well as the question of ... The signs and wonders confirmed God's message. Are there signs in life that tell us there's something more out there? When all of the outward and inward signs and feelings are gone?
Is God trying to speak to you about a situation in your life concerning the occult?

In 1815 Nathan Rothschild virtually bought the Bank of England.

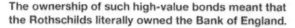

- After the battle of Waterloo, Nathan's own courier was the first to reach England, bringing news that Wellington had won the battle, and thus the war.

- Armed with this critical information, Nathan began selling up his British war bonds, fooling other traders into believing Napoleon had won instead.

- Panicked, those traders quickly began selling off their own near-worthless bonds, at which point Nathan ordered his workers to buy up as many of those bonds as they could.

- Once the news reached London that Wellington had won, Nathan's newly acquired bonds gained more value than they had before the entire war.

The ownership of such high-value bonds meant that the Rothschilds literally owned the Bank of England.

From that moment onwards, the interests of the British Crown and the Rothschilds became so entwined that the Rothschilds were given titles of nobility. Through inter-marriage the Rothschilds *became* royalty.

Nathan Rothschild. Born in Frankfurt.
1777 - 1836.

WHO REALLY RUNS THE WORLD?

COURTESY OF IN5D.COM
HTTP://IN5D.COM/WHO-REALLY-RUNS-THIS-WORLD/

HIGHEST LEVEL MALEVOLENT EXTRATERRESTRIAL(S) WHO LITERALLY EXIST AND FEED OFF OF FEAR, DEATH, PAIN, SUFFERING, MISERY, AND SACRIFICES; CONTROLLERS OF THE ARCHONS

1	1. ARCHONS & OTHER INVISIBLE MATTER
2	2. HIGHER LEVEL MALEVOLENT EXTRATERRESTRIALS (E.G. ANUNNAKI)
3	3. LOWER LEVEL MALEVOLENT EXTRATERRESTRIALS (E.G. DRACOS AND REPTILIANS)
4	4. THE VATICAN / ROMAN CATHOLIC CHURCH
5	5. THE BILDERBERGERS
6	6. BUSINESS ADVISORY COUNCIL
7	7. COUNCIL ON FOREIGN RELATIONS
8	8. UNITED NATIONS BANKING COMPLEX
9	9. FEDERAL RESERVE AND OTHER CENTRAL BANKS
10	10. UNITED NATIONS
11	11. COUNCIL OF 13
12	12. THE COMMITTEE OF 300
MDCCLXXVI	13. SECRET SOCIETIES

BELOW THE PYRAMID, YOU WILL FIND CORPORATIONS SUCH AS MONSANTO.
WOLRD LEADERS AND POLITICIANS ARE BELOW THEM.
AT THE BOTTOM, YOU'LL FIND US, THE 99.999% OF THE POPULATION.

Royal Secretion?

- The most wealthy bloodline in the world, bar none, and the leader of the Ashkenazi Jews in the world today, is the Rothschild family.

- As you will see in the timeline, the Rothschilds have obtained this position through lies, manipulation and murder.

- Their bloodline extends into the Royal Families of Europe, and the following family names: Astor; Bundy; Collins; duPont; Freeman; Kennedy; Morgan; Oppenheimer; Rockefeller; Sassoon; Schiff; Taft; and Van Duyn.

The TALMUD Is the book Of the scribes And Pharisees

- 1770: Mayer Amschel Rothschild draws up plans for the creation of the Illuminati and entrusts Ashkenazi Jew, Adam Weishaupt, a Crypto-Jew who was outwardly Roman Catholic, with its organization and development.

- The Illuminati is to be based upon the teachings of the Talmud, which is in turn, the teachings of Rabbinical Jews. It was to be called the Illuminati as this is a Luciferian term which means, keepers of the light.

Bill Gates

I am worth $61 Billion US Dollars

IMPRESSIVE

Evelyn De Rothschild

With the exception of 3 countries, every $ of currency on earth is an I.O.U. to my family

VERY IMPRESSIVE

Before 9/11 there were 7 countries without a Rothschild -Owned Central Bank:
Afghanistan, Iraq, Sudan, Cuba, North Korea & Iran

As of 2012 only 3 are left to invade, take over and aquire before the worlds wealth is controlled by a single family.

THIS SHOULD SCARE YOU

SIGNS OF THE TIMES

Common hand signs, where they came from and what they mean:

1. THE HORNS

Index finger and pinkie raised; thumb joins middle and ring fingers. See story at right for the many, many interpretations of this symbol.

2. "OK"

The modern interpretation of OK might come from President Martin Van Buren's nickname, Old Kinderhook. Another explanation comes from an 1839 Boston Globe misspelling of "all correct" as "oll korrect." Beware sending this sign in Germany, the Balkans, the Middle East and parts of South America, where it translates to "orifice."

3. "I LOVE YOU"

Raise index finger and pinkie finger with thumb extended. Drunken partyers posing for photos often mistakenly send this sign when trying to show "the horns." It's the official American Sign Language sign for "I love you" and is a combination of the letters, I, L and Y.

PAULO MARTINEZ MONSIVAIS AND J. SCOTT APPLEWHITE | ASSOCIATED PRESS

The Bush family are multigenerational fans of the University of Texas Longhorns — or quite possibly, Black Sabbath.

Lost in translation
The Bushes love the Longhorns . . . or is it SATAN?

KATHLEEN MURPHY COLAN
Special to The Plain Dealer

Does the Bush clan worship the devil? Signs here point to "not likely," but overseas, you might get a different answer.

During the inauguration festivities, the first family's "Hook 'em, 'horns" signal — right hand raised with the index and pinkie fingers extended — was interpreted as a salute to Satan and horrified thousands, especially in Norway.

The two-finger salute — flown by George, Laura, Jenna and even Grandma Barbara during inauguration festivities — has generated Internet chatter and news reports. For the record, the gesture is a sign of love for the University of Texas Longhorns, whose fans — whose numbers famously include the Bush family — often shout "Hook 'em, 'horns!" at sporting events.

It's easy to understand where the confusion comes in — this is, after all, a hand signal that is estimated to be 2,500 years old.

For much of that time, it's been associated with pagans and the occult, and today it's best known among heavy metal music fans.

In the beginning, though, it was about a bull.

Ancient people used the symbol to call on the great horned bull, which was a protective god, but "as Christianity gained momentum, this horned god grew to be thought of as the devil, so those who still practiced this gesture as a protective measure were actually calling on the devil to ward away evil," writes Nancy Armstrong and Melissa Wagner, authors of the "Field Guide to Gestures" (Quirk Books, 2003).

Evidence of these beliefs are seen today in the "horn" amulets worn by many Europeans as magical protection against the evil eye. Still other signs of the horn are known as the mano cornuto (literally "horned hand"), which implies a man has an unfaithful wife.

More commonly here, it implies a man — or a woman — likes to rock.

The symbol seen at every rock concert for the past 30 years is attributed to heavy-metal masters Black Sabbath. According to VH1's "100 Most Metal Moments," which aired in spring 2004, Sabbath's Ronnie James Dio came up with the sign, but Gene Simmons of Kiss and funkmaster George Clinton also claim ownership.

Dio says he learned the gesture from his Italian grandmother, who used it to ward off the "evil eye."

Want more? It's used as a curse in parts of Africa; and in Russia, it's a symbol for so-called New Russians, the newly rich, arrogant and poorly educated.

Perhaps most surprisingly, in American Sign Language, it's a sign for an abrupt barnyard expletive that translates roughly to "poppycock." That produced a surprised giggle from the first lady's press secretary when revealed to her last week.

With so many meanings for one simple hand gesture, no wonder people are confused. Follow our guide to make sure you're sending the right message next time you send up a sign.

Colan is a free-lance writer in Cleveland.

4. "PEACE"

The "peace" or "victory" sign was made popular by Winston Churchill during World War II. The 1960s generation appropriated it as a sign of peace during the Vietnam era. President Richard Nixon was famous for flashing the double "V."

5. "HANG LOOSE"

The pinkie and thumb are extended from a fist as the forearm twists, causing the hand to wiggle back and forth. This gesture has origins in Hawaii and translates to "relax" or "be cool." Popular among surfers and hipsters around the United States.

6. "LOSER"

An "L" is formed with the index finger and thumb and displayed on the forehead. The "loser" gesture first made the scene in the 1994 movie "Ace Ventura: Pet Detective." Jim Carrey's character used the sign as his trademark gesture for making sure that those who didn't measure up knew it.

7. FINGERS CROSSED

The index and middle fingers of one hand are crossed, with the middle finger being brought over top of the index finger. This gesture traditionally is associated with wishing for good luck or to show the closeness of a relationship.

8. "SHAME"

One index finger is rubbed across the other. This gesture, known only in the United States, symbolizes the friction between the shamer and shamee.

9. "LIVE LONG AND PROSPER"

The palm is held flat and facing out while the middle and ring fingers are splayed apart, with a space in-between. "Star Trek's" Mr. Spock made this gesture famous. Leonard Nimoy, who played Spock, came up with the "live long and prosper" sign based on the Hebrew letter "shin."

10. "THUMBS UP"

Modern-day hitchhikers, Arthur "The Fonz" Fonzarelli of "Happy Days" fame and ancient Romans gave meanings to the gesture to get their points across.

Text by Kathleen Murphy Colan
Illustrations by Milan Kecman

Signs of Satan says, and I quote, "If you think Miss Keller's hand sign is just a coincidence, then you are truly gullible. If you were deaf, and wanted to develop a hand sign to tell someone that you love them, what would it be? A hand over the heart would be reasonable. There is no way that any reasonable person would develop the hand sign that Keller invented, paralleling an existing hand salute to Satan. The above photo is one of Ozzy Osbourne's Rock-n-Roll album covers. It is abundantly clear to see that Keller's hand sign praises the Devil."

First of all, I don't think Helen Keller invented the I LOVE YOU sign language sign. But it wouldn't even matter if she did. The fact that she is thought to have been an occultist has no prevalence over what I'm about to show you.

The Devil's Horn

The devil's horn freemason hand signal, as contained in the Satanic bible.

The "devil's horn" signal signifies that satan rules. Remember that satan is called the "Horned God", and the hand signal is formed so as to resemble horns.

It is a universal hand signal used by politicians, celebrities as well as heavy metal bands, affirming their allegiance to satanic powers and a visual shorthand for "Hail, Satan." The devil's hand has been observed and photographed around the world, used by George Bush, Bill Clinton, Silvio Berlusconi, Elizabeth Taylor, Prince William, Paul McCartney, Metallica, Ozzie, Avril Lavigne, Stephen Dorff, Dave Navarro and many others.

Three versions of the *El Diablo*," the sign of Satan, the horned god. The hand sign at right is also the deaf's gesture, or signing, for "I love you," a fact which has many people confused.

facebook.com/OdysseyOfOddities

Helen Keller was a Theosophist (God Wisdom) Madame Helena Petrovna Blavatsky founded the Theosophical Society in 1875 & openly stated, "It is Satan who is the god of our planet and the only god."

The "devil's horn" hand sign often is confused with the deaf hand signal of the phrase, "I love you." While at first this appears an odd resemblance, we must remember that the person who invented the hand sign system for the deaf, Helen Keller, was herself an occultist. Did Keller purposely design the deaf's "I love you" sign to be such a remarkable imitation of the classic sign of Satan? Was Keller saying, basically, "I love you, Devil?"

https://veritas-vincit-international.org/2015/01/18/hand-signals-of-freemasonry-explained/

Self-proclaimed German vampire Manuela Ruda

The "El Diablo" hand sign often is con-fused with the deaf hand signal of the phrase, "I love you." While at first this appears an odd resemblance, we register an "ahh, I get it!" emotion when we discover that the person who invented, or created, the hand sign system for the deaf, Helen Keller, was herself an occultist and Theosophist. Did Keller purposely design the deaf's "I love you" sign to be such a remarkable imitation of the classic sign of Satan? Was Keller saying, basically, "I love you, Devil?" —Texe Marrs, **CODEX MAGICA**

https://warningilluminati.wordpress.com/hands-signs-signs-of-satan/

"You are a den of vipers and thieves. I have determined to rout you out, and by the Eternal, I will rout you out!"
~ *Andrew Jackson and the*
Bank of the United States

The final image shows us a baby covered in tattoos, which is one thing. The other thing you might not have noticed was one of the tattoos on the man holding the baby. Check out his bicep:

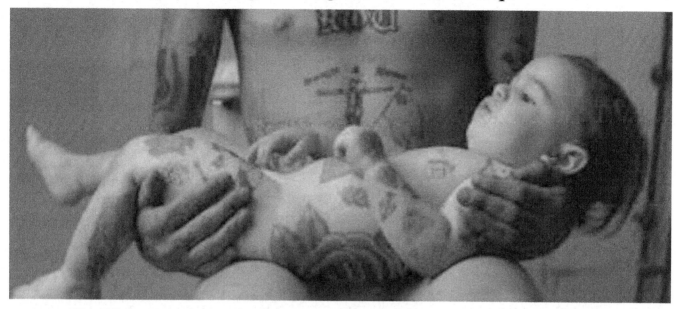

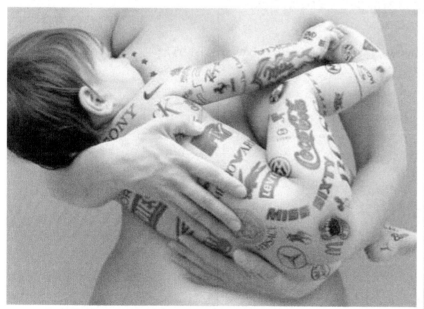

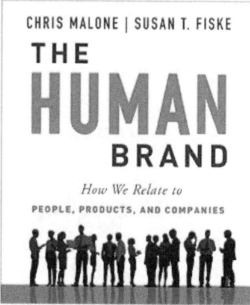

CHRIS MALONE | SUSAN T. FISKE

THE HUMAN BRAND

How We Relate to

PEOPLE, PRODUCTS, AND COMPANIES

"Impersonal forces over which we have almost no control seem to be pushing us all in the direction of the Brave New Worldian nightmare; and this impersonal pushing is being consciously accelerated by representatives of commercial and political organizations who have developed a number of new techniques for manipulating, in the interest of some minority, the thoughts and feelings of the masses."
– Aldous Huxley, Preface to A Brave New World

BRAVE NEW WORLD

ALDOUS HUXLEY

FIG. 34.

SIGN OF THE MASTER OF THE
SECOND VEIL.

Stalin and Washington – two opposing ideologies, one hand
gesture

*"Today's thinking toward a democratic world state is neither a new trend nor an
accidental circumstance; the work of setting up the background of knowledge
necessary to the establishing of enlightened democracy among all nations has been
carried on for many hundreds of years by secret societies."*
-Manly P. Hall, Secret Destiny of America

http://vigilantcitizen.com/vigilantreport/the-hidden-hand-that-changed-history/

Grand Master Jacques de Molay of the Knights
Templar, predecessor to today's Freemasonry and other
secret societies. Accused of blasphemy and of
worshipping the grotesque idol of Baphomet, the
horned goat-god, de Molay was burned at the stake by
the King of France on March 11, 1314. The sign he is
giving his captors seems clearly to be the vulgar and
obscene "up yours" gesture. Although de Molay was
reputed also to be a homosexual, today's international
Masonic Lodges honor their former Grand Master by
naming their youth groups the "de Molays."

"Our current economic crises stem, at least in part, from our
    inability to recognize the storage bias of the money we use.
    Since it is the only kind of money we know of, we use it for
    everything."

~Douglas Rushkoff

50

The Hidden Hand: http://vigilantcitizen.com/vigilantreport/the-hidden-hand-that-changed-history/

Occult symbolism in worldwide government architecture:

For the sake of time I took these from the same website I often refer to that does a series called Sinister Sites.

US Capitol Building: http://vigilantcitizen.com/sinistersites/mystical-sites-u-s-capitol/

Israel Supreme Court: http://vigilantcitizen.com/sinistersites/sinister-sites-israel-supreme-court/

The EU Parliament: http://vigilantcitizen.com/sinistersites/sinister-sites-the-eu-parliament/

Rockefeller Center: http://vigilantcitizen.com/sinistersites/sinister-sites-rockefeller-center/

Note the Rockefeller family is not the literal government but can be thought of as the shadow government - they pull the strings.

Here's a great article elaborating:
http://americaslastdays.blogspot.com/p/hidden-symbolism-of-dollar.html

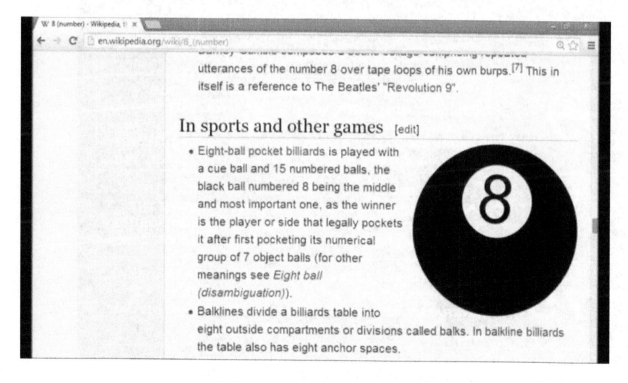

The Six Occult Sacred Numbers

1. <u>Three (3)</u> is the first sacred number, the first perfect number (Westcott, p. 41). Three represents the Pagan Trinity." (Westcott, p. 37). It is represented in the triangle, and spiritually as the Third Eye Of Hinduism. Occultists will multiply and add three to other sacred numbers to create new numbers. However, they also group threes in two's and threes, because they believe in the principle of "intensification", i.e., that greater power is achieved when a sacred number is grouped. In the case of three, greater intensification is achieved when it is shown as 33, or 333. 333 + 333 equals 666. Occultists have used 333 as the hidden symbol by which they present the more offensive number 666. When the details of an event are so arranged as to contain certain sacred occult numbers or numeric combinations, this is literally an occult signature on the event. Mathematically, 666 can be created when three pairs of threes are added. Thus, (3+3) + (3+3) + (3+3) = 666. Now, eliminate the parentheses and the plus sign, and you have 33 space, 33 space, 33, representing the number 666.

GEMATRIA (OCCULT NUMEROLOGY)	
NUMBER	**DERIVATION & MEANING**
93	θελημα - WILL (9+5+30+8+40+1 = 93); αγαπη - LOVE (1+3+1+80+8 = 93); ASCENSION OUT OF EGO / DUALITY, TO LOVE / WILL / UNITY CONSCIOUSNESS; REDUCES TO 3, SO EQUIVALENT TO 777.
77	77 OUT OF 777; 14 OUT OF 21; ⅔ = .666 INTELLECT COMBINED WITH EGOIC WILL BUT DEVOID OF COMPASSION; DUALITY X 7; ONE SHORT OF 78, NUMBER OF TAROT CARDS, BOOK OF TRUTH; DECEIT, SORCERY & CHAOS PREVAIL OVER TRUTH, LOVE, WILL
11	SIGNALING NUMBER OFTEN USED TO IDENTIFY OCCULTISTS TO EACH OTHER; REPRESENTS THE "GREAT WORK" OF SYNTHESIS BETWEEN OPPOSING FORCES; DUALITY; CHAOS; "THE FALL;" US VS. THEM.
175	REDUCES TO 13; EQUIVALENT TO 418, ABRAHADABRA, MANIFESTATION, WHICH ALSO REDUCES TO 13; GENERALLY REPRESENTATIVE OF MAGICK OR RITUAL WORKINGS.

2. <u>Six (6)</u> is the next sacred number, representing the number of the soul of man (Westcott, p. 66). This shows the omnipotent power of God, as this belief parallels Revelation 13:18, where God assigns 666 to man and to the beast. Six is also believed to be "all-sufficient". This parallels Biblical teaching, which states that man's great sin is pride in himself.

3. Seven (7) is a sacred number. Van Buren calls 7 "one of the most sacred of all the numbers...the Invisible Centre, the Spirit of everything" (p. 39). Since multiplication of seven creates an even more powerful sacred number, we should not be surprised that 3x7, or 21, is considered powerful. Thus, when Adam Weishaupt formed the Illuminati, he arranged the timing of the event by arranging the numbers in a manner which would add to powerful numbers. He chose May 1, because May, month #5, added to the first day, equals 6. Weishaupt chose 1776, because the four numbers of this year add up to 21 (1+7+7+6 = 21). Further, the number 6 + 21 = 27, another number of power, because it is formed by the multiplication of 3x9. This date was very carefully chosen by Weishaupt; he believed the greatest Plan is doomed to failure if it is not carried out in the most numerically advantageous time.

4. Nine (9) is sacred because it is the "first cube of an odd number (3)" (Van Buren, p. 40-41). The triple nine (999) is utilized to represent 666, because it is simply the inversion of 666.

5. Eleven (11) is a sacred number. When eleven is multiplied by the perfect number 3, the number 33 is produced, a number of tremendous occult importance. In 1933, Adolf Hitler and President Franklin Roosevelt came to power. Both these men were committed to the establishment of the New World Order, and their actions impacted humanity greatly. It was also in 1933 that the First Humanist Manifesto was issued. Do you see how Satan manipulated world history to produce three New World Order events in 1933? Thus, a powerful 333 served as a framework for world events in that year.

6. Thirteen (13) is deemed sacred. It was also no accident that Hitler chose the year 1939 to begin World War II, because 39 is formed by the multiplication of 13x3. Thus, you can see how human history has been shaped by the occult belief in the power of numbers. We have provided much detail as to how history has been shaped by this belief in the power of numbers. You can get this information in our Cutting Edge Radio Program dated May 9, 1992, entitled, "33 33 33 = 666 New Age Numerology".

Here's another article which covers a few more numbers:
http://helpfreetheearth.com/news565_numbers.html
Source:
http://www.cuttingedge.org/pages/seminar2/NUMBERS.htm

It all started shortly after 9/11 with the passing of the Patriot Act, which ushered in numerous violations on our Fourth Amendment protections against unlawful search and seizure. And most people supported it because, after all, we had to "go after the terrorists." And, hey, we had to give up our liberty for a time until the crisis passed.

Read more at http://thefreethoughtproject.com/tsa-wont-government-you/#iFyKT8aPuuRvEcef.99

Just consider the passivity with which most people accept "porn, perversion and pedophilia" – I wish I knew who said that first – in the name of "transportation safety". When you look at a nude photograph of a minor, it is child pornography. If someone else feels you up without your consent, it is sexual assault. (And if anyone did this to me under any other circumstances, it would take about one nanosecond for me to put the wretched little pervert's teeth on the ground.)

Read more at *http://thefreethoughtproject.com/tsa-wont-government-you/#iFyKT8aPuuRvEcef.99*

OCCULT MEANING AND PSYCHOLOGY OF 'CURRENCY' OR 'MONEY'
THE RELATION BETWEEN ENERGY AND CURRENCY

THE WORD CURRENCY ALSO SOUNDS SIMILAR TO "CURRENT-CHI." IN CHINESE, THE WORD CHI MEANS "NATURAL ENERGY," "LIFE FORCE," OR "ENERGY FLOW." BASED ON THESE DEFINITIONS, CURRENCY MEANS THE "FLOW OF ENERGY." WHEN YOU REALLY THINK ABOUT IT, CURRENCY IS A MEDIUM FOR EXCHANGING ENERGY.

IN LEGAL TERM, WHEN SOMEONE GETS BEATEN UP, THAT PERSON IS OFTEN REFERRED TO AS A "VICTIM OF BATTERY." IF THE VICTIM PRESSES CHARGES, THE PERSON WHO COMMITTED THE BATTERY WILL BE SUMMONED TO GO TO COURT TO FACE THE CHARGES. THE WORD BATTERY IS AN IMPORTANT WORD IN COMMERCE AND LAW, BECAUSE IT HAS TO DO WITH THE PROCESS OF HARNESSING THE ENERGY OF HUMANITY. - PL CHANG

STILLNESS&
Storm
SITSSHOW.BLOGSPOT.COM

Occultist Numerology (Numbers and Meanings) The most venerated occult numbers are: 3, 6, 9, 11, 13, and multiples thereof, especially 22, 33, 44, 55, 66, 77. A triplication of numbers is also considered sacred (possibly even more sacred) to the occultist: 111, 222, 333, and so fourth.

If nine is one
Ten is none
Here is all the mystery

Occultists place much faith in the inherent power of numbers (not to be confused with Numerology of the bible). No plan of action can be carried out without first determining two things:

1 Is the timing of this plan of action in accordance with the astrological lineup of the stars, moons, and planets?
2 Is the timing of this plan of action in accordance with the numbers it will produce?

This process is "Divination" and is specifically prohibited by God. (Deut 18:10-11)

Once you understand how occultists think and calculate, you will be able to see occultism in world events. This effort to determine the correct time for an action is carried out to precise days and times. A good example is the suicide of Adolf Hitler. Hitler chose the date, April 30, 1945, because it was the first day of the Pagan Spring Holy Days. He chose 3:30p.m. because, according to occult doctrine, this combination of three's presented to him the most favorable time to depart this life and reenter the reincarnation cycle. Note the triple 3's present here, April 30 as the first three, 3 o'clock in the afternoon as the second three, and 30 minutes past the hour is the final three. Hitler was engaging in typical occult behavior by arranging the timing of his death in a very precise, numeric manner. Hitler wanted to exit this life in such a proper time that he could come back quickly, as the real Anti-Christ. http://www.definemania.com/the-mania.html

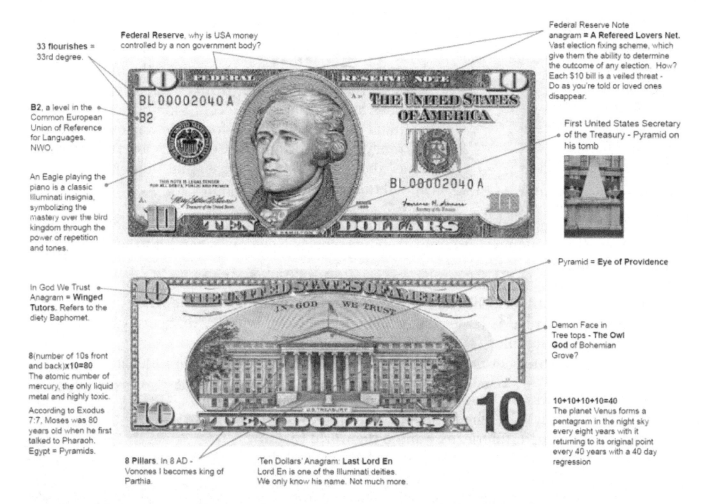

33 flourishes = 33rd degree.

Federal Reserve, why is USA money controlled by a non government body?

Federal Reserve Note anagram = A Refereed Lovers Net. Vast election fixing scheme, which give them the ability to determine the outcome of any election. How? Each $10 bill is a veiled threat - Do as you're told or loved ones disappear.

B2, a level in the Common European Union of Reference for Languages. NWO.

First United States Secretary of the Treasury - Pyramid on his tomb

An Eagle playing the piano is a classic Illuminati insignia, symbolizing the mastery over the bird kingdom through the power of repetition and tones.

Pyramid = Eye of Providence

In God We Trust Anagram = Winged Tutors. Refers to the diety Baphomet.

Demon Face in Tree tops - The Owl God of Bohemian Grove?

8(number of 10s front and back)x10=80 The atomic number of mercury, the only liquid metal and highly toxic.

According to Exodus 7:7, Moses was 80 years old when he first talked to Pharaoh. Egypt = Pyramids.

10+10+10+10=40 The planet Venus forms a pentagram in the night sky every eight years with it returning to its original point every 40 years with a 40 day regression

8 Pillars. In 8 AD - Vonones I becomes king of Parthia.

'Ten Dollars' Anagram: Last Lord En Lord En is one of the Illuminati deities. We only know his name. Not much more.

http://www.ridingthebeast.com/numbers/nu10.php

Symbolism: Symbol of the matter in harmony - 4 + 6.

Represent the Creator and the creation, 3 + 7, the Trinity resting in the expressed universe. For Pythagoras, 10 was the symbol of the universe and it also expressed the whole of human knowledge. Sum of 5 + 5, the number 10 represents the two opposite current directions of the conscience: involution and evolution. According to H.- P. Blavatsky, the 1 followed by 0 indicates the column and the circle, meaning the principle of the female and male, and this symbol would refer to the Androgyne nature and also to Jehovah, being at the same time male and female. The zero in the form of circle is a symbol of unit, completing then the meaning of the number 1 to show that the number 10 contains all preceding numbers as a whole contains its parts. Represent the first couple, the marriage: 1 = the man, 0 the egg fertilized by the 1. The ten gives the indication of a spiritual regression since the marriage is a consequence of the fall of the man. The number ten is regarded as the most perfect of numbers, because it contains the Unit that did it all, and the zero, symbol of the matter and the Chaos, of which all came out; it then includes in its figure the created and the non-created, the beginning and the end, the power and the force, the life and the nothing.

The use of the phrase "In God We Trust" in U.S. currency first appeared in 1864. Salmon P. Chase, Lincoln's Secretary of the Treasury in the middle of the Civil War, received a letter from a Pennsylvanian minister requesting some recognition of God in a national motto. The phrase found its way onto all U.S. currency in the thick of the Cold War (around the same time, and for the same reasons, that "under God" was added to the Pledge of Allegiance).

http://time.com/4179685/in-god-we-trust-currency-history/

As part of the cultural war on godless communism, a 1955 congressional vote elected to place the motto on all U.S. money. Certainly in some respects Newdow is correct to see the motto as a modern innovation.

If removing religious affiliations from U.S. currency is the goal, you have to wonder if Newdow has missed the 100-pound truncated pyramid in the room. The fairly innocuous phrase "In God We Trust" is far less specific than the occult imagery that currently adorns the common one dollar bill.

http://www.thedailybeast.com/articles/2016/01/24/dear-atheists-don-t-fear-in-god-we-trust.html

"In God We Trust" was first added to U.S. coins during the beginning of the Civil War, when religious sentiment was on an upswing and concerned Americans wanted the world to know what their country stood for. Many wrote to Secretary of the Treasury Salmon P. Chase on the matter, and he agreed with their arguments. Congress passed his act requesting the addition of "In God We Trust," adapted from a lesser-known verse of Francis Scott Key's "Star-Spangled Banner," and the first two-cent coin with the phrase was minted in 1864.

The writing ' In God we trust ' is seen on a dollar bill on August 14, 2015, in Berlin, Germany.

MASONIC SIGNIFICANCE OF THE GREAT SEAL

Not only were many of the founders of the United States government Masons, but they received aid from a secret and august body existing in Europe which helped them to establish this country for a peculiar and particular purpose known only to the initiated few.

The Great Seal is the signature of this exalted body— unseen and for the most part unknown— and the unfinished pyramid upon its reverse side is a trestleboard setting forth symbolically the task to the accomplishment of which the United States Government was dedicated from the day of its inception.

~The Secret Teachings of All Ages (1928)
Manly P. Hall (bold emphasis mine)

*Roosevelt, as he looked at the colored reproduction of the Seal, was first struck with the representation of the "All Seeing Eye," a **Masonic representation of The Great Architect of the Universe**. Next he was impressed with the idea that the foundation for the new order of the ages had been laid in 1776, but that it would be **completed only under the eye of the Great Architect**. Roosevelt like myself was a 32nd degree Mason. ~Wallace letters, 1951*

1). Novus Ordo Seclorum: A Latin phrase which means "a new order of the ages" is born. Literally, it is calling for a New World Order. – Dictionary.com

2). Annuit Coeptis: A Latin phrase which means "he has favored our undertakings". – Dictionary.com

3). The Egyptian Pyramid: One of the great Illuminati symbols, the triangle, representing the ancient wisdom of Egypt. In the bible, Egypt is always a type of the unsaved world rebelling against God.

4). The All-Seeing Eye Of Horus: Horus was worshipped in the ancient world as a god of protection, and was often depicted as a falcon swooping in to catch it's prey. Horus was the child of Isis and Osiris conceived through witchcraft in Egyptian mythology. The symbol of America – the swooping Bald Eagle – was patterned after falcon of Horus. The All-seeing-Eye is taken from the left eye, the "moon" or "sound" eye of Horus. Horus is a detestable pagan god, the son of Osiris and Isis. There is much pagan Egyptian mythology in the roots of Masonry and Mormonism. So why is it on our dollar bill?

5). 13 Levels: The pyramid has 13 steps, or levels leading up to the capstone. In the bible, 13 is the number for rebellion. America was created when our founding fathers rebelled against King George.

"SOME EVEN BELIEVE WE ARE PART OF A SECRET CABAL WORKING AGAINST THE BEST INTERESTS OF THE UNITED STATES, CHARACTERIZING MY FAMILY AND ME AS 'INTERNATIONALISTS' AND OF CONSPIRING WITH OTHERS AROUND THE WORLD TO BUILD A MORE INTEGRATED GLOBAL POLITICAL AND ECONOMIC STRUCTURE – ONE WORLD, IF YOU WILL. IF THAT'S THE CHARGE, I STAND GUILTY, AND I AM PROUD OF IT." "– DAVID ROCKEFELLER, FROM HIS BOOK "MEMOIRS".

6). MDCCLXXI: These Roman numerals refer to founding of the Illuminati as an organization on May 1, 1776. This is not a reference to our Independence Day of July 4th, 1776.

7). 13 Stars: Again, the biblical number for rebellion – 13 – forms the basis of the Great Seal. The number 13 is all over the dollar bill.

8). E Pluribus Unum: Another Latin phrase which means "from many, one". You will note that this phrase contains exactly 13 letters. Amazing coincidence.

9). A Spiders Web: When you look at the background pattern of the dollar bill, you will clearly see that it is a spider's web. The spider and the spider web in ancient cultures represented death, treachery and conquest.

10). Olive Leaves and Berries: You will note that the eagle is holding 13 olives leaves with 13 olive berries. The olive leaf is a sign of peace, but the eagle's claws are closed to represent that these things are being taken away, and not being offered.

"IT WAS NOT MY INTENTION TO DOUBT THAT, THE DOCTRINES OF THE ILLUMINATI, AND PRINCIPLES OF JACOBINISM HAD NOT SPREAD IN THE UNITED STATES. ON THE CONTRARY, NO ONE IS MORE TRULY SATISFIED OF THIS FACT THAN I AM. THE IDEA THAT I MEANT TO CONVEY, WAS, THAT I DID NOT BELIEVE THAT THE LODGES OF FREE MASONS IN THIS COUNTRY HAD, AS SOCIETIES, ENDEAVOURED TO PROPAGATE THE DIABOLICAL TENETS OF THE FIRST, OR PERNICIOUS PRINCIPLES OF THE LATTER (IF THEY ARE SUSCEPTIBLE OF SEPARATION). THAT INDIVIDUALS OF THEM MAY HAVE DONE IT, OR THAT THE FOUNDER, OR INSTRUMENT EMPLOYED TO FOUND, THE DEMOCRATIC SOCIETIES IN THE UNITED STATES,

MAY HAVE HAD THESE OBJECTS; AND ACTUALLY HAD A SEPARATION OF THE PEOPLE FROM THEIR GOVERNMENT IN VIEW, IS TOO EVIDENT TO BE QUESTIONED." (**GEORGE WASHINGTON**, SHORTLY BEFORE HE DIED, READ JOHN ROBISON'S BOOK PROOFS OF A CONSPIRACY AND IMMEDIATELY EXPRESSED HIS BELIEF TO THE PREACHER WHO HAD SENT IT TO HIM, THAT THE DESIGNS OF THE ILLUMINATI WERE INFECTING OUR COUNTRY. LETTER TO REVEREND G. W. SNYDER, **WRITINGS OF GEORGE WASHINGTON, P 518-519.)**

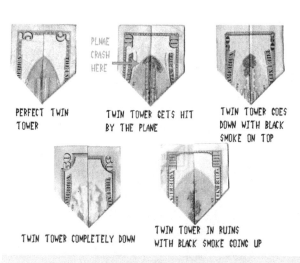

PERFECT TWIN TOWER

TWIN TOWER GETS HIT BY THE PLANE

PLANE CRASH HERE

TWIN TOWER GOES DOWN WITH BLACK SMOKE ON TOP

TWIN TOWER COMPLETELY DOWN

TWIN TOWER IN RUINS WITH BLACK SMOKE GOING UP

Remember...

- Symbols can be interpreted different ways by different people.
- The symbolism of an image can change over time.
- Symbols are a powerful way to express meaning without words.
- Symbols can only be powerful if you recognize them and know what the creators intended them to mean.
- Be careful of the symbols you choose to wear as you do not know how they could be interpreted by someone else.

The Classical Elements of the One-Dollar Bill

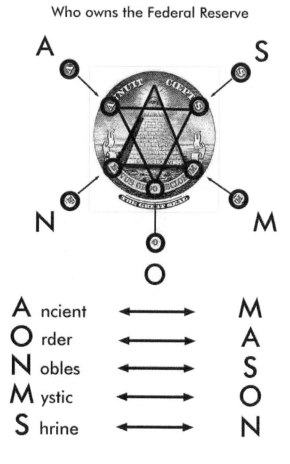

Who owns the Federal Reserve

A	ncient	⟷	M	
O	rder	⟷	A	
N	obles	⟷	S	
M	ystic	⟷	O	
S	hrine	⟷	N	

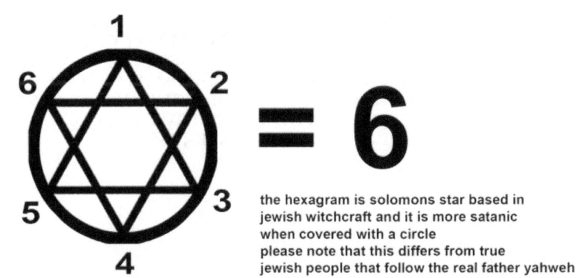

1
6 2
5 3
4

= **6**

the hexagram is solomons star based in
jewish witchcraft and it is more satanic
when covered with a circle
please note that this differs from true
jewish people that follow the real father yahweh

**3 hexagrams coverd with a circle form the
666 remember that no one may buy or sell
unless you have the cash in your hand**

this seal means

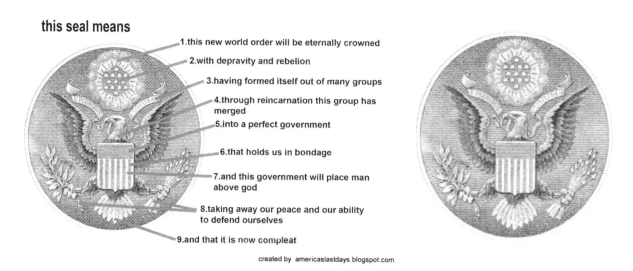

1. this new world order will be eternally crowned
2. with depravity and rebelion
3. having formed itself out of many groups
4. through reincarnation this group has merged
5. into a perfect government
6. that holds us in bondage
7. and this government will place man above god
8. taking away our peace and our ability to defend ourselves
9. and that it is now compleat

created by americaslastdays.blogspot.com

http://www.atlanteanconspiracy.com/2009/01/freemasonic-statue-of-liberty.html

The symbol for the U.S. dollar is $, sometimes with one or two vertical lines. The "S" and "I" have nothing to do with "dollars" and everything to do with "ISIS." The Egyptian Goddess of the Moon and Sirius was "ISIS" and this is the most common name for her used by the Brotherhood. The dollar sign is actually an occult talisman to this Illuminati Goddess. This is why both the Statue of Liberty/Isis and her dollars are both the same color green. The ancient roots of the word Moon were "mon" and "min" which is why we have "money" made at the "mint." The very idea of money and symbolic currency comes from ancient secret societies.

CURRENCY=CURRENTS=FLOOD
FINANCIAL CRISIS / CRY SEES / SEA RISES

DOLLAR
DOLOROSA
VIA DOLOROSA
"the way of sorrows"
(ALSO SYMBOL FOR YIN YANG / CADUCEUS / DNA ... ETC.)

VESICA PISCES
PISCES ♓ FISH SYMBOL
♓ = ⚹ = ⊕ EYE ALL SEEING
ZODIAC ELEMENT - WATER

$ = 9 | |

CURRENCY = RRUC-EN-CY = ROCK and SEA
ROCK and SEA = MOTHER & SON = SOLOMON

The dollar sign $ (I S I S)

Most of the explanations on the origin of the sign naturally refer to the serpentine shape. In connection with Isis quest to recover the scattered pieces of her husband and to reconstitute him, we may add, from the anecdotal point of view, another explanation about the dollar sign origin:

The vertical line represents the "World Axis", bridge between Heaven and Earth. The earlier drawing of the sign contained two vertical bars, instead of one, which referred to both ascending and descending phases alongside the axis.

The serpentine line symbolizes the cycling way around the axis as explained in the euro symbol part. For more details regarding this point, consult the double spiral.

"Silver was connected with the moon and therefore with the Goddesses of the moon, the most famous of which was and is ISIS. So her name became the symbol of money. We find this today in the cleverly camouflaged motif - $- which is nothing more than the sigil for the name of I-S-I-S, but fused together in an ingenious manner." -Michael Tsarion, **"Astrotheology and Sidereal Mythology"**

63

this seal means

1. ANOUNCCING THE BIRTH

2. OF A NEW WORLD ORDER

3. ITS HEAD WILL BE LUCIFER

4. IT WILL BE BASED ON DEPRAVITY AND REBELLION

5. birthed MAY 1ST 1776

created by americaslastdays.blogspot.com

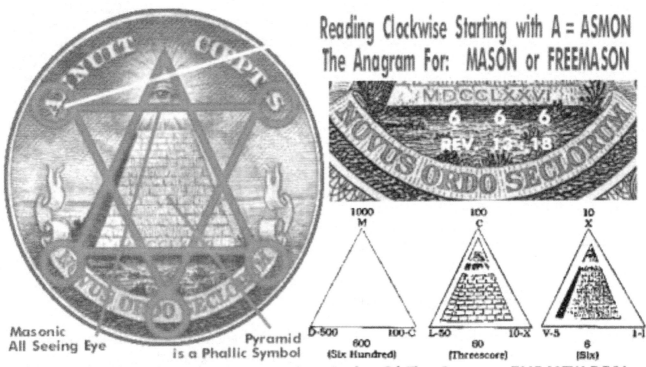

Reading Clockwise Starting with A = ASMON
The Anagram For: MASON or FREEMASON

666
REV 13 - 18

1000 M	100 C	10 X
D-500 100-C	L-50 10-X	V-5 I-I
600 (Six Hundred)	60 (Threescore)	6 (Six)

Masonic All Seeing Eye

Pyramid is a Phallic Symbol

NOVUS ORDO SECLORUM = A New Order Of The Ages = THE NEW DEAL
Understood by the Illuminati as: "The New World Order" under Their Control

64

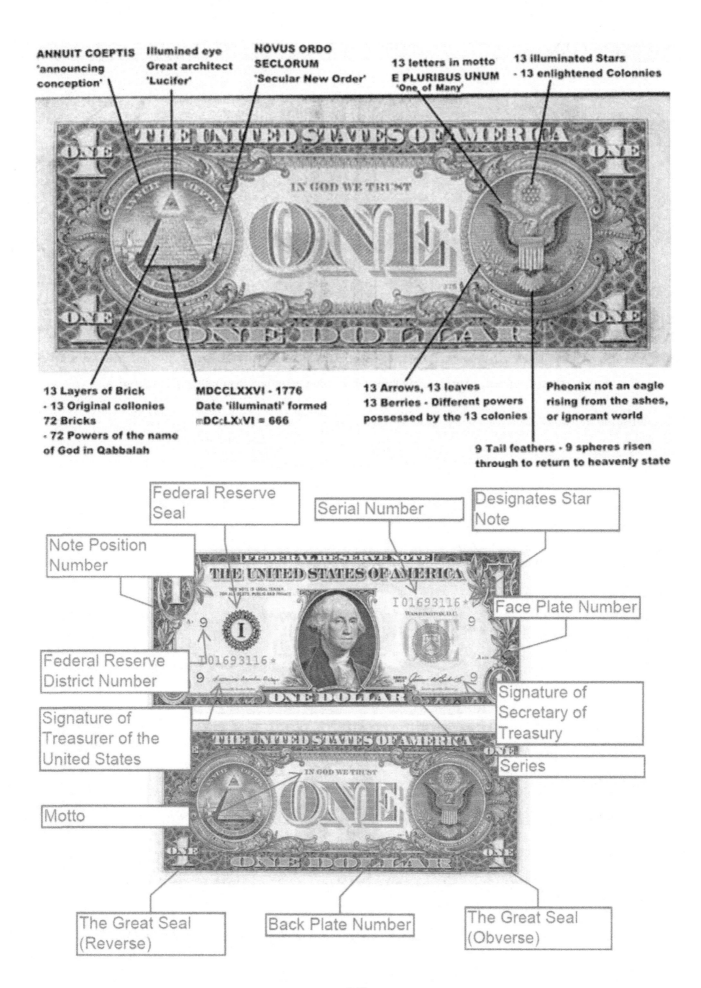

ANNUIT COEPTIS 'announcing conception'

Illumined eye Great architect 'Lucifer'

NOVUS ORDO SECLORUM 'Secular New Order'

13 letters in motto E PLURIBUS UNUM 'One of Many'

13 illuminated Stars - 13 enlightened Colonnies

13 Layers of Brick - 13 Original collonies **72 Bricks** - 72 Powers of the name of God in Qabbalah

MDCCLXXVI - 1776 Date 'illuminati' formed mDCcLXxVI = 666

13 Arrows, 13 leaves **13 Berries** - Different powers possessed by the 13 colonies

Pheonix not an eagle rising from the ashes, or ignorant world

9 Tail feathers - 9 spheres risen through to return to heavenly state

Federal Reserve Seal

Serial Number

Designates Star Note

Note Position Number

Face Plate Number

Federal Reserve District Number

Signature of Secretary of Treasury

Signature of Treasurer of the United States

Series

Motto

The Great Seal (Reverse)

Back Plate Number

The Great Seal (Obverse)

65

Secret Symbolism on the back of the US $1 bill

ANNUIT CŒPTIS : Latin words annuo (nod, approve) and cœpi (begin, undertake), is literally translated as "He approves (or has approved) [our] undertakings".

E pluribus unum is Latin for "Out of Many, One."

the ALL- SEING EYE : Representing the eye of God keeping watch on humankind

33 feathers symbolises the 33 degree of Masonry

Why so much Egyptology? **Isn't this America?**

Anagram : Mason

13 feathers

13 arrows

PYRAMID : Symbol representing the Illuminati

The number thirteen :

13 stars

13 stripes

Novus Ordo Seclorum : Latin meaning "New Order of the Ages".

The Eagle was chosen to represent the Egytian God RA symbolizing human Enlightenment.

ConspiracyCards.com © 2009

http://s589.photobucket.com/user/Ashalayah80/media/Dollar_Symbols_05-1.gif.html

Two is spelled out 6 times on the front of the dollar bill. The number two (2) appears 5 times. Repeating the number 6 five times gives us **66666**. That's **666** plus two more – which makes it 40% more powerful.

All Seeing Eye - In perfect proportion to ear, nose and forehead. Coincidence?

Jefferson - Was NOT a Freemason. But he was a member of the Bavarian Illuminati

Scale = Balance of power between the old world Illuminati and New World Brotherhood.

The shield contains a **key**. Keys represent the ability to unlock your mind, opening it to the influence of the Illuminati

Thomas Jefferson - Jefferson's ties to the number 6 are numerous and reveal his membership in the Illuminati. He had **six children**. His wife Martha dies on September 6th. His statue in the Jefferson Memorial is 19 feet tall – which converts to **6 meters** (Illuminati prefer the metric system).

13 Stars: 13 illuminated colonies. 13 Illuminati bloodlines.

Genisis 13:4: "Twelve years they served Chedorlaomer, and the thirteenth year they REBELLED.

1789: The Illuminati make a bold move towards world domination, installing George Washington as President - Starting French Revolution - Pope Pius VI appoints first Illuminati Catholic Bishop in US, John Carroll.

Stephen Hopkins: Note that he is the only one wearing a hat. Illuminati worshipful masters are the only men that wear hats at meetings.

George Clinton: George Clinton is the direct ancestor to President Bill Clinton, a known member of the Illuminati.

Why is **Baphomet** overlooking this monumental event?

23 = Eris, goddess of discord.

23 enigma refers to the belief that most incidents and events are directly connected to the number 23.

The anagram of Two Dollars is "**To Owls Lard**": code to subliminally recruit new members to the Illuminati, instructing them to go towards the owls to find the lard, which at the time of our nation's founding, was a sign of wealth. Owls are an Illuminati deity worshipped at the **Bohemian Grove**.

This image comes from a painting by **John Trumbull**. The original painting had 47 men, but the bill only has 42. Those five were known opponents of the Illuminati who mysteriously disappeared after the Declaration of Independence. The Illuminati removed their pictures from the two dollar bill in an attempt to remove all evidence of their existence.

Crossed legs - right over left. Known symbol of Conservative Illuminati dominating liberal common man. This is also a way to let other know "where you stand."

Illuminati hand signs.

Pillars of Solomons Temple on Throne. Why would this be represented in a New America? NWO

http://extremelifechanger.com/index.php?p=1_216_202-SECRETS-OF-THE-2-DOLLAR

66

The Colors of Money "The Wizard of OZ"

The Land of Oz is colorful, to say the least, and *The Wonderful Wizard of Oz* is replete with references to gold, silver, and green. A number of these references have been noted already, but the story makes several others. The references to gold and silver echo the prominence of monetary politics in the 1890s, especially the bimetallic crusade led by Bryan and the Populists. Moreover, gold and silver are often portrayed as working in combination. The Witch of the West conjures her minions with a silver whistle and a golden cap, and the Tin Man receives a new ax made of gold and silver, as well as a new oil can that contains both metals. Of course, there is Dorothy on her sojourn through Oz, "her silver shoes tinkling merrily on the hard, yellow, roadbed." The word *oz* itself is the abbreviation for an ounce of gold or silver. There are additional references to gold and silver, but the ones given here amply illustrate Baum's use of the monetary metaphor.

"It is the 'dark side' of the ego, and the evil that we are capable of is often stored there. Actually, the shadow is amoral-neither good nor bad, just like animals" ("Jung"), written in the "Carl Jung" web page.

"During the medieval times, money consisted of metal coins. Paper currency ... In the Byzantine Empire, gold, silver, and copper coins were minted and used.

Green, often in combination with gold, is also a recurrent image. Then as now, green was the color of paper money. The Greenback Party, a precursor of the Populists, advocated the expansion of the money supply via the increased circulation of "greenbacks." Jacob Coxey was a greenbacker, as was James B. Weaver, the Populist presidential nominee in 1892. Most of the green imagery in Oz is general in nature and does not appear to indicate specific parallels. Toto wears a green collar that fades to white (silver), and later he receives a gold collar, as does the Lion. In Emerald City, everyone is required to wear green glasses with golden bands, so that nearly everything appears in a resplendent green. The Lion's liquid "courage" is poured from a green bottle into a gold-green dish, and the Wizard's balloon is patched with green silk of various shades. As the spectacles create an illusion, the liquid courage is only a placebo, and the balloon is a mere patchwork, so the demand for paper money is exposed as a panacea for the farmers' woes.

At the end of the story, the Scarecrow supplants the Wizard as the ruler of Emerald City, the Tin Woodman is made master of the West, and the Lion is placed over the animals of the forest. Dorothy transports herself back to Kansas by clicking her silver shoes together three times. All this is achieved with the help of Glinda, the good Witch of the South. The message? Populism is triumphant, the goal of gaining political power is achieved. Or is it? Neither the Scarecrow nor the Tin Man nor the Lion truly lacked what each believed he was missing; the great Wizard's powers proved illusory; and Dorothy had the power to transform her condition all along. These features of the story point to a more ambivalent result. Indeed, Populism's outright failure is suggested when Dorothy's silver shoes fall off in the desert and are "lost forever." After Bryan's defeat in 1896, the free-silver movement went into rapid decline. McKinley's reelection and the statutory adoption of the gold standard in 1900 spelled political oblivion for the Populists. **http://www.independent.org/publications/tir/article.asp?a=504**

WANTED

FOR

TREASON

THIS MAN is wanted for treasonous activities against the United States:

1. Betraying the Constitution (which he swore to uphold):
He is turning the sovereignty of the U.S. over to the communist controlled United Nations.
He is betraying our friends (Cuba, Katanga, Portugal) and befriending our enemies (Russia, Yugoslavia, Poland).

2. He has been WRONG on innumerable issues affecting the security of the U.S. (United Nations-Berlin wall-Missle removal-Cuba-Wheat deals-Test Ban Treaty, etc.)

3. He has been lax in enforcing Communist Registration laws.

4. He has given support and encouragement to the Communist inspired racial riots.

5. He has illegally invaded a sovereign State with federal troops.

6. He has consistantly appointed Anti-Christians to Federal office: Upholds the Supreme Court in its Anti-Christian rulings. Aliens and known Communists abound in Federal offices.

7. He has been caught in fantastic LIES to the American people (including personal ones like his previous marraige and divorce).

(John F. Kennedy) Original "**Wanted for Treason**" Handbill. **John F. Kennedy** (1917-1963) 35th President. On November 21, 1963 "**Wanted for Treason**" handbills were distributed on the streets of Dallas, before **Kennedy's** scheduled visit. ... An original 9" x 12" "**Wanted for Treason**" handbill, has uneven toning and age spotting.

JANESVILLE DAILY GAZETTE

PRESIDENT KENNEDY IS SLAIN IN TEXAS!

Johnson To Take Helm

trea·son

noun: **treason**; noun: **high treason**; plural noun: **high treasons**

1   the crime of betraying one's country, especially by attempting to kill the sovereign or overthrow the government.the crime of murdering someone to whom the murc owed allegiance, such as a master or husband.

King James Version

Here is wisdom. Let him that hath understanding count the number of the beast: for it is the number of a man; and his number is Six hundred threescore and six. Both Kennedy and Lincoln had an idea of issuing bank notes or changing policies when it came to money.

It was a symbol used widely in the Roman Empire and it consists of rods bound together around an axe. This axe is the origin of the term Axis Powers for the fascist countries in the Second World War. The symbolism is of people and countries bound together under a common centralised dictatorship, the axe.

Not only was this used by Ancient Rome back in the day as one of its Symbols of "Supreme Authority", but also by the Original "Axis Powers" of Europe back in the first half of the 20th Century prior too and during WWII.

Numerous governments and other authorities have used the image of the fasces as a symbol of power since the end of the Roman Empire. It has also been used to hearken back to the Roman republic, particularly by those who see themselves as modern-day successors to the old republic. http://sosymbol.tumblr.com/post/9544645575/do-you-know-what-a-fasci-is

Fasci is the symbol from which we get the word, fascism.

And they had a king over them, which is the angel of the bottomless pit, whose name in the Hebrew tongue is Abaddon, but in the Greek tongue hath his name Apollyon. - Revelation 9:11

Occult Symbolism That is Hidden in Plain Sight

Tragic events have occurred, and were carried out carefully according to the sacred occult number 11, such as the 11th day, of the 9th month, in the year 2001 (9+1+1=11). The American Airlines flight #11 crashed into the world trade centre. United Airlines flight #77 crashed into the Pentagon (11x7=77). The north and south Twin Towers were 110 stories tall (11x10=110). It happened on the 254th day of the year (2+5+4=11). On September 11th, 1990, George W. Bush gave a congressional speech about moving towards a new world order. When President Bush visited New York after the attacks, he was pictured with a fireman with a helmet number, 164 (1+6+4=11). 9/11 is one of the biggest lying wonders of the world; unfortunately, delusion and illusion inhibit seeking after the real truth. **https://exemplore.com/misc/Occult-Symbolism-in-the-Music-Industry-that-is-Hidden-in-Plain-Site**

Fasces like the ones described above are a prominent feature of 'images of power in early America'. As Garry Wills, in writing on Jean-Antoine Houdon's famous statue of George Washington, notes in *Cincinnatus: George Washington and The Enlightenment (Images of Power in Early America)*, Doubleday, New York, 1984, pp. 227-228) notes:

America was the first "fascist" country of the modern world–the first, that is, to make wide use of this symbol [the fasces] of a revived Roman republic. The French revolutionaries enthusiastically followed suit–the relationship of Washington to the fasces in Houdon's statue partly resembles that of David's design for Hercules standing by a fasces in the fourth stop of the Procession for the Festival of Brotherhood in 1793. by Samir Chopra

The fasces were everywhere in early American art; and they are still encountered all over Washington– on bridges, on Lincoln's chair in his Monument on the frames that hold Trumbull's paintings in the Rotunda. Columbia holds the fasces in Fragonard's depiction of Franklin. by Samir Chopra

https://samirchopra.com/2016/05/12/fascism-in-american-iconography/

Note the Fasci making up the columns under Lincolns hands, Fasci need not always have the Axe head in it

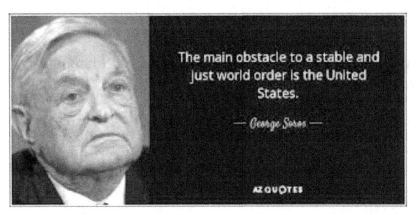

Lincoln-Kennedy Penny

ABRAHAM LINCOLN 1809-1865

JOHN F KENNEDY 1937-1963

This uncirculated Lincoln Head penny is stamped with a profile reproduction of John F. Kennedy looking-at-Lincoln. This unusual commemorative piece is truly a collector's item.

Shortly after noon on November 22, 1963, President John F. Kennedy was assassinated as he rode in a motorcade through Dealey Plaza in downtown Dallas, Texas. By the fall of 1963, President John F. Kennedy and his political advisers were preparing for the next presidential campaign.

LINCOLN'S ASSASSINATION WAS THE RESULT OF A **CONSPIRACY** OF POWERFUL INTERNATIONAL BANKERS. This theory is that **Abraham Lincoln** was killed as a result of his monetary policies. John Wilkes Booth would be seen as a hired gun. In its simplest terms, the theory is that **Lincoln** needed money to finance the Civil War.

September 22 marks the 150th anniversary of Abraham Lincoln's preliminary Emancipation Proclamation, in which he declared that as of January 1, 1863, all slaves in states in rebellion against the Union "shall be then, thenceforward, and forever free." To commemorate the occasion, we invite you to consider some surprising facts about Lincoln's views on slavery, and the complex process that led him to issue the document he later called "the central act of my administration, and the greatest event of the 19th century." http://www.history.com/news/5-things-you-may-not-know-about-lincoln-slavery-and-emancipation

List describes a number of amazing coincidences that can be found between the assassinations of Abraham Lincoln and John F. Kennedy.

http://9gag.com/gag/62161/creepy-facts-about-jfk-and-lincoln

- Abraham Lincoln was elected to Congress in 1846. John F. Kennedy was elected to Congress in 1946.
- Abraham Lincoln was elected President in 1860. John F. Kennedy was elected President in 1960.
- Both were shot in the back of the head in the presence of their wives.
- Both wives lost their children while living in the White House.
- Both Presidents were shot on a Friday.
- Lincoln's secretary was named Kennedy.
- Both were succeeded by Southerners named Johnson.
- Andrew Johnson, who succeeded Lincoln, was born in 1808. Lyndon Johnson, who succeeded Kennedy, was born in 1908.
- Lincoln was shot in the Ford Theatre. Kennedy was shot in a Lincoln, made by Ford.
- Lincoln was shot in a theater and his assassin ran and hid in a warehouse. Kennedy was shot from a warehouse and his assassin ran and hid in a theater.
- Booth and Oswald were assassinated before their trials.

http://www.school-for-champions.com/history/lincolnjfk.htm#.WJ0RqxiZMyc

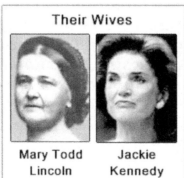

Their Wives

Mary Todd Lincoln

Jackie Kennedy

WHY DO PRESIDENTS ON THE QUARTER DIME NICKEL; FACE OPPOSITE OF LINCOLN ON THE PENNY?

Why does the portrait of Abraham **Lincoln** on the penny **face** to the right when all other portraits of presidents on U.S. circulating coins **face** to the left? The likeness of President **Lincoln** on the penny is an adaption of a plaque executed by Victor David Brenner, an outstanding portraitist and sculptor.

There are many theories out there but following are the most popular. . At the end I select the one that makes most sense to me; but you decide—Tell us which one you agree with...and feel free to add your theory if it's not included below:

1. The likeness of President Lincoln on the penny is an adaption of a plaque executed by Victor David Brenner, an outstanding portraitist and sculptor. President Theodore Roosevelt was so impressed with Mr. Brenner's design of a Lincoln plaque that he recommended to the Secretary of the Treasury that the design be placed on a coin to be issued in the Lincoln Centennial Year, 1909.
2. The other presidents are turning their back on Lincoln because he freed the slaves.
3. The direction that Lincoln faces on the cent was not mandated — this was simply the choice of the designer.
4. It is because he died in office. He is shown as looking back rather than forward because we don't know what his future would have been, or the future of the country if he had lived and served out his second term. As said in his eulogy, "Now he belongs to the ages."
5. Because he turned his back on his country men. He allowed this country to be divided and go to war with it's self.
6. He faces right because he was a Republican.
7. He was assassinated so he faces the opposite way of the other presidents. (This obviously ignores the fact that Kennedy on the half dollar faces left)
8. Lincoln's Best Side: **Because he has a big scare on the left side of his face.**

https://melaniannews.net/2012/07/08/why-do-presidents-on-the-quarter-dime-nickel-face-opposite-of-lincoln-on-the-penny/

According to the late occultist John Todd, Unocal's 76 brand refers to 1776, the year Adam Weishaupt founded the Bavarian Illuminati. The Union Oil Company of California was founded by Thomas Bard, and Wallace Hardison, and Lyman Stewart in 1890.

The 76 brand was created in 1932 at the suggestion of Robert Matthews. It's a reference to the Spirit of 76, which coincidently was the octane rating for the company's high-performance gasoline. The company was swallowed up by Chevron in 2005. Phillip 66 now owns the 76 brand. *http://illuminatisymbols.info/latest/*

We take authority in the name of Jesus Christ and through the power of His shed blood and bind the demonic forces in this filth of Satan.

Thank you, Lord, for setting me free.

There shall not be found among you anyone...that useth divination...or a witch; ...or a consuler with familiar spirits, or a wizard....For all that do these things *are* an abomination unto the Lord. Deut. 18:10-12

JOHN TODD

The "NEW WORLD ORDER" is the GLOBAL TOTALITARIANISM dream that a BANKER called Mayer Amschel Rothschild, helped revive in 1760's to protect his private bank from global government regulation. His grand blue print is best described by his paid social engineer called Dr. Adam [Spartacus] Weishaupt, Professor of Canon Law in the university of Ingolstadt. Weishaupt adopted the term "Illuminati." This nightmare is still sought after today by their family's decedents. Below is the 'outline' Weishaupt set out for his banker financier master! Carefully notice the similarities between Karl Marx's 10 Plank's of his Communist Manifesto and Weishaupt's outline.

Also, please read Communism & The New World Order.

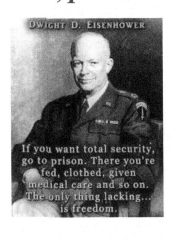

DWIGHT D. EISENHOWER

If you want total security, go to prison. There you're fed, clothed, given medical care and so on. The only thing lacking... is freedom.

The blue print for the NWO is:
* Abolition of all ordered governments
* Abolition of private property
* Abolition of inheritance
* Abolition of patriotism
* Abolition of the family
* Abolition of religion
* A global population of 500 million
* Creation of a world government

COMMUNISM
...there are some lies that lodge so deep in the hopes of man that they can never be killed no matter how many are executed to make the lie true. -Gerard Vanderleun

Most Oil Company Logos...

...Are Actually Pre-Existing, Powerfully-Charged Ancient Pagan / Masonic Symbols

The big 7 Oil Company's were known as "The Seven Sisters." Keep that in mind.

Many remember the Chevron Gas Station logo being different from what it is today.

Which do you remember? The current Chevron logo has BLUE sitting atop RED. I remember the RED sitting atop the BLUE.

"Occult Oil". You will see how large corporations place occult talismans (or symbols) on their logos, to empower themselves, and how all the founders have taken part in secret societies. All the major oil company's and other industry logos are taken from ancient solar cults, or secret society symbology.

3RD DEGREE

My Mind playing Tricks on Me
Mind Control in america

My Mind playing Tricks on Me
Mind Control in america
Operation Mind Control 9 "I know of no safe depository of the ultimate powers of society but the people themselves, and if we think them not enlightened enough to exercise their control with a wholesome discretion, the remedy is not to take it from them, but to inform their discretion by education." -- Thomas Jefferson

ed·u·ca·tion

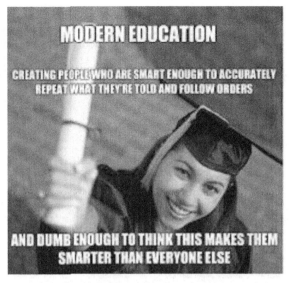

noun: education; noun: an education

1.
the process of receiving or giving systematic instruction, especially at a school or university. "a new system of public education"

Among other contrasts he points out the following: http://www.yourarticlelibrary.com/difference/difference-between-propaganda-and-education/24317/

(i) Education is the indoctrination of children, propaganda that of adults;

(ii) Education is what schools do, propaganda is any other effort to mould thinking;

(iii) Education consists of teaching truth, propaganda of teaching lies;

(iv) Education is rational, propaganda is irrational;

(v) The contents of education are desirable, those, .of propaganda are undesirable;

(vi) Education promotes general welfare, propaganda supports special interests;

(vii) Education supports the moral values and standards of the society, propaganda always attacks them;

(viii) Education is open minded, propaganda is narrow minded;

(ix) Education is a counter-argument against propaganda.

In pointing out the above differences between education and propaganda Woddy has used the word propaganda in a bad sense.

According to Lass-well, education seeks to promulgate a skill, mental or physical, as its primary objective while propaganda regards its content as always secondary, a means to the end of securing some immediately desired kind of behaviour.

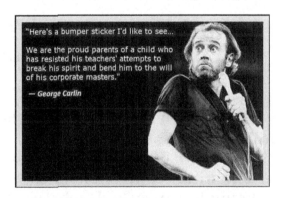

According to Bird, propaganda proceeds primarily by the use of suggestion toward an emotional objective, while education uses, principally, the mental process of inquiry or investigation of detail. Obviously, education aims at clarification, not persuasion.

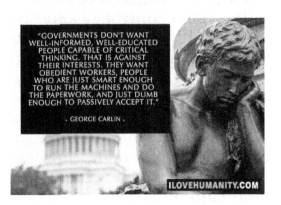

Silent Weapons for Quiet Wars (Excerpt and Introduction)

EDUCATION: Planned Enslavement Through Lack of Knowledge

"The aim of public education is not to spread enlightenment at all, it is simply to reduce as many individuals as possible to the same safe level, to breed and train a standardized citizenry to put down dissent and originality." H. L. Mencken (1880-1956)

"I don't want a nation of thinkers, I want a nation of workers." — John D. Rockefeller

"Silent Weapons for Quiet Wars"
EXCERPT FROM Page 7
"The quality of education given to the lower class must be of the poorest sort, so that the moat of ignorance isolating the inferior class from the superior class is and remains incomprehensible to the inferior class. With such an initial handicap, even bright lower class individuals have little if any hope of extricating themselves from their assigned lot in life. This form of slavery is essential to maintain some measure of social order, peace, and tranquility for the ruling upper class."

Read "Silent Weapons for Quiet Wars"
www.StopTheCrime.net/source.html

Operations Research Technical Manual (TM-SW 7905.1)
War is merely the act of destroying the creditor, and the politicians are the publicly hired hit men that justify the act to keep the responsibility and blood off the public conscience.
The silent weapon is a type of biological warfare. It attacks the vitality, options and mobility of the individuals of a society.

If the people really cared about their fellow man, they would control their appetites (greed, procreation, etc.) so that they would not have to operate on a credit or welfare social system which steals from the worker to satisfy the bum. Since most of the general public will not exercise restraint, there are only two alternatives to reduce the economic inductance of the system:

(1) Let the populace bludgeon each other to death in war, which will only result in a total destruction of the living earth.

(2) Take control of the world by the use of economic "silent weapons" in a form of "quiet warfare" and reduce the economic inductance of the world to a safe level by a process of benevolent slavery and genocide.

Mind Control and Brainwashing of Children

http://www.mall4us.com/mindcontrol.htm

There are a number of ways children can be brainwashed. It is often accomplished by a parent or other trusted caregiver. Simplified, the process follows these steps:

1. The mind controller is a trusted, loved, and important person to the child.
2. The mind controller hates the person/concept/item who/which the child is being brainwashed to hate. (for example: The mind controller hates dad. or The mind controller hates religion. or The mind controller hates kittens.)
3. The child must agree with the mind controller because the child believes that to not do so might lose the support, love or acceptance of the mind controller. (The child hates dad because to not do so would mean losing mom's love. or The child hates religion because to not do so might cause mom to not love the child anymore.)

In the above example, the term Mind Controller may be replaced by the words <u>mom, dad, grandmother, the elder, the teacher,</u> or any other significant individual in the life of the child.

WARNING, READ THIS FIRST BEFORE READING THE BOOK.

IF THERE IS ANY CHANCE you the reader have had mind-control done to you, you must consider the following book to be **DANGEROUS**. If you are consulting a therapist for DID (also known as MPD), it is recommended that you consult your therapist before reading this book. The complications that could result for those under mind control learning the truth--could be fatal. The co-authors take no responsibility for those who read or misuse this information.

The reader's mind is like a garden. It may not be time to plant the truth in your mind. Perhaps you need some weeding or ground preparation, before the garden of your mind is ready. Perhaps the weather is too stormy to plant the truth.

The blessings that flow from planting the information of this book in your mind, will require the presence of living waters of love. If you do not have love in your heart, this book is not for you. The information contained in this book is the biggest news-story of the 20th century, and still the biggest secret. It will challenge you, shock you, horrify you and hopefully motivate you to redouble your **efforts to humble yourself and seek strength from God.** http://www.theforbiddenknowledge.com/hardtruth/illuminati_formula_mind_control.htm

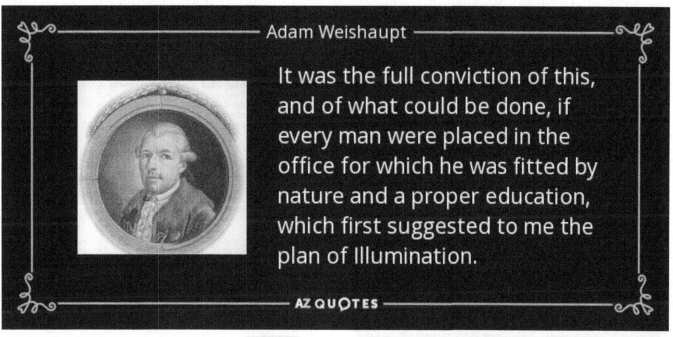

Adam Weishaupt

It was the full conviction of this, and of what could be done, if every man were placed in the office for which he was fitted by nature and a proper education, which first suggested to me the plan of Illumination.

AZ QUOTES

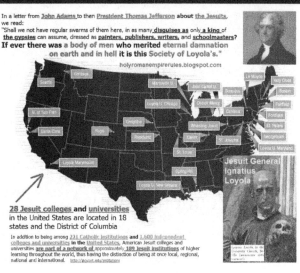

In a letter from John Adams to then President Thomas Jefferson about the Jesuits, we read:
"Shall we not have regular swarms of them here, in as many disguises as only a king of the gypsies can assume, dressed as painters, publishers, writers, and schoolmasters? If ever there was a body of men who merited eternal damnation on earth and in hell it is this Society of Loyola's."
holyromanempirerules.blogspot.com

28 Jesuit colleges and universities in the United States are located in 18 states and the District of Columbia

In addition to being among 231 Catholic institutions and 1,600 independent colleges and universities in the United States, American Jesuit colleges and universities are part of a network of approximately 189 Jesuit institutions of higher learning throughout the world, thus having the distinction of being at once local, regional, national and international. http://jesuit.edu/institutions

Jesuit General Ignatius Loyola

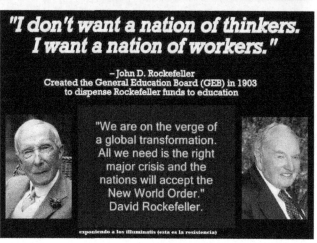

"I don't want a nation of thinkers. I want a nation of workers."

– John D. Rockefeller
Created the General Education Board (GEB) in 1903 to dispense Rockefeller funds to education

"We are on the verge of a global transformation. All we need is the right major crisis and the nations will accept the New World Order." David Rockefeller.

exponiendo a los illuminatis (esta es la resistencia)

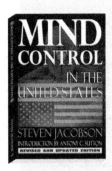

1. Introduction

The most effective way to protect yourself from subconscious manipulation is to be aware of how it works.

Steven Jacobson, author of Mind Control in the United States, is a film technician experienced in subliminal techniques used in the communication media.

Subliminal perception is a process, a deliberate process created by communications technicians, by which you receive and respond to information and instructions without being consciously aware of the instructions.

Scary? You bet your life it is. And as Jacobson details in this book it is happening in America today.

Mind Control in the United States is an introduction to the history and practice of subliminal communication. It outlines the principles of mental programming, i.e., that an initial distraction must be followed by repetitive commands, and it tells you how these ideas are implemented.

Further, the book tells you when and where it has been used. Jacobson's examples range from In Flight Motion Pictures, Inc. and its on-board films to general audience movies such as Reefer Madness, The Exorcist, and My World Dies Screaming. The effects on audiences are graphically described.

The case of the movie The Exorcist is specially interesting. William Peter Blatty, author of the book and producer of the movie, is a former CIA operative. Blatty had an extensive career in government psychological manipulations. One has to be pretty naive to argue there is no connection between Blatty's CIA career and his choice of communications techniques.

"People shouldn't be afraid of their government. Governments should be afraid of their people." ~ V, V for Vendetta (2006)

Symbols of Masonic Degrees

Destructive Education

The intellectuals will teach all of the "false information from science" which our agency specialists have cunningly pieced together for the purpose of educating their minds in the direction we want. Darwinism, Marxism, Nietzsche-ism.

The Black Cube of Saturn

THE WOMAN'S DICTIONARY OF SYMBOLS AND SACRED OBJECTS

Kaaba

BARBARA G. WALKER

Illustrated by the Author

HarperSanFrancisco
A Division of HarperCollinsPublishers

SCHOOLS, CHURCHES, AND COURTS: THE CULT OF SATURN

SUBVERTING EDUCATION

• 2) The faculties of colleges and universities were to cultivate students possessing exceptional mental ability belonging to well-bred families with international leanings, and recommend them for special training in internationalism, or rather the notion that only a one-world government can put an end to recurring wars and strife. Such training was to be provided by granting scholarships to those selected by the Illuminati.

MORTARBOARD
Derived from a cap worn by the Roman Catholic clergy, the mortarboard is now a symbol of erudition.

:We see this Saturn symbolism all around us including black school gowns worn at graduation with a square (*think cube) mortarboard hat

I WAS BORN INTELLIGENT, BUT EDUCATION RUINED ME

If you don't **CONTROL YOUR MIND,** someone else will.
~John Aliston

The university graduate wears the black robe of the god Saturn and the mortarboard of Freemasonry. Both are very ancient symbols.

The holiday of Saturnalia was established by the Romans, as discussed in the post on Occult & Illuminati holiday traditions:

The Saturnalia festival featured human sacrifices and ran from December 17th-23rd. There would be gladiator battles and the deaths would be considered more sacrifices to the deity Saturn. There were also concepts of role reversal; with masters feeding their slaves (still practiced today at work Christmas parties when the bosses feed the workers).

The Romans also participated in a festival called Dies Natalis Solis Invicti, or "Birthday of the Unconquered Sun" on December 25th. Sol Invictus was a Roman god of the sun, which could be yet another retelling of Nimrod and Semiramis. The depictions of Sol Invictus appear to mirror that of the Statue of Liberty, who was designed after the Roman goddess Libertas:

CUBE WORSHIP IN THE KABAH, IN MECCA

Masonic Keystone

Kabah Allah or Cube God represents Saturn and it's color, Black. Chuin is Rempha who is Moloch who is Saturn, who is Satan.

The Black Eyed Peas ironically sing a song called Third Eye with lyrics like,

"I got three eyes, one look from the left side, the other from the right side, got one eye on the inside, and I can see you outside, plottin' to come in."

Schools, Courts, Churches, and the Cult of Saturn

"When you graduate from high school you come out processionally with a black robe, which is black for Saffron, the *God* of the Hebrews, requiring that you wear the square mortarboard on top of your head. The square mortarboards are, of course, used by the Freemasons for their plaster, so that is why you wear a square mortarboard when you graduate, ultimately becoming an Alumni. It all has to do with Freemasonry; it all has to do with the control of education in this country."

Jordan Maxwell, "Matrix of Power"

First you pay out your "tuition" to get into "universe"ity where they strip you of your Intuition and give you an Indoctrination. Then you receive a "MaStars" Masonic "degree," while wearing a Masonic mortar board cap and Cult of Saturn black robes to become an Alumni/Illumini. Graduation means to increment or retard progress. As **Jordan Maxwell** says, "the true meaning of Graduation is *gradual indoctrination.*"

Is Western Higher Education Really Relevant in The African Context?

By Ochieng' Maddo

As early as 1935 Kwame Nkrumah, the revered father of independent Ghana sailed from Liverpool to the United States and attended Lincoln University in Pennsylvania where he received a Bachelor of Sacred Theology in 1942. He proceeded to earn a Master of Science in education the same year, a Master of Arts in philosophy the following year and a PhD in 1943. He led his country to independence in 1956 but his degrees failed to yield for Ghana. His unpopular leadership led to his overthrow in 1966. He lived in Romania until his death in 1972.

https://maddopinions.wordpress.com/2013/08/06/is-western-higher-education-really-relevant-in-the-african-context/

Libya's Muamar Gaddafi went to the United Kingdom in 1966 for further military training, where he underwent an English-language course at Beaconsfield, Buckinghamshire and a Royal Air Corps signal instructor course in Bovington Camp, Dorset. He also took an infantry signal instructor course at Hythe, Kent. Gaddafi is reported to have been unable to adjust to the Country's culture. He would assert his Arab identity while in London by walking around Piccadilly wearing traditional Libyan robes. However, he returned home more confident and proud of British values, ideals and social character. ***Gaddafi would later turn one of the world's worst dictators, culminating in his shameful killing in 2011. (please reference the following books to get an accurate account)***

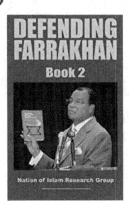

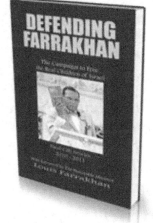

Defending Farrakhan is a 368-page collection of articles written by the scholars of the Nation of Islam and published by The Final Call newspaper. The foreword is written by the Honorable Minister Louis Farrakhan.

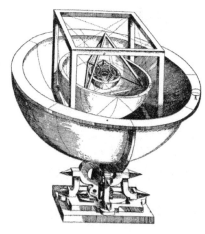

Kepler's planetary orbits in The Polyhedra using Platonic solids– note Saturn's cube

The Beast Aleister Crowley left a heritage of Thelema followers and one of them was the Brotherhood of Saturn. This magical order was similar to the other occult groups, whether it be New Age, Freemasonry or Thelema; they all revolve around the idea of mastery of occult knowledge (e.g. axioms like "As above, so below" which emphasize the duality aspects of man and world) in order to advance and evolve one's self in a series of steps and rituals.

The Brotherhood of Saturn incorporates 33 steps to achieve the full spectrum of enlightenment, similar to Scottish Rite of Freemasonry who also incorporates 33 degrees. The end of the path for a member of the Brotherhood of Saturn is self-deification, an important concept in Thelema and seen in the realm of music with musicians making themselves god-like (e.g. Kanye West = Yeezus, Jay-Z = Hova, Beyonce = Beysus, etc.).

Thus it can be said they are "circling the square." Masons are also constantly referring to "circling the square" and "squaring the circle."

For instance, this is why a "boxing" match is fought for "rounds" in the "ring" but it is actually a 4 sided square arena with corners.

http://www.bibliotecapleyades.net/sociopolitica/
atlantean_conspiracy/atlantean_conspiracy37.htm

Why is it called a boxing ring?

The name **ring** continued with the Jack Broughton rules in 1743, which specified a small circle in the centre of the fight area where the boxers met at the start of each round. The first **square ring** was introduced by the Pugilistic Society in 1838. That **ring** was specified as 24 feet (7.3 m) **square** and bound by two ropes.

TEXAS MESSES WITH SCHOOL HISTORY BOOKS!

FORGET ABOUT THAT THOMAS JEFFERSON GUY FOR STARTERS!

WE'RE CHANGING THE NAME DEMOCRACY! IT SOUNDS LIKE DEMOCRATS!

IT'S HIGH TIME WE LEARN ABOUT OUR CHRISTIAN LEADERS AND THE NRA!

OUR NEW NAME FOR THE USA IS CONSTITUTIONAL REPUBLIC!

© Original Artist
Reproduction rights obtainable from
www.CartoonStock.com

Oct 21, 2015 - McGraw-Hill **Education**, the publisher of the **textbook**, has since ... But it will **take** more than that to fix the way slavery is taught in **Texas** ... What those people, especially the **slave** owners, are doing is clear:

The page in a McGraw-Hill Education geography textbook that refers to Africans brought to American plantations as "workers," rather than slaves.
Credit Coby Burre

HOUSTON — *Coby Burren, 15, a freshman at a suburban high school south of here, was reading the textbook in his geography class last week when a map of the United States caught his attention. On Page 126, a caption in a section about immigration referred to Africans brought to American plantations between the 1500s and 1800s as "workers" rather than slaves.*

He reached for his cellphone and sent a photograph of the caption to his mother, Roni Dean-Burren, along with a text message: "we was real hard workers, wasn't we."

Their outrage over the textbook's handling of the nation's history of African-American slavery —

"The most common characteristic of all police states is intimidation by surveillance. Citizens know they are being watched and overheard.

Their mail is being examined. Their homes can be invaded."
~ Vance Packard

"We should create media outlets that help to educate our people and our children and not annihilate their minds."
~UNKNOWN

THIS IS THE NEW CHILDHOOD IN AMERICA:

1 in 3 is overweight
1 in 6 has learning disabilities
1 in 9 has asthma
1 in 10 has ADHD
1 in 12 has food allergies
1 in 20 has seizures
1 in 54 males have autism
1 in 88 has autism

50% (half) of all children have chronic illness or are overweight

This is the new normal in our country.

Are you concerned yet?!

Because if you're not, then you are not paying attention!!!

Mind Control Techniques

Mind Control Techniques are the most powerful self improvement tool that you can use to change your life.

Instantly control your own mind or the minds of others...

Mind Control Techniques are so powerful because they are a powerful combination of Hypnosis, NLP, Seduction and persuasion.

*What is Mind Control?

*Mind control is also known as brainwashing, re-education, coercive persuasion, thought control or thought reform. It outlines many key elements that need to be controlled: Behavior, Information, Thoughts and Emotions. If these four components can be controlled, then an individual's identity can be systematically manipulated and changed.

Media & Thought Control

All freedom will be in our hands, since the laws will abolish and will create only what is desirable for us. The majority have no idea what ends the press really serves.

We shall inflict fines without mercy on those who attack us. Among those who attack us will be groups ESTABLISHED BY US. They will only attack what we already need to alter.

NO NEWS WILL REACH THE PUBLIC WITHOUT OUR CONTROL. All news items are received by a few agencies (Associated Press, Reuters) in all parts of the world.

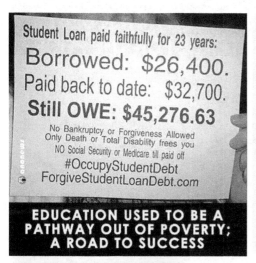

In his 1996 book Mass Control Jim Keith meticulously lays out the factual and documented ground work for mass mind control through network television and exposes now declassified CIA and Nazi mind control operations such as Project Monarch and Project Paperclip. The book also exposes the "culture creation" industry from the minds of the social engineers themselves, from Manchurian candidates and eugenics to secret satanic cults.

A must read for anyone interested in the history of social engineering from the mouths of the elite.

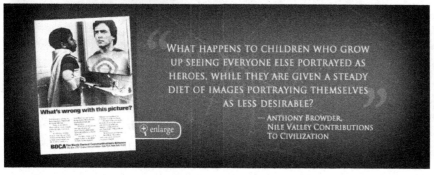

"The whole educational and professional training system is a very elaborate filter, which just weeds out people who are too independent, and who think for themselves, and who don't know how to be submissive, and so on -- because they're dysfunctional to the institutions."
- Noam Chomsky

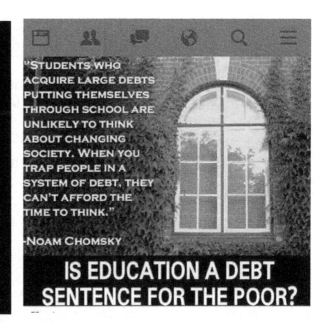

"STUDENTS WHO ACQUIRE LARGE DEBTS PUTTING THEMSELVES THROUGH SCHOOL ARE UNLIKELY TO THINK ABOUT CHANGING SOCIETY. WHEN YOU TRAP PEOPLE IN A SYSTEM OF DEBT, THEY CAN'T AFFORD THE TIME TO THINK."

-NOAM CHOMSKY

IS EDUCATION A DEBT SENTENCE FOR THE POOR?

GMAIL LOGO MASONIC APRON

GMAIL LOGO

Royal Arch Apron

Royal Arch Masonry is the 7 degree for master masons who chose to join (or work in masonspeak) the York Rite. Mason must first complete these four level before proceeding to the next set of York Rite degrees.

 =

 =

Even before Snowden's allegations that the NSA intercepted data between data centers, Google has frequently been accused of spying for the Illuminati. Some researchers have even pointed out the possibility that the logo for Google's browsing software, Chrome features the numbers 666.

Chronology of Education
With Quotable Quotes

Dennis Laurence Cuddy, Ph.D.

• He advised how he had been a high degree mason in the Scottish Rite of Freemasonry, and had been invited by Adam Weishaupt to Europe, where he had been given a revised copy of Weishaupt's conspiracy. However, although he pretended to go along with it, Professor Robison did not agree with it and therefore published his informationed book included details of the Bavarian governments investigations into the illuminati and the French Revolution.

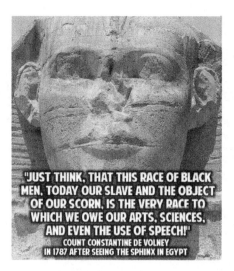

"JUST THINK, THAT THIS RACE OF BLACK MEN, TODAY OUR SLAVE AND THE OBJECT OF OUR SCORN, IS THE VERY RACE TO WHICH WE OWE OUR ARTS, SCIENCES, AND EVEN THE USE OF SPEECH!"
COUNT CONSTANTINE DE VOLNEY IN 1787 AFTER SEEING THE SPHINX IN EGYPT

THE RUINS OF EMPIRES
BY C.F. VOLNEY

From first-hand observations and study, Volney demonstrates that early Nile Valley Africans provided a basis for the civilization of his time.

Dr. John Henrik Clarke
{A Great Mighty Walk}

To control a people you must first control what they think about themselves and how they regard their history and culture. And when your conqueror makes you ashamed of your culture and your history, he needs no prison walls and no chains to hold you.

Psi E's Lamp Club pledging Omega Psi Phi, 1949.

We have compiled a list of 28 rare pictures of what pledging a Black Greek fraternity/ sorority looked like back in the day. Please share this gallery with as many people as you can on social media. We feel that these pictures honor NPHC history and give you a good look into the past. Enjoy!

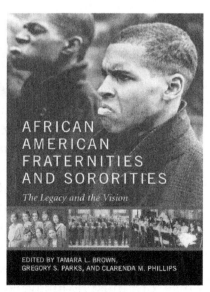

AFRICAN AMERICAN FRATERNITIES AND SORORITIES
The Legacy and the Vision

EDITED BY TAMARA L. BROWN, GREGORY S. PARKS, AND CLARENDA M. PHILLIPS

http://www.watchtheyard.com/uncategorized/28-rare-pictures-pledging-black-greek-org-looked-like-back-day/

We must overstand that greek mythology is just that... a myth!

VERSUS ← GOTO VS INDEX
HISTORY VS OURSTORY SERIES

MENTOR AND TELEMACHUS

JEGNA VS. MENTOR
THE STORY OF MENTOR AND TELEMACHUS
BY M'BWEBE AJA ISHANGI

http://daghettotymz.com/current/mentor-jegna/mentor-jegna.html

The word 'Mentor' is defined as an *"adviser, guide, guru, counselor, consultant; confidant."* Look at the last word in the definition... 'confidant'.
Now let's look that definition up: *"a person with whom one shares a secret or private matter, trusting them not to repeat it to others."* Now let's look at the history of the word 'Mentor' again.

In Greek *myth*ology, Mentor was the son of Alcumus and, in his old age, a friend of Odysseus aka Ulysses. When Odysseus left for the Trojan War he placed Mentor in charge of his son, Telemachus, and of his palace. Mentor, however, apparently had other plans that went beyond the mere development of Telemachus' cognitive skills—Mentor, like many a societal norm of greece, was a homosexual who preyed on young boyz to be used in their queer escapades. Mentor carefully cultivated a sexual relationship with Telemachus.

Many are not aware that greece was a society where homosexuality was the norm. Men took great pride in feelin' the greatest love could only be experienced between two men—and women were only used for procreative purposes. The excuses given for this imbalanced, yet societal acceptance of sexual misconduct, was often explained as a man literally injecting male principles into the child through his buttocks—and we can see figuratively the sick pleasure a predator has in "having his way" with a child never thinking of the natural *dis*pleasure and residual damage done to said child.

This is the source of the modern use of the word mentor: a trusted friend, counselor or teacher; usually a more experienced person. Some professionz have "*mentor*ing programz" in which newcomerz are paired with more experienced people in order to obtain examples and advice. Schoolz also have *mentor*ing programz for new students who are having difficulties. Even apprentices often refer to superior's and even Elder's as their *mentor*. This word must be analyzed, historically processed, and frankly, removed from Afrikan vocabulary.

http://daghettotymz.com/current/mentor-jegna/mentor-jegna.html

This is key for when we use this word, we are unknowingly honoring and condoning the acts of a predator, something that's been widely accepted even in the perceived "holiness" of the Roman Catholic Church.

The history of the hedz who created the english language have a completely different value system than us. That's why it's important we get in the practice of using the right terminology.

Author of 'African Psychology', Dr. Wade Nobles introduced a more suitable word when referring to those who've been an influence. The word is **Jegna** (Jenoch, plural form) are those special people who have

1) been tested in struggle or battle
2) someone who demonstrates fearlessness
3) one who has the courage to protect their people, culture and way of life
4) shown diligence and dedication to our people
5) produced an exceptionally high quality of work, and
6) dedicated themselves to the protection, defense, nurturance and development of our young by advancing our people, place and culture.
"Jegna", yeah, that's more appropriate...

I highly recommend reading 'Homosexuality and the Effeminization of Afrikan Males', by Mwalimu Baruti

Greek men were not shy in showing their sexual desire for intimacy with other males. If you ever wondered why when looking at greek art, you rarely see women, it's because they were not the preference of greek men; they were only used for the procreation. In fact, a man's status was based on how many young male loverz he had, not women!

Men with their boyfriends — ca. 540 BCE, from Vulci, Italy. British Museum, London.
Attic black-figure amphora by the Painter of Berlin
Men shown giving gifts, enticing, and making love to youths. The man without a partner pleasures himself.
http://www.gay-art-history.org/gay-history/gay-art/greek-love-homosexual-art/homosexual-greek-pelike-sex.html

[O]ne of the thingz the NAACP is most notably known for is initiating the Anti-Lynch Bill during the 1910s, where they called for the government to pass a bill prohibiting the lynching of American-Afrikanz. What many don't know is the bill did not pass congress until 1959, about 50 yearz later! What's even more interesting were conditionz YT required from the NAACP. The U.S. government, in exchange for such a bill, would oblige only if the NAACP reported "Black Intelligence" to them.

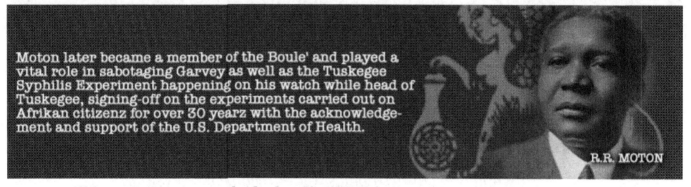

The Boule' was utilized effectively to limit the power and influence of Marcus Garvey. A meeting of all the prominent Black newspaper families and editorz from The Amsterdam News, The Chicago Defender, The Pittsburgh Courier, The Baltimore and Washington Afro-American Newspaper took place in Washington, D.C. where Masonic orderz were given to either not discuss Garvey or deem him persona non grata, so that no one would follow him and his Back to Africa Movement.

MARCUS GARVEY

BLACKS UNDER THE SPELL...

By the Greek definition, the word, "Boule'" was the lower house of the greek parliament or Adviserz to the king. There is also a French version of the word, which defines a conclave or coming together. Allegedly, this is the version sororities like Alpha Kappa Alpha who call their convention the Boule'. Using the Greek definition these career and socially successful Blacks are under the control of the larger <u>Masonic</u> society of secrets that round up America's doctorz, lawyerz, real estate ownerz, and celebrities commandeering the agenda of the black masses who look to these successful Blacks for influence and direction. Over the yearz and many discussionz about the Boule', people have asked if the word "Boule'" meanz "Adviser", one would think they're actually giving advice instead of taking direction. Well, we all know english is a bastard language where some even say it's the language of confusion. The word "Adviser" is also spelled, "Advisor" and when you look up the definition, we find, *"the spellings adviser and advisor are both correct. Adviser is the more common spelling in North America; advisor is more common in Britain. In both places, however, the adjectival form is advisory. In the U.S., adviser may be seen as less formal, while advisor often suggests an official position."* — Websters Dictionary **http:// daghettotymz.com/rkyvz/articles/bouleseries/boule1-3roster/boule4/boulept4.html**

Moton later became a member of the Boule' and played a vital role in sabotaging Garvey as well as the Tuskegee Syphilis Experiment happening on his watch while head of Tuskegee, signing-off on the experiments carried out on Afrikan citizenz for over 30 yearz with the acknowledgement and support of the U.S. Department of Health.

R.R. MOTON

It was well known that Garvey had a lot of respect for Washington and Tuskegee, so once Washington passed, the government used that to their advantage when Moton took over the school.

Moton, now a mole "Gay" Edgar Hoover would've had wet dreamz about, started attending Garvey's meetingz and would brief the government on the detailz. His reward? He got the 1st Black Veteranz hospital at Tuskeegee; the infamous place where the Syphilis Experiments were conducted, all on Moton's watch. Although history has been kind to Moton because of this government conspiracy, he and memberz of the staff at Tuskegee knew what was going on.

Researcher Steve Cokely (1952-2012) is the ultimate source of the information on the Boule. You can find his <u>lectures on YouTube</u>. His persistent theme is that the Jewish financial elite had put a phoney black leadership class in a position of influence and wealth.

Their role is to protect their sponsors and perpetuate their hegemony. Genuine leaders like MLK and Malcolm X, who forget their "place," are eliminated. Ironically, when Steve was hospitalized in 2012 he <u>expressed fears that they would kill him in the hospital.</u> This appears to have taken place. He was married and had three children.

- See more at: <u>http://henrymakow.com/2016/04/Boule-Black-Elite-Betrayed-their-Brothers%20.html#sthash.nxsyWyVO.dpuf</u>

I was forwarded a quote that's allegedly taken directly from the Phi Beta Sigma history book -- of which Moton was also a member -- <u>'Our cause speeds on: An informal history of the Phi Beta Sigma fraternity'</u>,
by W. Sherman Savage:

"Many Americans, in and out of the military, felt that the "social equality" of the contacts of the Negro soldiers and French individuals and families would ruin the black Americans for their place in American society... Brother R.R. Moton was sent over on one of his special missions to prepare the black troops so that they might return to life in America properly."

In other wordz, Moton's job was to keep these Afrikanz in check, for returning *"to life in America properly"* meant them still being treated as subhuman. It should not surprise you that a Black man would agree to do such a job when you realize this is the nature of the Boule' man, one who wishes, as said on page 28 of the Boule's history book, *"create an organization which would partake in the tenants* (basis, or root) *of Skull & Bones at Yale."*

The Boule – Skull and Bones Society

http://daghettotymz.com/current/mentor-jegna/mentor-jegna.html

Henry McKee Minton
1871-1946

FOUNDER OF THE **BLACK** *BOULE*

Grand Sire Archon Harris noted this historic visit marked the Boule' had taken a significant step toward achieving its vision of being *"the preeminent fraternity for African American men of achievement"* by becoming *"better informed about, and taking appropriate action on, major public policy issues of concern to the community, and by supporting or providing social action programs that benefit disadvantaged African Americans"* -- a major part of Harris' alleged focus on the importance of public policy in shaping the quality of life for American-Afrikanz. *"This meeting with White House officials speaks to the wisdom of our Fraternity's vision and its strategic plan,"* he noted.
(from http://www.sigmapiphi.org/home/boul-leadership-meetsh-white-house

In 1904, the first African -American Greek Secret Society was formed in Philadelphia, by Dr. Henry Minton and five of his colleagues. The Boule, (an acronym for Sigma Pi Phi) and pronounced "boo-lay"), was formed to bring together a select group of educated Black men and women.

Fashioned after Yale's Skull and Bones, the Boule historically takes pride in having provided leadership and service to Black Americans during the Great Depression, World Wars I and II, and the Civil Rights Movement. What could the Boule offer America's Blacks in the early 20th century? Joining the exclusive secret society offered advancement and perks to select Blacks in return for loyalty to its objectives.

W.E.B. Dubois
http://secret--societies.blogspot.com/2013/12/the-boule-skull-and-bones-society.html

W.E.B. Dubois, founding member of the NYC chapter of the Boule said, "The Boule was created to keep the black professional away from Marcus Garvey". The remaking of the House Negro was necessary to institute a group of Blacks who had a vested interest in protecting the Elite White System. It was about selling out brothers and sisters for power and money. The majority of Black lawyers, doctors, engineers and accountants were members of this secret club.

The Boule recruits top Blacks in American Society into its ranks. Today, 5000+ Archons, (male Boule members) and their wives, (Archousais), with 112 chapters, make up the wealthiest group of Black men and women on the planet. "Archon" means "demon" – the kind that like to keep hidden.

Now! If Henry Minton, who was black, wanted to create a black secret society based on these beliefs and customs, what type of devil is he? If you were to look on page 38 of the Boule's history book, it also says,

"In the building of the organizations plan, reliance was placed upon Greek history and tradition. The reasons of this action are not difficult to discover, for it is well known that the study of Greek civilization was basically an acquaintance with western civilization, although Greek culture had relationships with the culture of the orient."

http://secret--societies.blogspot.com/2013/12/the-boule-skull-and-bones-society.html

My next incision will go a level deeper. I will perform open heart surgery and split open the aorta of these so-called black Greeks; I will define the meaning of the Boule's logo — the Sphinx; their colors; and more of their connection with masonry. Let's start with their logo.

According to the Greeks, this beast was a guardian of the city of Thebes. She sat on a cliff on the only path leading to the city. Anyone that wanted to enter Thebes had to first confront the sphinx. The sphinx would ask one simple riddle and if you didn't know the answer, she would devour you, tearing you to pieces. The king, Creon, was upset that many people were unable to enter his city. He consulted a homosexual named Oedipus (NOTE: homosexuality was a norm for the Grecian culture).

The king offered his crown and his daughter if he could kill the sphinx. So he bounced to where she was and she asked him the riddle, "What has one voice, and goes on four feet on two feet and on three, but the more feet it goes on the weaker it be?" Oedipus responded, "Man — who crawls on all fours as a baby, then walks on two as an adult, and walks with a cane in old age." After answering the riddle correctly, the sphinx committed suicide by jumping off the cliff and Oedipus was claimed king of Thebes for outsmarting the beast.

They could never understand what Her-Em-Akhet means. The statue faced the east because our ancestors knew the pineal gland is the seat of the Afrikan soul and when the sun rises in the east, it hits the forehead (pineal gland), suppressing the beastly nature of man. As author Tony Browder puts it,

"Symbolically, the body represents the animal nature which exists in woman, and the lion exemplifies the royalty and power of the divine spirit that exists in its lower physical form. The head of a man symbolizes the intelligence of the mind which must be cultivated in order to elevate the consciousness into a higher spiritual state so that it may become divine. Metaphorically speaking, it is the suppression of the lower animal nature and the refinement of the thought process that leads to the spiritual evolution of man. Spiritually speaking, it is only by conquering the "beast" within that one is capable of truly knowing God."

http://secret--societies.blogspot.com/2013/12/the-boule-skull-and-bones-society.html

"When we look at the Boule' closely, we find a confusion of values. Black men who felt that their advancement was edged upon a positive relationship with wealthy and influential white peop¹ᵉ

In 1953, the same year the **CIA/MK ULTRA** program was formed, **Dick (Richard Claxton) Gregory** left college to join or was drafted into the **U.S. Army**, where his commanding officer (Ft. Hood, Texas, Ft Lee, Virginia or Ft. Smith)[1] designated and assigned him as a black "comedian" to host and perform comedy routines in military shows. [2] That's interesting that the U.S. Military will make you a "**comedian**", too.

In 1953, **Hugh Hefner** setup **Playboy**, which was eventually revealed to be banked by the **CIA**.[3] Sometime before 1961, **Dick Gregory** formed some type of special personal relationship with **Hefner (Mythological PUCK)**. In 1961, **Hefner** put **Gregory** on the payroll of his **Chicago Playboy Club** that opened the door to his HollyWeird career. It is more accurate to say that the "Gates of Hell" had opened upon him.

In order to join **Hefner's** elite secret satanic circle at that high **CIA** level of secrecy, **Gregory** had to have been initiated by a blood sacrifice (late 2 month old, Richard Claxton Gregory, Jr.?) into a subservient lower ranking black Luciferian group like the Prince Hall Freemasons or one of the Greek Hellenized societies.

Gregory is openly known to be a **Hellenized** Negro, an **Alpha Phi Alpha** (secret Boule) man. **Gregory's X** signal not only represents Skull & Bones and the Brotherhood of Death, it is a sign of the **Royal DRAGON** race of Old England. [4]

"The whole world is lying in the power of the wicked one."

(1John 5:19)

http://daghettotymz.com/current/heremakhetsphinx/heremakhetsphinx.html#riddle

For the record, as far as Dick Gregory's good friend **Bill Cosby** is concerned, both are absolutely blood oath obedient to the secret elite **Global Satanic Cabal**, CIA and Hugh Hefner as no more than their mere black mind control attendants and recruiters. Dick Gregory is way out on the limb and on the bandwagon of the changing of the guard of America's **Black Satanic Cabal**; and the ILLUMINATI movie, Selma. His well wishes to the new order, Welcome and thank you Oprah!

Aldous Huxley, MK ULTRA, the Dionysian Cult & Black Folk

Some of the symbols **Dick Gregory** hides behind strongly suggest that he is also a blood oath secret **Prince Hall**, **York Rite** or **Scottish Rite 33 degree Master Mason**. An **Official MASONIC Portrait** of Norman Vincent Peal 'Cutting' of two secret **Masonic** signal signs visible Crossed Arms = 'Skull & Crossbones and "Hidden Hand."** Both Peale and Gregory- **'Blue Tie for 'Blue Lodge'**[5] In 1962, **Hefner** wrote the introduction to **Gregory's** book, **From the Back of the Bus.**[6]

Operation Mind Control 9 "I know of no safe depository of the ultimate powers of society but the people themselves, and if we think them not enlightened enough to exercise their control with a wholesome discretion, the remedy is not to take it from them, but to inform their discretion by education."

    -- Thomas Jefferson

1% CONTROL THE WORLD

4% ARE SELLOUT PUPPETS

90% ARE ASLEEP

5% KNOW AND ARE TRYING TO WAKE UP THE 90%

THE 1% DON'T WANT THE 5% WAKING UP THE 90%

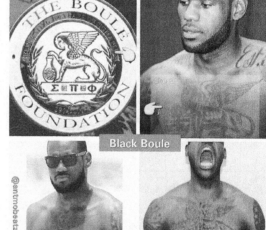

Black Boule

Griffins are a symbol of the sun, wisdom, vengeance, strength, and salvation ... (thanasis.com)

Griffin Symbolism

A very protective and vigilant Spirit Guide, the Griffin (also spelled gryphon or griffon) is a master of astral workings and a guardian of the Soul and Life-essence. It appears as a creature with the head & wings of an eagle and the body of a lion.

The griffin is a mythical creature with the face, beak, talons and wings of an eagle and the body of a lion. At times, it is portrayed with a long snake-like tail. In some traditions, only the female has wings. Its nests are made of gold and its eggs resemble agates. Pliny believed griffins came from Northern Russia; Aeschylus thought they originated in Ethiopia; and Bullfinch wrote that their native country was India. In its body, the griffin is blessed with the speed, flight, and penetrating vision of the eagle and the strength, courage, and majesty of the lion.

In symbolism, the griffin combines the symbolic qualities of both the lion and the eagle. It is the king of birds and lord of the air united with the king of beasts and lord of the earth.

But to who does the Boule really serve? The Satanic (mostly white) global elite! As long as the Black member conforms to the rules, the riches will be in abundance; if not, down comes the hatchet. Blackmail is part of the deal. This Masonic secret society has a pyramid style like all the rest. The lower ranks are kept from knowing what the upper ranks are doing. The early 20th century was a period of reconstruction.

Skull and Bones Society Members | Because Geronimo isn't a fossilized arrowhead or a muddy moccasin ... | Pinterest | Geronimo, Skull And Bones and .

George W. Bush's grandfather, Prescott, and fellow Bonesmen reportedly robbed Geronimo's grave and stole the Apache chief's skull and some bones and other personal relics.

"Black public outcry against lynching, bordering on what some authorities considered to be "unpatriotic" expression in a time of war, was a domestic "nuisance" which might well hinder prosecution of U.S. war aims overseas. Though generally supportive of the use of black troops to further the defined interests of the country abroad, the AfroAmerican press was nevertheless quite given to providing front-page coverage to these almost daily atrocities committed against black Americans.

With support from what appears to have been only a handful of colleagues in the Military Intelligence Branch, [Joel E.] Springarn [a Jewish U.S. Military Intelligence Officer (Negro Subversion Division) who doubled as head of the Jewish founded and led NAACP understood full well that any unilateral attempt to suppress publication of such stories, while at the same time allowing lynch mobs of white Americans to continue a favored pastime, would, at the very least, lead to further disaffection within the Afro-American national community. Consequently,

Major Springarn, aided by Emmett J. Scott, evolved a plan to appease the most prominent and powerful molders and shapers of "black public opinion." On 5 June, Scott and Springarn drafted 'a letter to George Creel, chairman of the federal Committee on Public Information, requesting that the Committee sponsor, "at an early date," a conference of approximately twenty Afro-American editors and about "a dozen or so other influential leaders among the Negro people....

" That three-day conference was convened in Washington, D.C. on 19 June. The thirty-one persons in attendance included John H. Murphy of the Baltimore Afro-American; Robert L. Vann, Pittsburgh Courier; Fred R. Moore, New York Age; Benjamin J. Davis, Atlanta Independent; Robert R. Moton of Tuskegee Institute; Archibald H. Grimke, president of the Washington branch NAACP; P. B. S. Pinchback, former governor of Louisiana; Kelly Miller, Howard University dean; Robert S. Abbott of the Chicago Defender; and W. E. B. DuBois. When the conference opened Wednesday morning, 19 June, the overall atmosphere seemed calculated to play upon the bourgeois sensibilities of black leaders in attendance. "To enliven the occasion for the visitors," reported the New York Evening Post.

Dick Gregory is just as dual natured **(Satanic Principle)** as his friend, **Bill Cosby**. Like his friend, there are always by his own admission two sides to **Dick Gregory**, (Light vs. Dark) Good and diabolical **EVIL** that transcend the moral boundaries of original men. These kind of shadow people give me the creeps and nightmares.

https://mindcontrolblackassassins.com/2015/01/27/bill-cosby-part-iv-selma-the-illuminati-movie-rise-of-the-black-lesbianic-satanic-cabal-dick-gregory-huey-p-newton/

Greek art depicting anal sex

Whether it is a woman inserting her finger up there or a man inserting his penis, many men feel violated, especially by the latter because it involves allowing someone else to experience pleasure and release inside of your body. Even women feel this way about anal sex despite being accustomed to vaginal penetration. There is just something about anal penetration that is so intimate and visceral it makes one feel like a completely helpless child.

WHY THIS IS RELEVANT

To want to segregate ourselves in an already segregated world is insane! With all these thousandz of successful men who are in the Boule', fraternities or even Masonry, or any other part of these elite social clubz, they have yet to present a black agenda, nor at the very least, formidable Black-owned corporationz. Where are our Black businesses? They too busy licking boots of our collective oppressor!

All of this stemz from Afrikanz being stripped of the knowledge of our past which became lost and now distorted through the many invasionz in the Nile Valley. Instead of realizing the tenacious power we possess collectively, having no cultural base has left us with little to any hope when it comes to self-reliance.

All this is maintained systematically using the 10 Areas of People Activity (Economics, Education, Entertainment, Labor, Law, Politics, Sex, Religion, War, and Health).

Instead of dealing with the real perpetrator/culprit, we fight ourselves leaving YT to enjoy the fruits of our ignorance. When will we wake up and realize if you're not trying to be Afrikan, you're emulating someone else?!

Mass Mind Control

The June-July, 1989 issue of the West German scientist publication, Raum & Zeit *carried an article by Dr. W. Volkrodt, titled: "Can Human Beings Be Manipulated By ELF Waves." The article stated:*

The technical principal of receivers for electromagnetic waves is fully analogous with biological information and communications systems. If several thousand of the hundreds of billions of nerve cells in our brain resonate with man-made centimetre waves, the carrier frequency has to be suppressed when the signal is passed on to the synapses.

To overcome cell membranes, living organisms use electrochemical processes involving sodium and potassium ions. This suppresses the carrier frequency in the high-frequency range just as the demodulation circuit does in man-made receivers. What remains is the signal impressed on the carrier frequency, e.g. in the low frequency ELF range. This is also the frequency range at which our own nervous system normally works.

Using these frequencies, the nerve fibres convey pain sensations, the feeling of hungry, tiredness, nausea, and signals on the sense of balance to points in the brain which invoke these stages in a awake consciousness.

If interference signals are superimposed on the natural signals generated by the body, e.g. by using artificially created centimetre waves as a carrier, the brain could be presented with simulated states that we consciously perceive, but which do not appear as reality.

A state of disturbed sense of balance, which seems to us to be real, is enough to stop people from being able to run or make them feel dizzy even when they are lying down.

In a 'psychotronic war' using microwaves modulated using ELF waves, it would no longer be necessary to kill whole armies by inducing cardiac or respiratory irregular signals. The enemy can simply be incapacitated by disturbing their states of balance or confusing the ability to think logically. ...The manipulation of human beings, by means of ELF waves is relatively easy to perform.

Government authorities and the military would have to overcome no insurmountable difficulties to modulate carrier frequencies with ELF signals in existing centimetre radio-relay links. ...an army of occupation could then manipulate a nation's ability to make decisions in confusing political situations or disable undesirable activities. ELF-modulated microwave transmitters employed in this way could also serve to obviate the use of force (non-lethal weapons).

An entire nation can be gradually subjugated psychically by the means of long-term radiation using ELF-modulated centimetre waves. ...Once any kind of desire to defend or capacity to resist has been dispelled, political activities by negotiation are sufficient to incorporate into one's power a nation subjugated in this way.

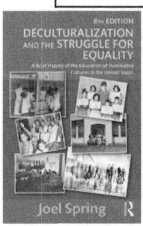  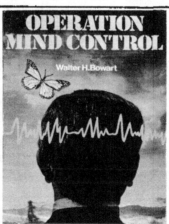 

The most virulent viruses today are composed of information. In this information-driven age, the easiest way to manipulate the culture is through the media. A hip and caustically humorous McLuhan for the '90s, culture watcher Douglas Rushkoff now offers a fascinating expose of media manipulation in today's age of instant information.

David, Young Air Force Sergeant: He Was One Of The Victims.

"Ever since I got out of the service I haven't been able to give a day-by-day account of what happened to me during those four years. The scary thing is that I still have a horrible fear of talking. I have a tendency to speed up my speech when I'm being pressed on something; and I get very tense when anyone asks me about my service duties.

"Something has happened to my mind. . ."

"The phones are smarter but we are dumber."
~Douglas Rushkoff

4TH DEGREE

E-Pluribus Unum

(one out of many)

entertainment

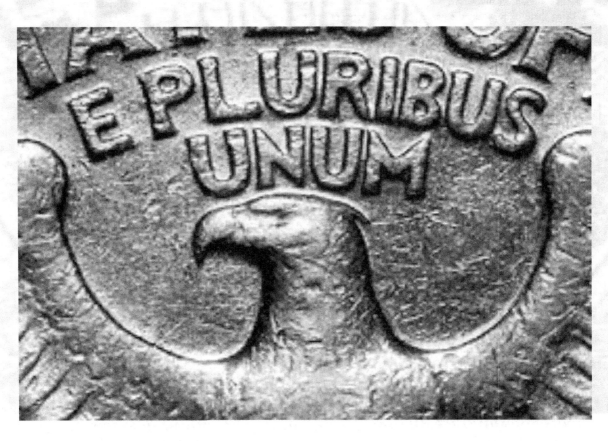

E- Pluribus Unum (one out of many)

*A motto of the United States; Latin for "Out of many, one." It refers to the Union formed by the separate states. **E pluribus unum** was adopted as a national motto in 1776 and is now found on the Great Seal of the United States and on United States currency.*

A motto of the United States; Latin for "Out of many, one." It refers to the Union formed by the separate states. **E pluribus unum** was adopted as a national motto in 1776 and is now found on the Great Seal of the United States and on United States currency.

"The phones are smarter but we are dumber."
~Douglas Rushkoff

"The media's the most powerful entity on earth. They have the power to make the innocent guilty and to make the guilty innocent, and that's power. Because they control the minds of the masses."

~Malcolm X

http://www.bibliotecapleyades.net/ciencia/code_matrix/
codematrix101-125.htm

Again, there is no limit to how many people will join *the Illuminati Circus* if they are given the opportunity.

As I said before once you are in "the know" you will see it everywhere. Imagine, these two artist both released CD's related to the Circus, the home of the Animist. One is called Womanizer, clearly a term that should not be respected and yet thousands of women bought the CD upon its release.

T-Pain whose name is enough explanation shows the "33" on his cover and of course the Skull.

All this is looked over by the fan who just wants to hear the tunes. Pan and his flute win again. All this is for a reason. Stay Alert Since this Matrix is based on Colors, Sounds, Shapes, and Numbers you have an opportunity to "view" the program.

Thousands if not millions of Americans faced heavy levels of mind control in the 80's and 90's just by leaving their T.V. on after the last show and falling asleep for a good 3 hours of low vibration frequency which was the prolonged sound you would hear before the station went off the air. It is of value to also point out that these Entities are not ignorant, doomed possibly, but not ignorant.

They have been here for Eons and carry the wisdom of Eons and many in exchange for that wisdom have sold their very souls.

http://www.bibliotecapleyades.net/ciencia/code_matrix/
codematrix101-125.htm

Rupert Murdoch's News Corporation is a behemoth: it is the largest media company in the world by market capitalization ($38 billion). For most people, the conservative news channel Fox comes foremost to mind when asked what they think of Murdoch's media empire – but the company's holding is far larger: it includes Asia's Star TV Network, the National Geographic Channel and even the iconic TV Guide network.

Don't watch TV? Even if you prefer to browse the Internet, most likely you've visited News Corp's property, which include Hulu (owned in partnership with GE through its subsidiary NBC Universal) and the social networking giant MySpace.

Dow Jones & Company, Inc.
Fox Television Stations
The New York Post
Fox Searchlight Pictures
Beliefnet
Fox Business Network
Fox Kids Europe
Fox News Channel
Fox Sports Net
Fox Television Network
FX
My Network TV
MySpace
News Limited News
Phoenix InfoNews Channel
Phoenix Movies Channel
Sky PerfecTV
Speed Channel
STAR TV India
STAR TV Taiwan
STAR World
Times Higher Education Supplement Magazine
Times Literary Supplement Magazine
Times of London
20th Century Fox Home Entertainment
20th Century Fox International
20th Century Fox Studios
20th Century Fox Television
BSkyB
DIRECTV
The Wall Street Journal
Fox Broadcasting Company
Fox Interactive Media
FOXTEL
HarperCollins Publishers
The National Geographic Channel
National Rugby League
News Interactive
News Outdoor
Radio Veronica
ReganBooks
Sky Italia
Sky Radio Denmark
Sky Radio Germany
Sky Radio Netherlands
STAR
Zondervan

Floor of the house

The mosaic pavement of the lodge is discussed in the lecture of the first degree. This is commonly described as the checkered carpet which covers the floor of the lodge. The lecture says that the mosaic pavement "is a representation of the ground floor of King Solomon's Temple" and is "emblematic of human life, checkered with good and evil."

http://freemasoninformation.com/2009/03/the-checkered-flooring/

In the account of King Solomon's Temple in the Bible, the ground floor is said to be made of pine or fir, depending on which translation of the Bible that you read (1 Ki 6:15). It is hard to imagine that pine or fir flooring would be particularly mosaic in nature. However, it can be agreed that the mosaic pavement represents the ground floor of King Solomon's Temple in the Entered Apprentice degree because that ceremony symbolically takes place in that location.

 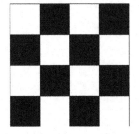 

Symbolism really does represent duality and change in consciousness which is monarch mind control. And Aleister Crowley used the checkerboard symbolism for human/animal sacrifice rituals. Just like any other illuminati symbolism has a meaning like the all seeing eye isn't just an eye but its Checkboards is one eye only representing the eye of Horus which is Satan. **http://exposingthematrix.blogspot.com/2012/03/masonic-checkerboardduality-symbolism.html**

While these facts may not be particularly intriguing, the symbolism of the checkered carpeting presents some interesting concepts.

Mackey's Encyclopedia of Freemasonry discusses the symbol of the the mosaic pavement.

"The mosaic pavement in an old symbol of the Order. It is met with in the earliest rituals of the last century. It is classed among the ornaments of the lodge along with the indented tassel and the blazing star. Its party-colored stones of black and white have been readily and appropriately interpreted as symbols of the evil and good of human life."

So from this information, it can be understood that the concept of duality has played a part in Masonic symbolism since the early days of the fraternity. While duality is not often discussed in the ritual of the Blue Lodge, the Scottish Rite mentions this concept numerous times. The Rite makes the ideas of dualism, or opposition, in the universe an important part of its theme. Indeed, the ideas of the Kabbalah and the Alchemists are used in the Scottish Rite to discuss this concept in several of the degrees. 2

The lecture pertaining to the 15th Degree, Knight of the East and West, discusses the idea of duality or good and evil as a conflict. Pike writes "God is great, and good, and wise. Evil and pain and sorrow are temporary, and for wise and beneficent purposes... Ultimately, Good will prevail, and Evil be overthrown."3

Masonic Checkerboard/ Duality Symbolism

The Masonic Checkerboard is one of the most important symbols to the Illuminati, for it is used in ritualistic ceremonies. This is used because black and white is a symbol for duality, or the base of consciousness. Base consciousness is important, because it is where all other states of mind arise. Personally, I like to think that checkerboards are also symbols for the celebrities being pawns.

Duality patterns, such as checkerboards, stripes or zebras, are also commonly used as triggers for mind control slaves in order to reach specific alters. I didn't add too much stripes symbolism-wise in this post because I was overwhelmed with checkerboards alone.

Michael Jackson - The Illuminati like to blueprint their plans in plain site before they follow through, and this is a perfect example. Michael is in red, which is symbolism for sacrifice, while standing over the Masonic checkerboard.

explains the events leading up to the Superbowl and the ritual that took place before Whitney Houston's death

Whitney Houston and Michael Jackson

Whitney Houston

Nicki Minaj, with the title A Star is Born. Right over the checkerboard.

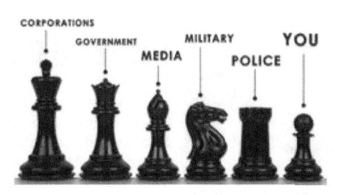

WE'RE ALL BEING PLAYED.

107

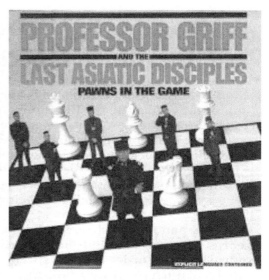

Ephesians 6:10-12, "Finally, my brethren, be strong in the Lord, and in the power of his might. Put on the whole armour of God, that ye may be able to stand against the wiles of the devil. For we wrestle not against flesh and blood, but against principalities, against powers, <u>against the rulers of the darkness of this world</u>, against spiritual wickedness in high places."

Interestingly, Nebuchadnezzar used an image (Daniel 3:5-7) and demanded worship **at the sound of the music**. That's very interesting. Everyone was told to bow to the 90 x 9 foot golden obelisk (which symbolizes an erect male penis) when they heard the music (Daniel 3:5). Why did king Nebuchadnezzar tell the people from all nations to worship the image instead of him directly? It's because the image projected the man. That's very important to understand. The Great Pyramid and the All-Seeing Eye are iconic images used to represent the coming Antichrist and his kingdom, called the New World Order. Whereas there are 7,000 languages upon the earth, images and symbols transcend all languages, being understood by everyone, regardless of the native language they speak. As you can see, images therefore, can be very powerful.

The Word Became flesh John 1:14

13 children born not of blood, nor of the will of the flesh, nor of the will of man, but born of God. 14 The Word became flesh and made His dwelling among us. We have seen His glory, the glory of the one and only Son from the Father, full of grace and truth.

"The Illuminati refers to a tightly organized network of family dynasties representing Anglo American and European aristocracy and Jewish finance joined by intermarriage, belief in the occult, and hatred of Christianity. Freemasonry is their instrument. They care nothing for their non-Illuminati brethren, Jewish or not. They will destroy billions as they create a neo feudal world characterized by the superrich, their support staff, soldiers and serfs."

"Masonic lodges are established all over the world to help us achieve our independence. Those pigs, the non-Jewish Masons, will never understand the final objects of Masonry."

Theodor Herzel
1897 Switzerland

Predicted 9/11 weeks before it happened on his radio show.

"Whatever is gonna happen that they are gonna blame on Osama Bin Laden, don't you even believe it."
William Cooper JUNE 2001

"I didn't make these predictions because I'm some kind of psychic...as a member of the Intelligence Briefing team on the staff of the commander- in-chief of the United States Pacific Fleet, I saw a plan called Majesty 12 which contained an operation called Operation Majority. And that plan outlined all of these things that were to happen from that time into the future, and all I've done is research"
"Read everything, listen to everybody, don't trust anything unless you can prove it with your own research"- William Cooper

Audience member: "Why haven't you been assassinated?"
Bill: "If they were to kill me right now, what would you think?"
Bill Cooper (May 6, 1943 – November 5, 2001)
R.I.P.

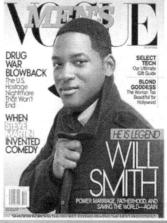

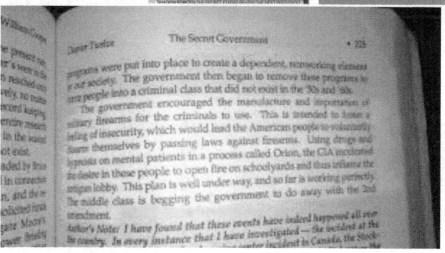

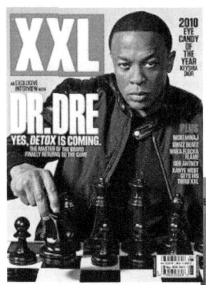

Dr. Dre, a known handler, playing chess. He's also moving a pawn. This symbolizes the playing of his many slaves, such as Eminem, 50 Cent, etc.

Dr. Dre 666 Commercial

Singer Lauryn Hill dared to speak out against the Illuminati in the music industry.

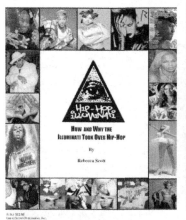

A court has ordered she must undergo counselling because of her "conspiracy theories".

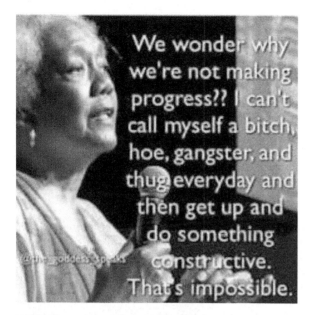

We wonder why we're not making progress?? I can't call myself a bitch, hoe, gangster, and thug everyday and then get up and do something constructive. That's impossible.

"We're the only people on this entire planet who have been taught to sing and praise our demeanment. 'I'm a bitch. I'm a hoe. I'm a gangster. I'm a thug. I'm a dog.' If you can train people to demean and degrade themselves, you can oppress them forever. You can even program them to kill themselves and they won't even understand what happened."
Dr. Frances Cress Welsing

If there was ever any doubt that the music industry has strong ties to the occult, the 2012 Grammy Awards performance by Nicki Minaj should put those doubts to rest. This was a prime example of an occult ritual, being passed off as entertainment on prime time network television

E PLURIBUS UNUM
FEDERAL ENDORSEMENT OF A DEITY OR RELIGION VIOLATES THE U.S. CONSTITUTION
BillStamp.com

Placing idolatry on Government issued money violates the Constitution. It elevates those that Thomas Jefferson labeled as "the real anti-Christ"- the clergy - and promotes *The Greatest Fraud*, their sacred, organized ignorance, arrogance and intolerance.

The Greatest Fraud: http://pinterest.com/holyheretics/the-greatest-fraud/

Luke 16:13 No servant can serve two masters: for either he will hate the one, and love the other; or else he will hold to the one, and despise the other. Ye cannot serve God and mammon.

http://stopbarackobama.drboydreviews.com/id46.htm

Kirk Franklin

KIRK FRANKLIN THE ILLUMINATI & FREEMASONRY MEMBER WITH HOMOSEXUAL TENDENCIES! KIRK FRANKLIN SOLD HIS SOUL

Vogue magazine cover featuring LeBron James and model Gisele Bundchen is causing quite a disturbance around the internet. The photograph is by Annie Liebovitz. Mrs. Liebovitz did the cover that Jennifer Hudson was on an some people questioned that cover.

LeBron is a muscular and handsome black man, while Gisele is a frail looking white woman. LeBron is being compared to a King Kong ape ready to pounce on the poor little maiden in distress on the cover. I made a comment on The Field - Negro site that I didn't see a problem but, when you see the poster and cover together you have too ask that question. LeBron has made a statement that he has no problem with the picture. I don't know if he has seen it side by side or not.

It's true we see things differently in America weather it be race or anything else. Some people see this as racist and some don't. After seeing the side by side shot my question is it a coincidence that the cover looks like the poster? Maybe Mrs. Liebovitz had that image in her head but didn't mean for it to be taken that way. What Do You See?

Lady Gaga allegedly left "large amounts of blood" in a hotel bath.

The eccentric singer reportedly shocked staff when she checked out of London's lavish Intercontinental Hotel last summer and they discovered a pool of red liquid in the tub of her suite. One housekeeper claimed the pop superstar was "bathing in blood as part of a Satanic ritual". Other sources believe Gaga could have been using the red liquid as part of a "weird" stage costume or prop.

112

Jack Black leads a prayer to the Devil at the 2009 MTV Awards

The 40-year-old "comedian" Jack Black went on the "dark side" during the MTV Awards praying to the devil. Black, who was promoting a heavy metal video game called Brütal Legend, asked the "Dear Dark Lord Satan" to bless the rock star nominees with "continued success in the music industry." "I was mortified when Jack Black lead everyone in a prayer to satan. It was no joke," said Samantha Taylor of California. "The audience held hands and did it. I was a fan, but not anymore."

Black made his grand entrace wearing extra muscles and a battle axe.

"During the Awards, I seriously felt as if I were watching a big party celebration that was taking place in satan's den," said the viewer. "It sickened me. I'll never watch anything on MTV channel again. First and last time," said Taylor.

"In reality, television, film, and radio are powerful electronic forces that saturate the mind and body with sights and sounds that influence psychological, emotional, and spiritual well-being. Its effects can be controlled by acknowledging its existence and learning to neutralize the negative influences it projects."

~Anthony Browder

"SOLD MY SOUL TO THE DEVIL, MADE A PROFIT"
-LIL WAYNE

The music industry, and the occult

Tupac Shakur was fatally shot in Las Vegas when he was going to a night club. He succumbed to injuries after six days. Some people claim that Sean Comb was involved in Shakur's murder. But, no one has ever been charged for the murder.

Man lives in an environment of symbols, and it is extremely important to understand something about the symbol-making process because symbols are the raw material of human thought and all communication. Superficially we think that words are the only form of communication, because we live in such a highly verbal atmosphere. Yet in actuality there is a far greater amount of nonverbal communication going on all the time through the use of other symbols than words.

http://www.newparadigm.ws/suppressed-forbidden-knowledge/10-celebrities-killed-by-the-ruling-elite-for-exposing-the-global-conspiracy/

The FBI War on Tupac Shakur and Black Leaders

U.S. Intelligence's Murderous Targeting of Tupac, MLK, Malcolm, Panthers, Hendrix, Marley, Rappers & Linked Ethnic Leftists

by John Potash   Foreword by Pam Africa with Mumia Abu-Jamal
Afterword by Fred Hampton, Jr.

https://savedbyfaithinchrist.com/2012/02/18/the-music-industry-and-the-occult/

ROB BROTHERTON

SUSPICIOUS MINDS
Why We Believe Conspiracy Theories

"Illuminati want my mind, soul, and my body / Secret society trying to keep they eye on me," rapped Mobb Deep's Prodigy, in a 1995 remix of LL Cool J's "I Shot Ya." The same year, "Cell Therapy" by Goodie Mob painted a bleak picture of what society will look like under the coming New World Order, invoking conspiracy tropes like martial law, concentration camps, and black helicopters: "Time is getting shorter / If we don't get prepared, people, it's gonna be a slaughter." Also released in 1995, "We Can't Win" by AZ begins with a monologue explaining how society is *really* structured: "This world is ruled and controlled by societies that exist within societies, that exist within societies, you understand? These secret societies is maneuvering within society to control society. That's why society is outta control. Thirty-third and one third, I heard, the Illuminated ones."

Over the next year or so, Ras Kass, the Wu-Tang Clan, and Dr. Dre all mentioned the Illuminati or the New World Order. Canibus went even further down the rabbit hole with his 1998 single "Channel Zero," which begins by claiming the government is covering up visits by super-intelligent aliens, and explains that Roswell, cattle mutilations, and even astronomer Carl Sagan were part of the plot.

After a while, hip-hop's paranoia turned in on itself. Rumors emerged suggesting that certain artists might be part of the conspiracy. The first to come under suspicion was Jay Z. His immense success, the conspiracists theorized, couldn't have been earned through talent, hard work, or luck. He must have sold his soul to the Illuminati. One of the first and most vocal proponents of this theory was none other than Prodigy. Jay had sampled Prodigy's line about the Illuminati on "D'Evils" from his 1996 debut album. But by 2008, Prodigy was convinced. In a letter penned from prison, he accused Jay Z himself of being a puppet—wittingly or unwittingly—of the Illuminati, writing "J.Z. conceals the truth from the black community and the world and promotes the lifestyle of the beast instead."

How the Illuminati Stole the Mind, Soul, and Body of Hip-Hop
The true story of how an 18th-century secret society came to dominate today's music industry (allegedly). ROB BROTHERTON

The accusations spread far and wide, first to Kanye West and Rihanna when they appeared in the video for "Run This Town" with Jay—which had a distinctly spooky secret-society vibe, to be fair— and then to Nas, J Cole, Kendrick Lamar, Nikki Minaj, and virtually every major hip-hop figure. The rumors have transcended genre—Lady Gaga, Madonna, Bob Dylan, and Justin Bieber are all alleged to be card-carrying members of the Illuminati. YouTube is flooded with videos deconstructing lyrics, music videos, and interviews looking for hidden meaning, some with view counts in the millions.

Most hip-hop artists don't buy into the Illuminati theories, of course. Tupac Shakur was an early critic. He titled an album *Killuminati*, released posthumously in 1996, explaining in an interview recorded shortly before his death that "I'm putting the 'K' because I'm killin' that shit." Referring to people who claim to know the truth about the Illuminati, Tupac asks rhetorically, "How did he know? How'd it leak to him? Who told him? Who told him? The pope? Who? 'Cause they like, 'the pope' and 'the money.' Aw c'mon man, get the fuck outta here."

Black people can't worship Satan?

Famous crooner Sammy Davis, Jr with "Church Of Satan" leader Anton Lavey
His most famous disciple was Sammy Davis, Jr., who later regretted experimenting with Satanism. LaVey's church (The Church Of Satan) had 5,000 members.

"The Poor Devil" 1973

http://thekoolskool.blogspot.com/2010/02/esoteric-and-occult-themes-in-rap.html

Peak Illuminati was achieved in 2011, and as Genius.com's Rap Stats feature attests, the trend hasn't let up. Virtually every major hip-hop star has dropped an Illuminati reference into their music—mostly to deny their membership and mock the rumors. In his 2010 track "Gasoline," for example, Meek Mill referenced the influential Prodigy line, joking "Illuminati wanted my mind, soul, and body / They ask me would I trade it for all Maserati / I told him 'no,' he said 100 million, I said 'probably.'"

Here's John Lennon with Yoko on Andy Warhol's knee , they are gearing up for some group action obviously, probably also involving whoever the photographer was and whoever else was there. Recall that Lennon lived in The Dakota when Rosemary's Baby was filmed there in the same apt. (cum three floor mansion) atop The Dakota which John and Yoko bought five years later. Anyone not asleep should recall that Rosemary's Baby was about a satanic cult into group sex (there's a reason they are ALL naked in the ritual rape scene, btw)

http://letsrollforums.com//lady-diana-spencer-limo-t28930p88.html?
s=3db6c5fa659716da02b2cf787008588e&

Here are examples of celebrities said to have been killed by the ruling elite for exposing the global conspiracy.

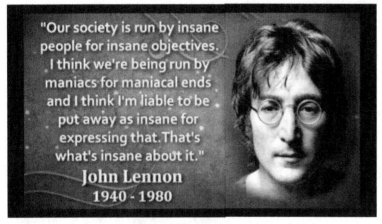

"Our society is run by insane people for insane objectives. I think we're being run by maniacs for maniacal ends and I think I'm liable to be put away as insane for expressing that. That's what's insane about it."

John Lennon
1940 - 1980

***John Lennon** spoke out against the ruling elite on a number of levels, including the evils connected to the entertainments industry. He was under surveillance by the FBI...*

He had befriended and funded a number of individuals labelled as 'subversives' who were regarded as political enemies by concerned governmental agents for the ruling elite.

His untimely end on December 8th 1980 was caused by Mark Chapman shooting him dead (incidentally, the Beatles song John wrote called *"Come Together"* recorded in 1969 has his vocals repeating the words *'shoot me...'*). The official story claimed that Chapman was a crazed fan, but this account does not add up. It has been said that Chapman was a mind controlled assassin.

-John's wife Yoko and son Sean are convinced that his killing involved the ruling elite...

Michael Jackson

In only a matter of days before his comeback concert tour Michael Jackson died on June 25, 2009.

Speaking of her brother Michael, La Toya Jackson has been known on a number of occasions to insist that *"they were trying to kill him."*

"I need you to know that this is very important what we are fighting for, because.. I'm tired. I'm really tired of manipulations. I'm really tired on how the press is manipulating everything that has been happening to the situation. They do not tell the truth... They're lying... they manipulate our history books. The history books are not true, it's a lie. The history books are lying, you need to know that, You must know that.

MICHAEL JACKSON
1958 - 2009

Not wanting to be part of the illuminati Michael claimed that there was a plan in operation to defame him with false allegations related to molesting children and that he was a freak... He had planned to speak out against the illuminati and their evil machinations in the music industry and expose much more.

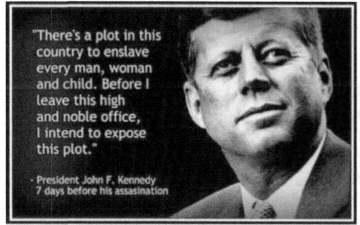

"There's a plot in this country to enslave every man, woman and child. Before I leave this high and noble office, I intend to expose this plot."

- President John F. Kennedy 7 days before his assasination

John F. Kennedy

JFK was said to have been an illuminati member, but as president decided to go against their wishes. -Many conspiracies have used this to explain his assassination on November 22nd 1963

http://www.newparadigm.ws/suppressed-forbidden-knowledge/10-celebrities-killed-by-the-ruling-elite-for-exposing-the-global-conspiracy/

'THROUGH MUSIC YOU HYPNOTIZE PEOPLE & WHEN YOU GET THEM AT THEIR WEAKEST POINT YOU CAN PREACH INTO THEIR SUBCONSCIOUS WHAT WE WANT TO SAY.' -JIMI HENDRIX

Jimi Hendrix

The US government had called Jimi a "subversive. " He was known for making comments regarding his fear of dying before he would reach 30 years old. For example, he told film director Chuck Wein

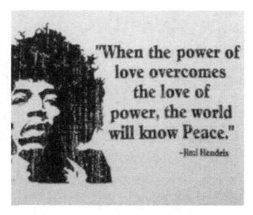

"When the power of love overcomes the love of power, the world will know Peace."
~Jimi Hendrix

"The next time I go to Seattle will be in a pine box" only 2 months before his death. He choked on his own vomit on September 18th 1970 aged 27 years.

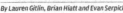
Rolling Stone

Jay-Z rocks Roc gesture, remains icy and aloof.

By Lauren Gitlin, Brian Hiatt and Evan Serpick

Diamond Dallas Page flashes the Diamond Cutter, growls.

Jay-Z Samples Wrestler's Act

Pro wrestler Diamond Dallas Page is suing Jay-Z, claiming that the Roc hand sign is in fact a copy of the Diamond Cutter he invented in 1996. Settle it in the ring!

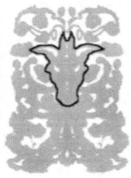

From saying "I don't pray to God, I pray to gotti" to calling himself Jahova, a name people have taken to mean Jehovah (one of the Hebrew names for God) Even Beyonce is not left out of all of this, her alter ego; Sasha Fierce has been said to be Beyonce possessed by a demon. Not to mention the Goat head ring she's been sporting recently which conspiracy theorists are calling the head of Baphomet which is notably the symbol of the church of satan.

In a midrash (Genesis Rabbah 19) Samael, the lord of the satans, was a mighty prince of angels in heaven. Satan came into the world with woman, that is, with Eve (Midrash Yalkut, Genesis 1:23), so that he was created and is not eternal. Like all celestial beings, he flies through the air (Genesis Rabbah 19), and can assume any form, as of a bird (Talmud, Sanhedrin 107a), a stag (ibid, 95a), a woman (ibid, 81a), a beggar, or a young man (Midrash Tanchuma, Wayera, end); he is said to skip (Talmud Pesachim 112b and Megilla, 11b), in allusion to his appearance in the form of a goat.

JAY-Z
the hits collection • volume one

Jay Z calls his label Roc-a-Fella obviously because of the Rockefeller Family one of the main ten banker families in the world, but also refers to it as the roc, when the actual Rock or Stone is Yahushúa.

Jay-Z's "Decoded" Book Cover

- The official cover for **Jay-Z's** upcoming book "Decoded" has hit the net.
- As previously **reported**, "Decoded" will be a book about the rapper's lyrics and the stories that have inspired them over the years.
- Jigga also plans to appear at the New York public library on Nov. 15 to give fans a preview of his new literature penned by author Dream Hampton.
- The cover for the book features an image made byAndy Warhol.

Freemason Handshake

As Nas himself said it "it ain't hard to tell", they are part of this secret society. Next, you'll see the pictures of them doing the hand shakes of the first 3 degrees of the blue lodge, those who barely know a thing, on the first degree the thumb presses on the first knuckle, for second degree the thumb is placed in between the first and second knuckle and for the third degree on the second knuckle.

Masonic Handshake

Hova has long been rumored to be a member of the Freemasons, the fraternal organization known for their deep political ties and use of signs (gestures) and grips (handshakes).

Jay-Z Caught Using Secret Handshake

The Freemason rumor gained popularity after Hov was photographed in a similar handhold with <u>Nas</u> when they squashed beef onstage in October, 2005.

Jay has been throwing up the Rocafella diamond for over a decade, which internet theorists believed to be connected to the Masonic "All seeing eye" pyramid symbol and Square and Compasses. He also referenced the illuminati and secret society back in 1996 on the hook of "D'evils."

<u>Kanye West</u>, another artist who has achieved great success since throwing up the Roc (Bleek where you at?), produced the song "Lucifer" for his big brother Jay, using Max Romeo's vocal sample "Lucifer son of the morning" which appears to be a direct reference to a Masonic text: "Lucifer, the Son of the Morning! Is it he who bears the Light, and with its splendors intolerable, blinds feeble, sensual, or selfish souls? Doubt it not!" [Albert Pike, Morals and Dogma of the Ancient and Accepted Scottish Rite of Freemasonry, p. 321, 19th Degree of Grand Pontiff].

Three Snakes One Charm Egyptian goddess religion associated with Osiris the horned god. It is also another form of 666

6
6
6

But of course Jay-Z and Beyonce are far from alone. All over America, prominent celebrities are gladly embracing the Illuminati and the New World Order. By doing so, they are sending a message to future generations of Americans that being a part of these things is trendy and cool.

For example, just check out some of the celebrity members of the Council on Foreign Relations...

George Clooney,Angelina Jolie,Oprah Winfrey,Michael Douglas
Jimmy Iovine,Rick Warren,Michael Bloomberg
Richard Branson,Katie Couric
Brian Williams,Fareed Zakaria,Erin Burnett
Rupert Murdoch,Les Moonves,Paul Krugman
Joe Biden,John Kerry,Newt Gingrich,John McCain
Dick Cheney,Bill Clinton,Hillary Clinton

It's funny – just about the only thing that Republicans and Democrats can agree upon is that joining the Council on Foreign Relations is a good thing to do. The mainstream media would have us believe that they are mortal enemies, but the reality is that they are really all working for the same side.

Rapper Tupac, was pursued by promiscuous Madonna, who introduced him to Kabbalah and her Illuminati beleifs. The two did a song together. Tupac then began writing music about the Illuminati and renamed himself "The don K-illuminati." The album features a sacrilegious cover, which Madonna and Kabbalah often do, depicting Tupac as Jesus on the cross. It caused great offense among Christians.

http://judiciaryreport.com/celebrities_who_suffered_tragedy_in_the_occult.htm

Baphomet the God of the Freemasons

WASHINGTON   BAPHOMET

"Lucifer, the Light Bearer! Strange and mysterious name to give to the Spirit of Darkness! Lucifer, the Son of the Morning! Is it he who bears the Light and with its splendors intolerable blinds feeble, sensual or selfish Souls?

The creature that you can see in the beginning of the video is called Baphomet, another name for Lucifer, that is the "god" the masons started worshiping when they were still called "The Knights Templar", according to the book "Morals & Dogma" written by Albert Pike, co-founder of the KKK and pioneer of Freemasonry in the United States, the god of Freemasonry is Lucifer.

http://thedoggstar.com/articles/secret-societies/freemasonry-in-hip-hop/

Albert Pike issued this statement on July 14, 1889 to the 23 Supreme Councils of the World:

"That which we must say to the crowd is: We worship a God, but it is the God one adores without superstition. To you, Sovereign Grand Instructors General, we say this, that you may repeat it to the Brethren of the 32nd, 31st, and 30th degrees: The Masonic Religion should be, by all of us initiates of the high degrees, maintained in the purity of the Luciferian doctrine." -Albert Pike

"The Blue Degrees are but the outer court or portico of the Temple. Part of the symbols are displayed there to the Initiate, but he is intentionally misled by false interpretations. It is not intended that he shall understand them; but it is intended that he shall imagine he understands them. Their true explication is reserved for the Adepts, the Princes of Masonry. The whole body of the Royal and Sacerdotal Art was hidden so carefully, centuries since, in the High Degrees, as that it is even yet impossible to solve many of the enigmas which they contain. It is well enough for the mass of those called Masons, to imagine that all is contained in the Blue Degrees; and whoso attempts to undeceive them will labor in vain, and without any true reward violate his obligations as an Adept. Masonry is the veritable Sphinx, buried to the head in the sands heaped round it by the ages. "

"Masonry, like all the Religions, all the Mysteries,... conceals its secrets from all except the Adepts and Sages, or the Elect, and uses false explanations and misinterpretations of its symbols to mislead those who deserve only to be misled ..."

"The Blue Degrees are but the outer court or portico of the Temple. Part of the symbols are displayed there to the Initiate, but he is intentionally misled by false interpretations. It is not intended that he shall understand them; but it is intended that he shall imagine he understands them. Their true explication is reserved for the Adepts, the Princes of Masonry." - (pp. 104, 105 & 819)

General Albert Pike wrote those words in a work called <u>Morals and Dogma of the Ancient and Accepted Scottish Rite of Freemasonry</u>, 1871

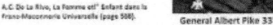

"That which we must say to the CROWD is: we worship god, but it is the god that one adores without superstition. To YOU Sovereign Grand Inspectors General, we say this, that you may repeat it to the brethren of the 32nd, 31st and 30th degrees- the MASONIC RELIGION should be, by all of us initiates of the high degrees, maintained in the purity of the LUCIFERIAN doctrine. If Lucifer were not god, would Adonay [Jesus]... calumniate [spread false and harmful statements about] him?... YES LUCIFER IS GOD..."

A.C. De La Rive, La Femme et l' Enfant dans la franc-Maconnerie Universelle (page 588).

General Albert Pike 33'

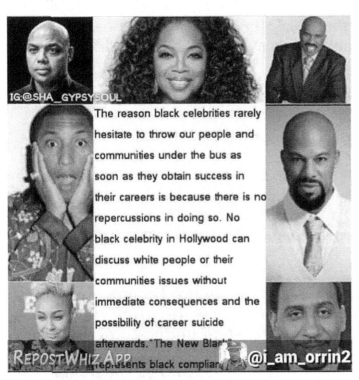

IG:@SHA_GYPSYSOUL

The reason black celebrities rarely hesitate to throw our people and communities under the bus as soon as they obtain success in their careers is because there is no repercussions in doing so. No black celebrity in Hollywood can discuss white people or their communities issues without immediate consequences and the possibility of career suicide afterwards."The New Black" represents black complian...

REPOSTWHIZ APP   @i_am_orrin2

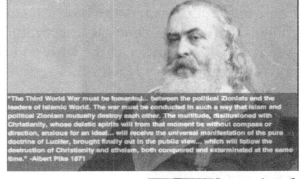

"The Third World War must be fomented... between the political Zionists and the leaders of Islamic World. The war must be conducted in such a way that Islam and political Zionism mutually destroy each other. The multitude, disillusioned with Christianity, whose deistic spirits will from that moment be without compass or direction, anxious for an ideal... will receive the universal manifestation of the pure doctrine of Lucifer, brought finally out in the public view... which will follow the destruction of Christianity and atheism, both conquered and exterminated at the same time." -Albert Pike 1871

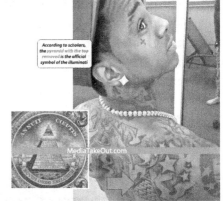

According to scholars, the *pyramid with the top removed is the official symbol of the illuminati*

MediaTakeOut.com

THE DEVIL MADE ME DO IT

"When you're talking about Afrika Bambaataa, first of all, you're talking about the person who invented hip-hop," KRS-One said in the sit-down.

This masterpiece takes its readers from Hip Hop's ancient origin, to its modern day Matrix. Never before has a book been written about Hip Hop through the spiritual scope of the culture, or has examined the culture from a mystical perspective. The Black Dot cleverly accomplishes both, while providing plenty of fuel for conspiracy theorist.

Hip Hop Decoded reveals that Hip Hop is far deeper than just beats and rhymes, and masterfully illustrates that each element of Hip Hop (Graffiti, DJ, Emcee, and B-Boy) has an ancient origin (hieroglyphics, drummer, oracle, and dancer), as well as, spiritual significance (earth, air, fire, and water). Knowledge is the fifth and most sacred element of Hip Hop, however, the most misunderstood.

The Black Dot has compiled the most comprehensive study of the subject in book form. Hip Hop Decoded is the red pill for those looking to escape from the Matrix of Hip Hop, and begin the journey to uncover the truth about the culture. The foreword to the book was written by legend and Live Rhyme Master, Grandmaster Caz.

Warning: this book will not be conventional in the sense that it will try to provide politically correct answers to the problems that we are facing in urban America. A subject of this matter requires a deeper analysis that goes well beyond the scope of one's typical way of thinking, so I wrote this book as a starting point in an attempt to address such matters. We must explore unconventional solutions, or at least view the situation from an unconventional standpoint if we want to make any true breakthroughs. If we are going to deal with the core of the problems that we as an urban society are faced with in regards to our youth, we must be open and honest about the current state that they live in. While it is important that we address the cause of the situation, it is also equally important that we look at the affects of living in an artificial environment plagued by violence, drugs, unemployment, discrimination, and police brutality. How could one not be violent in the face of all the violence that we have endured over the last 400 years? How could one not want to use drugs as an escape from all of the hardships related to living in such conditions?

When faced with the option of being hungry and unemployed, or hitting the streets to sell drugs, how could one not make the choice of getting paid? This is a no-brainer when the concept of survival is on the line. The million- dollar question is, what if the same things that plagued us could save us? This generation has learned to embrace the unbearable. That old saying, whatever doesn't kill you will only make you stronger rings true with this generation. Drugs and alcohol, which have caused so much damage to the previous generation, has almost had the reverse affect on this generation. They have become immune to the negative affects.

They have become stronger than ever before. They celebrate life in what appears to be the direst situations, leaving even their oppressors confused. They have created an entire culture based on the type of music that they listen to, the type of drugs and alcohol that they use, and their sexual behaviors. While most will view them as violent, lost, and confused troublemakers with no regard for life, in my humble opinion, they are the most advanced, enlightened, and spiritual beings on the planet. They just lack the knowledge, wisdom, and understanding of who they really are. As a result, their actions are in contrary of such divine principles. They have bottomed out, and are now using the very vices that were meant to weigh them down, to uplift them. I call this urban alchemy. To the parents, teachers, and elders who have all but given up on this generation, and scoff at the notion that they are an asset, I have but a few questions to ask you, have you taught them about sex magic and the power of using their creative energy to activate their spirituality? Have you taught them about the use of certain drugs that could assist them in seeing beyond this so-called reality and their connection to everything in the universe? Have you taught them about the power of music and sound vibration, and its ability to heal and open up their spiritual centers? If you have answered no to any of these questions, then it is you who are out of touch with the current reality that they reside in. They are in the process of a metamorphosis unlike what we have ever witnessed before. If your response is, this is just some mumbo jumbo new Age nonsense, then it shows that you are really out of touch with the transformation that we are all making, which is being led by this cast of rebellious, misunderstood youth. Some of you may have already put the book down, for those who are still with me, strap on your seatbelt because we are about to go on one hell of a ride.

Roc-a-Wear t-shirt, illuminati's "all seeing eye", pyramid symbol (hands), in the small round things around the pyramid symbol are; masonic handshake (second right) the rest isn't easy to see in this pic.. pyramid also seems to "illuminate".. Putting the Pyramid Hand Symbol on this (and other) shirts in his clothing line SHOWS this is exactly what he means when he throws the sign.

"Do what thou wilt", one of the *"commandments" of Aleister Crowley's Occult book Thelema.. Jay why wear this shirt when your no satanist as you say?*

(line on shirt 'Masters of the Craft' a masonic line)

The I-Ching
3 stripes also represent Ch'ien in the Taoist I-ching symbology "CH'IEN, The Creative, represents pure Yang, the primal creative power which exists before all created things. It is therefore called Heaven, the Father, the strong, the life force, and the swift and tireless horse." – www.zianet.com

One of the 9 primary signs of the Ninja Kujin   Dora making a triangle   Feminist Gloria Steinem   Diamond Sign Dallas Page

Screenshots: http://www.illuminatirex.com

Hebrew high priests throwing a Roc   Sign for Toblerone's triangular shape or shout out to illuminati

And saith unto him, All these things will I give thee, if thou wilt fall down and worship me. - Matthew 4:9

124

*"When I'm onstage I'm aggressive and strong and not afraid of my sexuality. **The tone of my voice gets different, and I'm fearless. I'm just a different person."***

"I have someone else that takes over when it's time for me to work and when I'm on stage, this alter ego that I've created that kind of protects me and who I really am".-Beyonce

"I understand Beyoncé was making hand symbols of, what else, a pyramid, or triangle if you will, which is a sign of the Illuminati and the New World Order, at the end of the show," Fawell told US News & World Report in an email Monday.

"[Beyoncé] has a long history of serving the godless Illuminati and their Satanic cult."

http://vigilantcitizen.com/musicbusiness/jay-zs-run-this-town-and-the-occult-connexions/

125

Rhianna bent over inside a pyramid in the Umbrella music video. The videographers obviously doctored this scene to extend Rhianna's neck—creating the snout—and to create the eyes at her shoulders—stylized after the Baphomet head on the right. In real time, this particular scene flashes by rather quickly to give it a subliminal effect.

http://beforeitsnews.com/gulf-oil-spill/2012/06/the-hollywood-kabbalah-cult-unmasked-2283356.html

Origins of the Name

Monarch mind control is named after the Monarch butterfly – an insect who begins its life as a worm (representing undeveloped potential) and, after a period of cocooning (programming) is reborn as a beautiful butterflies (the Monarch slave). Some characteristics specific to the Monarch butterfly are also applicable to mind control.

Method

The victim/survivor is called a "slave" by the programmer/handler, who in turn is perceived as "master" or "god." About 75% are female, since they possess a higher tolerance for pain and tend to dissociate more easily than males. Monarch handlers seek the compartmentalization of their subject's psyche in multiple and separate alter personas using trauma to cause dissociation.

Monarch mind control is covertly used by various groups and organizations for various purposes. According to Fritz Springmeier, these groups are known as "The Network" and form the backbone of the New World Order.

The following is a partial list of these forms of torture:

1. Abuse and torture
2. Confinement in boxes, cages, coffins, etc, or burial (often with an opening or air-tube for oxygen)
3. Restraint with ropes, chains, cuffs, etc.
4. Near-drowning
5. Extremes of heat and cold, including submersion in ice water and burning chemicals
6. Skinning (only top layers of the skin are removed in victims intended to survive)
7. Spinning
8. Blinding light
9. Electric shock
10. Forced ingestion of offensive body fluids and matter, such as blood, urine, feces, flesh, etc.
11. Hung in painful positions or upside down
12. Hunger and thirst
13. Sleep deprivation
14 Compression with weights and devices
15. Sensory deprivation
16. Drugs to create illusion, confusion, and amnesia, often given by injection or intravenously
17. Ingestion or intravenous toxic chemicals to create pain or illness, including chemotherapy agents
18. Limbs pulled or dislocated
19. Application of snakes, spiders, maggots, rats, and other animals to induce fear and disgust
20. Near-death experiences, commonly asphyxiation by choking or drowning, with immediate resuscitation
22. Forced to perform or witness abuse, torture and sacrifice of people and animals, usually with knives

23. Forced participation in slavery

24. Abuse to become pregnant; the fetus is then aborted for ritual use, or the baby is taken for sacrifice or enslavement

25. Spiritual abuse to cause victim to feel possessed, harassed, and controlled internally by spirits or demons

26. Desecration of Judeo-Christian beliefs and forms of worship; dedication to Satan or other deities

27. Abuse and illusion to convince victims that God is evil, such as convincing a child that God has abused her

28. Surgery to torture, experiment, or cause the perception of physical or spiritual bombs or implants

29. Harm or threats of harm to family, friends, loved ones, pets, and other victims, to force compliance

30. Use of illusion and virtual reality to confuse and create non-credible disclosure [8. Ellen P. Lacter, Ph.D., Kinds of Torture Endured in Ritual Abuse and Trauma-Based Mind Control]

Media Conspiracy & Manipulation

Illuminati and Satanic Manipulation In the Music and Film Industry, TV and mainstream media. Illuminati Symbols in movies, music videos, album covers. Hollywood artists and celebrities, singers, bands, actresses and actors. Mind Control, MK Ultra. Manipulación Illuminati Satánica en la Industria Musical, Películas, Televisión y medios de comunicación. Símbología en películas, videos y albumes musicales. Artistas y celebridades de Hollywood, cantantes, bandas, actrices y actores.

http://media-conspiracy-manipulation.blogspot.com/2011/10/butterfly-symbolism-illuminati-mind.html

128

Rihanna wears a shirt with an upside down cross that says "Control Minds". This is a reference to the satanic MK-Ultra mind control program. Is Rihanna a beta sex kitten? She does get around. She doesn't seem dissociative like Nicki Minaj though and she wasn't abused as a child.

This symbol is not just a fashion icon, but has its own history going back to the time before Christ when St. Peter was crucified. When Peter was sentenced to death by the Emperor, he requested to be hung upside down on the cross. He believed that he could not die upright on the cross because Jesus did. He felt he was not worthy to die the same way.

Designing Eden, a fashion blog, said that later in the Christian religion the upside down cross was adopted as a symbol of the church. The blog said in recent years, Satanists use the symbol as a way to show their anti-Christian beliefs. Today, the upside down cross is highly unaccepted by Christian organizations and considered to be satanic.

The V-Sign is the Sign of the occult, satanic Sabbatean/Frankists

http://okkulte-nazis.blogspot.com/2011/02/it-began-in-germany_24.html

http://www.whale.to/b/v_s.html

Vulcan was a sun deity who was associated with fire, thunderbolts, and light. The festival in honour of him was called the Vulcania in which human sacrifices were offered. "According to Diel, he bears a family relationship to the Christian devil." It is fascinating to know that he married Venus, another name for Lucifer or the devil. What is even more interesting is that Vulcan is adored in Masonry under the name of Tubal Cain. In the Masonic Quiz Book the question is asked: "Who was Tubal Cain?" The answer is: "He is the Vulcan of the pagans."

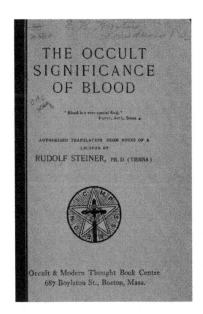

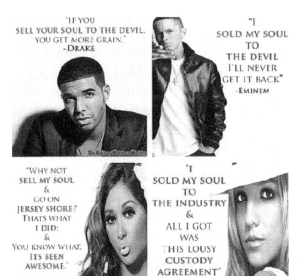

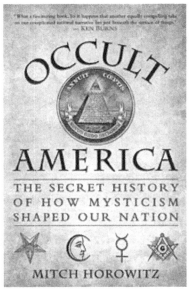

To become the wealthiest ($20 million+ club) for a higher position and royalty from the elite, you need to make a human (blood **sacrifice**).

The Illuminati and Michael Jackson

So you are probably wondering at this point what does this secret society known as the Illuminati have to do with the entertainer Michael Jackson and why would they want him dead? As I said, a few seconds ago the entertainment industry is one of the conduits that the Illuminati use to carry out their agenda. In regards to the entertainment industry this is carried out in the form of brainwashing and propaganda that is transmitted through the music and images of popular culture. Their goal is to hook the masses of people into a maze of satanic decadence that distracts them from thinking about important issues that affect the world today. It is through this distraction that the Illuminati are able to run amok and create chaos throughout the world without encountering any real resistance.

The Illuminati control the entertainment and music industries lock, stock and barrel and if an artist wants fame and fortune they must sell their souls to the powers that be who control these particular industries. No one will ever debate that Michael Jackson's ascent to the top of these industries were a result of his immense incomparable talents. However, to reach the status of "King of Pop" and the status of being the number 1 entertainer in the world he had to first get the blessings and approval of the Illuminati power structure.

1. The monkey represents man, before he was corrupted by the Illuminati. He is on a path to enlightenment, but as you can see by the pirate above the door, the Illuminati took over.

2. The All-Seeing Eye of Providence. The Dajjal or the Anti-Christ. One of the most sacred signs of the old world Illuminati.

3. The skeleton shows what happens to those who oppose the illuminati. The baby Michael shows that only Michael was able to enter the innermost chamber of the Illuminati and emerge alive.

4. Baphomet, the most evil of all Illuminati Deities looks down upon his work.

5. Alien hidden within the animal kingdom. Illuminati bloodlines descended from aliens?

6. Half of this statute is black and half is white, symbolizing the mixing of the Illuminati bloodlines. Many scholars have theorized that this is what Michael was trying to attempt as his skin got lighter through the years.

7. These crowns show the battle between the primate, dog, and bird kingdoms. Birds have long been known to be representations of the Illuminati (bird on $10 bill, owls). The human in the fish tank attached to the bird (10) represents humans being held in captivity by the Illuminati.

8. DANGEROUS - This is Michael's recognition that he was putting himself in danger by exposing the Illuminati, a risk he was willing to take.

9. The Illuminati are on a quest to turn our world up-side-down. They plan to reverse the magnetic poles using H.A.A.R.P.

10. Man and woman - the original Adam and Eve trapped inside of a transparent 'apple' and forced to watch the world descending into evil.

11. Anubis - Egyptian jackal-headed god of the dead. Later replaced by Osiris. One of the Illuminati's primary gods.

12. Connecting the three monkey heads creates a pyramid. While Illuminati pyramids have one eye, this one has both of Michael's eyes, serving as a message to the illuminati that MJ is watching.

13. The anagram from Michael Jackson is "Lone Scam Hijack" = MJ is the only one willing to expose the scam that is the Illuminati.

14. Johann Adam Weishaupt, founder of the Bavarian Illuminati. Based on the ancient Illuminati and Egyptian gods.

15. The right and left pillars of King Solomon's Temple with skulls on the top.

16. A Nubian (Africa/Egypt) child holds the skull of a dragon/dinosaur. Impressing upon the viewer that the Illuminati have been here since antiquity and even control the children.

17. White Elephants refer to a valuable possession which it's owners cannot dispose of. MJ knew about the Illuminati, but he could not get the information out for fear of his life being threatened.

18. A monkey with a crown. Puppet world leaders will be installed and controlled by the Illuminati.

19. There are many strange and fantastic animals pictured. A dog with a lizard tail, etc. Exposing the dangers of genetic engineering as practiced by the New World Order.

20. A road paved with rockets and stars - a clue to man's extraterrestrial origins?

21. The pentagram inside of a pyramid...

22. A hand holding a child and a skull - The Illuminati control the past and the future.

23. Egyptian god Horus, the god of creation and rebirth - represented by a figure with the head of a bird.

24. The Industrial Revolution - taking man backwards. Cutting off all communications and knowledge. Keeping man in the dark while only the Illuminati are enlightened.

25. MJ is trying to show us that everything is a 'mask.' His eyes were looking through the false world into the real. The world as we see it isn't real. It's being controlled by unseen forces and he was trying to show us that. And they stopped him - but not before his coded messages were released.

Michael Jackson became the most successful disciple of the occult, since Aleister Crowley, who died in 1947. For those of you who have never heard of Aleister Crowley, he was known as "the father of modern satanism". Yes, he would dress in black robes and perform sexual ritual orgies and blood sacrifice. He is also famous for spending the night in the Pyramid of Giza and channeling the "Book of Law". You might have even seen Jay-Z wearing a black hoodie with the number one law of the book, "Do what thou wilt". If you have not, please Google it.

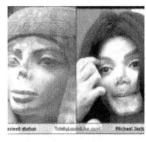

Recently, unearthed is a statue, it was carved between 1550-1050 BC and depicts a woman. It looks just like Michael Jackson and remember he had his face cut to look like a vision of who he wanted to be. Or was it his vision at all? I can not say this 100% true; but, the evidence is certainly compelling, right?

Michael Jackson

Jackson Calls Sony Music Chief 'Racist' and 'Devilish'
July 8 - Michael Jackson blasted the music industry — and Sony Music chief Tommy Mottola in particular — calling him "racist and very, very, very devilish."

June 25th, 2009 is remembered for the deaths of Michael Jackson, Farrah Fawcett, and Sky Saxon. Careful planning was carried out according to the correct numbers if their ritual sacrifices were to be successful. In the occult, human sacrifice is part of the ceremony.

Sony Buys Michael Jackson's Stake In Lucrative Music Catalog

March 15, 2016 9:59 PM ET

ELIZABETH BLAIR

For what is a man profited, if he shall gain the whole world, and lose his own soul? or what shall a man give in exchange for his soul? - Matthew 16:26

MICHAEL JACKSON
1958 - 2009

SINGER ACCUSES SONY MUSIC CHAIRMAN OF CONSPIRING AGAINST BLACK ARTISTS

Most of Jackson's comments were constrained to the overall treatment of black artists, the struggle of whom he said he shared. The pop star compared his troubles with his record company to those of artists who struggled financially, saying that there was an "incredible injustice" taking place.

"The recording companies really, really do conspire against the artists," Jackson said. "They steal, they cheat, they do everything they can, especially [against] the black artists. ... People from James Brown to Sammy Davis Jr., some of the real pioneers that inspired me to be an entertainer, these artists are always on tour, because if they stop touring, they would go hungry. If you fight for me, you're fighting for all black people, dead and alive."

But Jackson may have taken a wrong turn when he turned the fight for him into a fight against Mottola. Claiming that Mottola had used the "N-word" to refer to an unidentified black Sony artist, Jackson singled out the company chairman for being "mean ... a racist ... and very, very, very devilish."

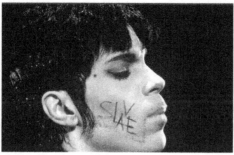

Prince is the name that my mother gave me at birth. Warner Bros. took the name, trademarked it, and used it as the main marketing tool to promote all of the music that I wrote. The company owns the name Prince and all related music marketed under Prince. I became merely a pawn used to produce more money for Warner Bros...

PRINCE AND THE PINEAL GLAND & THIRD EYE

Prince was obviously a complex man and artist. Throughout his career he kept us guessing as to whether or not he was an "Illuminati" occultist or if he was hip to the conspiracy and tried to reveal it to the masses. His artwork and symbolism suggests he was interested in Eastern occultism concepts such as the pineal gland-third eye; yet his religion remained to be that of a Jehovah's Witness.

The **pineal gland**, also known as the **pineal** body, conarium or epiphysis cerebri, is a small endocrine **gland** in the vertebrate brain. It produces melatonin, a serotonin derived hormone, which affects the modulation of sleep patterns in both seasonal and circadian rhythms.

L.A. Reid Says Prince Thought Elevators 'Were the Devil', Finds Friend's Death 'Haunting'

Prince's friend L.A. Reid is pretty "spooked" that the 57-year-old musician was found dead in an elevator.

Reid also recalled that Prince once brought up elevators to him in conversation. "One time when I was with him privately, he said, 'You know what the elevator is, right?' I said, 'No, what's the elevator?' He said, 'Well, the elevator is the devil,'" Reid shared. "It scared me. I don't like to talk like that, but he said that. So, for me, it was like really haunting when I read that he was found in an elevator."

133

DESTROYING THE EGO AND ALTERS

When it comes to the idea of using alter egos; Prince takes the cake. Before Nicki Minaj and Jhene Aiko touted multiple personalities and names, Prince was rotating through various personas- suggesting he was either channeling spiritual energies, or experimenting musically. This concept was also featured in my hip hop conspiracy book *SACRIFICE: MAGIC BEHIND THE MIC*:

We've explored the power of rituals and also the magical laws of names and words. This shows us the importance in selecting a good name. This could explain why rappers change their names from their "governments" into aliases and alter egos. Many will claim the stage names are a tradition handed down through the hip hop culture since its inception, but one has to wonder where this concept originated. Practically every rapper or R&B artist has at least one alias stage name; many have more than one (with Prince the reigning champ with over seven aliases):

- *Shawn Carter = Jay-Z = Hova = Jigga = Iceberg Slim*
- *Marshall Mathers = Eminem = Slim Shady*
- *Cordozar Calvin Broadus = Snoop Doggy Dogg = Snoop Dogg = Snoopzilla = Snoop Lion*
- *Dwayne Carter Jr. = Lil Wayne = Young Weezy = Young Tuneche = Weezy F. Baby*
- *Curtis Jackson = 50 Cent*
- *Sean Combs = Puff Daddy = P. Diddy = Diddy*
- *William Roberts = Rick Ross*
- *Cameron Thomaz = Wiz Khalifa*
- *Tauheed Epps = Tity Boi = 2 Chainz*
- *Onika Maraj = Nicki Minaj = Roman Zolanski = The Harujuku Barbie*
- *Rakim Mayers = A$AP Rocky*
- *Ben Haggerty = Macklemore*
- *Jhene Aiko = J. Hennessy*
- *Tracy Marrow = Ice T*
- *Janet Jackson = Damita Jo*
- *Prince Rogers Nelson = Prince = Jamie Starr = Alexander Nevermind = Joey Coco = Paisley Park = The Purple One = The artist formerly known as Prince*
- *Beyoncé Knowles = Beyoncé = Sasha Fierce = Yonce = Beezus*
- *Will Smith = The Fresh Prince*
- *O'Shea Jackson = Ice Cube*
- *Robert Diggs = The Rza = Bobby Digital*
- *Taalib Johnson = Musiq Soulchild = Purple*
- *Justin Bieber = Shawty Mane*
- *Mariah Carey = Mimi = Bianca*

"Sometimes your brain kind of splits in two — your ego tells you one thing, and the rest of you says something else. You have to go with what you know is right.

Even him, whose coming is after the working of Satan with all power and signs and lying wonders, And with all deceivableness of unrighteousness in them that perish; because they received not the love of the truth, that they might be saved. And for this cause God shall send them strong delusion, that they should believe a lie: - 2 Thessalonians 2:9-11

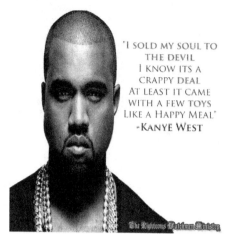

"I SOLD MY SOUL TO THE DEVIL I KNOW ITS A CRAPPY DEAL AT LEAST IT CAME WITH A FEW TOYS LIKE A HAPPY MEAL" -KANYE WEST

The Righteous Watchmen Ministry

"IF YOU SELL YOUR SOUL TO THE DEVIL, YOU GET MORE GRAIN." -DRAKE

"I SOLD MY SOUL TO THE DEVIL I'LL NEVER GET IT BACK" -EMINEM

"WHY NOT SELL MY SOUL & GO ON JERSEY SHORE? THATS WHAT I DID; & YOU KNOW WHAT, ITS BEEN AWESOME." -NICOLE POLIZZI "SNOOKI"

"I SOLD MY SOUL TO THE INDUSTRY & ALL I GOT WAS THIS LOUSY CUSTODY AGREEMENT" -BRITNEY SPEARS

"A nation can survive its fools, and even the ambitious. But it cannot survive treason from within. An enemy at the gates is less formidable, for he is known and he carries his banners openly. But the traitor moves among those within the gate freely, his sly whispers rustling through all the alleys, heard in the very halls of government itself. For the traitor appears not traitor, he speaks in the accents familiar to his victims, and he wears their face and their garments, and he appeals to the baseness that lies deep in the hearts of all men. He rots the soul of a nation, he works secretly and unknown in the night to undermine the pillars of a city, he infects the body politic so that it can no longer resist. A murderer is less to be feared." - Cicero, 42 B.C.

This is what they did in the next picture. The word sex is written hundreds of times all over the image. I've highlighted some of the embeds just to give you a clue where to look. Also look at the shadow on her right thigh - it was doctored to look like a huge spiky cock with scrotum.

Harry Potter and the Half-Blood Prince – word 'sex' dissimulated in ceiling lights

Promotional poster for Harry Potter and the Order of the Phoenix - 'sex' dissimulated in border decoration

136

What one symbol is most typical of Freemasonry as a whole? Mason and non-Mason alike, nine times out of ten, will answer, "The Square!" Many learned writers on Freemasonry have nominated the square as the most important and vital, most typical and common symbol of the ancient Craft.

Carved into a foundation stone in England. The **Square** and Compasses (or, more correctly, a **square** and a set of compasses joined together) is the single most identifiable symbol of **Freemasonry**. Both the **square** and compasses are architect's tools and are used in **Masonic** ritual as emblems to teach symbolic lessons.

Masonically the word "square" has the same three meanings given by the world:
(1) The conception of right-angled-ness -our ritual tells us that the square is an angle of ninety degrees, or the fourth part of a circle;
(2) The builder's tool, one of our working tools, the Master's own immovable jewel;
(3) That quality of character which has made "a square man" synonymous not only with a member of our Fraternity, but with uprightness, honesty and dependability.
The first of the three meanings must have been the mathematical conception and we should reflect upon the wisdom and reasoning powers of men who lived five thousand years ago, that they knew the principles of geometry by which a square can be constructed.
The square is the symbol of regulated life and actions. It is the masonic rule for correcting and harmonising conduct on principles or morality and virtue, and as a symbol, it is dedicated to the Master. We also identify ourselves with this symbol, because we are taught that squares, levels and perpendiculars are the proper signs to know a mason.
We are surrounded by squares in our Lodge and the Immediate Past Master and the Past Masters wear it most obviously. It stands, as one of the Great Lights, in the centre of all our activities. It is repeated in our F.C. salute, our feet positions, our way of moving around the Lodge and our legs when at the altar in our Fellow Craft obligation.
History tells us that the square, which is an upright with a right top arm, is the Greek letter gamma. In the construction trade, the square is used for "trueing" stones and "proving" them correct. We can see how easily, the association with truth and virtue could arise. There was the historical belief that the shape of the ancient world was an oblong square and this is represented in our "squared Lodge."
There have been references to the square's meaning as a symbol long before the start of Masonry, as we know it. The Egyptians, Confucius and Aristotle refer to 'square actions' and associate this with honest dealings, high morality and virtue. The symbol is not original, it is certainly far from new, but it seems to have a remarkable consistency of meaning.
If we move on to the Immediate Past Master's jewel for a moment it is normally identical to the Master's in shape except that pendant from it is the 47th problem of Euclid. It is important to remember that Euclid only proved the Pythagorean theorem of about 300 years earlier. When you consider what the theorem shows it is a multitude of further squares. Squares on sides, mathematically 'squared' numbers and a central closed square, about which all the 'proof' stands. As an emphasis of the square symbol we could see nothing which could do it better. We should know that the properties of this triangular arrangement were first thought to be magical in the relationship they demonstrated. We should always marvel that such a simple figure could have had such impact on our world and still has today

http://www.themasonictrowel.com/Articles/degrees/degree_2nd_files/ meaning_of_the_square.htm

137

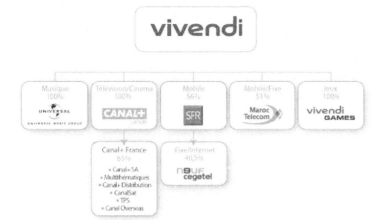

A letter has surfaced claimed to be written by a former music executive who says he witnessed a secret meeting in 1991 where the prison industrial complex encouraged the music industry to promote rap artists who glorify crime with the goal of encouraging listeners to get locked up in prison, so the private prisons could make more money. It's a very interesting read, but unless others come forward and confirm his story, there is no way to verify whether or not this meeting took place. I do believe that such a plan was put in motion, but whether or not this man was a part of that plan is not conformed. This letter first surfaced on HipHopisRead.com after the admin claims he received it in his email anonymously on April 24, 2012. Here is a link to the entire text of the letter: http://www.markdice.com/index.php?option=com_content&view=article&id=...

Vivendi Worksheet
all figures in euros

Shares Outstanding		**1,229,000,000**
Share Price (per share)		20.78
Market Value		**25,538,620,000**
euro conversion rate		1.33

Asset	Stake	Value Estimate (€)
NBC Universal		**2,800,000,000**
Activision Blizzard	60%	**6,750,000,000**
Universal Music	100%	3,750,000,000
Canal+ Group	100%	2,250,000,000
Canal+ France	80%	**6,400,000,000**
SFR	56%	11,275,000,000
Maroc Telecom	53%	**6,300,000,000**
GVT	100%	**3,000,000,000**

Note: Value estimates in **BOLD** print are based on observable market prices OR recent transactions

Figures in RED indicate stakes that Vivendi is seeking to increase to 100%

Asset Value	42,525,000,000
minus NET Debt	8,900,000,000
Value Estimate	33,625,000,000
Price target (per share)	27.36

The Definitive Guide to Illuminati Symbolism in Music Videos:

Rap and R&B Music

By Isaac Weishaupt, the IlluminatiWatcher

Swank Motion Pictures provides both public performance licensing rights and licensed movies to numerous non-theatrical markets, including U.S. colleges and universities, K-12 public schools and libraries, American civilian and military hospitals, motor coaches, Amtrak trains, correctional facilities and other markets such as parks, museums and businesses. Major Hollywood and independent movie studios have appointed Swank as their exclusive licensing and distribution partner to offer their box-office hits for public performance in non-theatrical markets (markets outside of the theaters). Swank represents **Paramount Pictures, Warner Bros., Sony Pictures, NBC Universal, DreamWorks Pictures, New Line Cinema, Lionsgate, MGM, Columbia Pictures, Tri Star Pictures, The Weinstein Company, Focus Features, Warner Independent Pictures, Paramount Classics, Paramount Vantage, Fine Line Features, Relativity, Samuel Goldwyn Films, Hallmark Hall of Fame, United Artists, National Geographic, Magnolia Pictures, Image Entertainment, Picturehouse Films, IFC Films, Millennium Entertainment, Cohen Media, Miramax, Monterey Media, eOne Entertainment, Vivendi Entertainment** and many other independent studios.

Mass Control, By Jim Keith

"If you tell a lie big enough and keep repeating it, people will eventually come to believe it. The lie can be maintained only for such time as the State can shield the people from the political, economic and/or military consequences of the lie. It thus becomes vitally important for the State to use all of its powers to repress dissent, for the truth is the mortal enemy of the lie, and thus by extension, the truth is the greatest enemy of the State." - **Joseph Goebbels, Nazi propaganda minister**

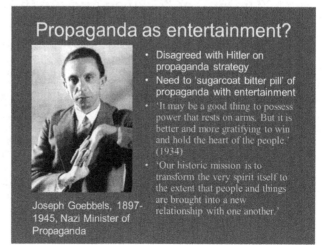

Propaganda as entertainment?

Joseph Goebbels, 1897-1945, Nazi Minister of Propaganda

- Disagreed with Hitler on propaganda strategy
- Need to 'sugarcoat bitter pill' of propaganda with entertainment
- 'It may be a good thing to possess power that rests on arms. But it is better and more gratifying to win and hold the heart of the people.' (1934)
- 'Our historic mission is to transform the very spirit itself to the extent that people and things are brought into a new relationship with one another.'

The occult sign language used since ancient times

The most prominent feature of the art productions of the Initiates of the Mystery Schools were the hand signs and this was known as the Ancient Sign Language which was transmitted from Age to Age, culture to culture. J.S.M. Ward made a thorough study of this secret sign language and in his book, "The Sign Language of the Mysteries," he identifies several of these hand signs and gestures to be found mostly in Christian art although by no means limited to Christendom. In his book Ward offers many instances of each sign. He explains that these hand poses are to be found all over Europe, Africa, Asia, India, Oceania, the Americas, ancient Crete, Polynesia, Babylonia, etc., in short, all over the world. Among the hand signs that he discusses are:

http://waitingtorot.blogspot.com/2007/11/17-occult-hand-signals-used-since.html

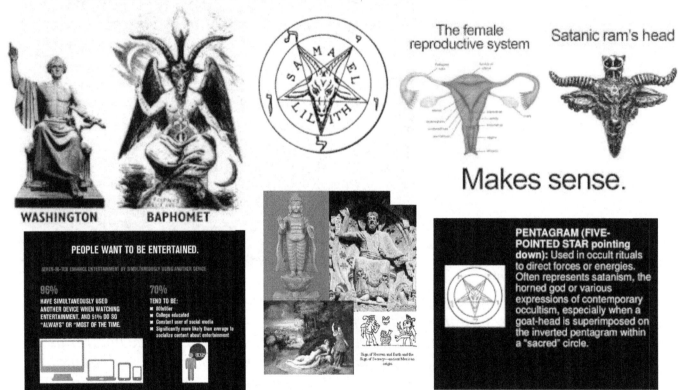

The sign of "Heaven and Earth" is often associated with the theme of resurrection or with deities sent to earth for a special mission, like Buddha, Christ, Quetzalcoatl etc.

The Secret Meeting That Changed Rap Music Forever

5TH DEGREE

US Vs USA

(Stocks and Bondage) American Governance

Labour/Work

US Vs USA (Stocks and Bondage)*American Governance*

Both systems concurrently exist today. However, the corporate system has been gaining predominance in the last 70 years. Many Sovereigns (We the people) have contracted with the corporate system unknowingly, unintentionally, and or without full disclosure given. The elite of the "One World government" corporate system want and need to have power and control over the population (masses) they call "Human Resources."

American Governance

Both systems concurrently exist today. However, the corporate system has been gaining predominance in the last 70 years. Many Sovereigns (We the people) have contracted with the corporate system unknowingly, unintentionally, and or without full disclosure given.

Once you learn the difference, you may have to make a decision for yourself, family, and posterity. That decision may require changes in how you conduct yourself. You will have to undo what has been done to make your Sovereign status known. This is not taught in the corporate government's public school system, because you are not to know.

The elite of the "One World government" corporate system want and need to have power and control over the population (masses) they call "Human Resources." *http://www.usavsus.info*

In the *National Security Strategy* of the United States President **Bush** stated: "America must stand firm for the nonnegotiable demands of human dignity: the rule of law; limits on the absolute power of the state; free speech; freedom of worship; equal justice; respect for women; religious and ethnic tolerance; and respect for private property."

142

The Flag

"Symbols are very important. If you don't think so, put a swastika on your arm, walk into a synagogue, and see the kind of response you get. Symbols elicit and bring out emotional responses in people. Even more importantly, symbols have their own spiritual presence. They tell you things." -Jordan Maxwell, Ancient Symbols and Hidden Meanings Lecture

The United States of America Military Flag

plain and simple--no gold fringe or other ornaments and symbolism attached

Prior to the 1950's, state republic flags were mostly flown, but when a USA flag was flown it was one of the following:

1 **Military flag** --Horizontal stripes, white stars on blue background
2 Has <u>no</u> fringe, braid (tassel), eagle, ball, spear, etc.

The Gadsden Flag

The rattlesnake was the favorite animal emblem of the Americans even before the Revolution. In 1751 Benjamin Franklin's *Pennsylvania Gazette* carried a bitter article protesting the British practice of sending convicts to America. The author suggested that the colonists return the favor by shipping "a cargo of rattlesnakes, which could be distributed in St. James Park, Spring Garden, and other places of pleasure, and particularly in the noblemen's gardens." Three years later the same paper printed the picture (as seen above) of a snake as a commentary on the Albany Congress. To remind the delegates of the danger of disunity, the serpent was shown cut to pieces. Each segment is marked with the name of a colony, and the motto "Join or Die" below. Other newspapers took up the snake theme.

By 1774 the segments of the snake had grown together, and the motto had been changed to read: "United Now Alive and Free Firm on this Basis Liberty Shall Stand and Thus Supported Ever Bless Our Land Till Time Becomes Eternity."

Other authors felt the rattlesnake was a good example of America's virtues. They argued that it is unique to America; individually its rattles produce no sound, but united they can be heard by all; and while it does not attack unless provoked, it is deadly to step upon one.

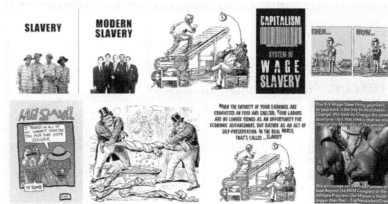

143

Don't Tread on Me The history of the Gadsden flag and how the rattlesnake became a symbol of American independence

[Benjamin Franklin's woodcut from May 9, 1754. Newspaper Serial and Government Publications Division,Library of Congress.]

The meaning of Old Glory can get mixed up with the rights and wrongs of the perpetually new-and-improved government. The meaning of "Don't Tread on Me" is unmistakable.

http://www.foundingfathers.info/stories/gadsden.html

Don't Tread On Me Flag - 666

The flag is 666 which is the number of the antichrist. Coincidence? Nope.

[The Gadsden flag: Don't Tread on Me]

The rattlesnake (serpent) became a symbol of "American independence."

"To accompany the Navy on their first mission, Congress also authorized the mustering of five companies of Marines. The Alfred and its sailors and marines went on to achieve some of the most notable victories of the American Revolution. But that's not the story we're interested in here."

"What's particularly interesting for us is that some of the Marines that enlisted that month in Philadelphia were **carrying drums painted yellow, emblazoned with a fierce rattlesnake, coiled and ready to strike, with thirteen rattles**, and **sporting the motto "Don't Tread on Me."**
Source: http://www.foundingfathers.info/stories/gadsden.html

After the 9/11 attacks, all U.S. Navy ships of war were ordered to return to the traditional "Don't Tread On Me" rattlesnake design for the duration of the "**war on terror**."Navy SEALS ordered to remove 'Don't Tread On Me' symbol from uniforms November 2, 2013

http://www.bizpacreview.com/2013/11/02/navy-seals-ordered-to-remove-dont-tread-on-me-symbol-from-uniforms-86391

King James Version

Here is wisdom. Let him that hath understanding count the number of the beast: for it is the number of a man; and his number is Six hundred threescore and six.

- George J. Laurer an employee of the Rothschilds controlled IBM, invents the UPC (Universal Product Code) barcode which will eventually be placed upon every item traded worldwide and bear the number, 666. The Book of Revelation, Chapter 13, Verse 17 through 18, states the following in relation to this number,

- "And that no man might buy or sell, save he that had the mark, or the name of the beast, or the number of his name.

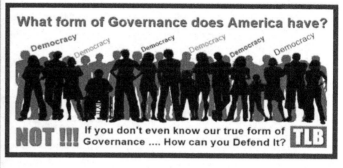

Samuel Adams said, *'When the people fear the government they have tyranny, when the government fears the people they have freedom.'*

This considered, we must realize using historical lessons that *in any republic, when government is not held in check by its true governing body, the people, it will naturally seek to accumulate and consolidate power and wealth unto itself, or its masters, eventually evolving into an autocratic entity to fill this vacuum.* Massive expansion of government and its intrusion into our freedoms by opportunistic entities is always a direct result of this evolution.

http://www.thelibertybeacon.com/most-americans-cant-even-tell-you-our-intended-form-of-governance-so-how-can-they-defend-it/

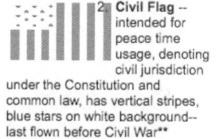

2. **Civil Flag** -- intended for peace time usage, denoting civil jurisdiction under the Constitution and common law, has vertical stripes, blue stars on white background-- last flown before Civil War**

The Esoteric Symbolism of the Confederate Flag Part I

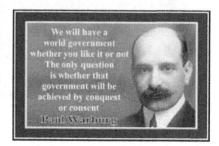

"You know, the Confederate flag represented slavery in a way – that's my abstract take on what I know about it," he said, according to People. "So I made the song 'New Slaves.' So I took the Confederate flag and made it my flag. It's my flag. Now what are you going to do?"– Kanye West

"Racism...is a universal operating system of white supremacy and domination in which the majority of the world's white people participate."

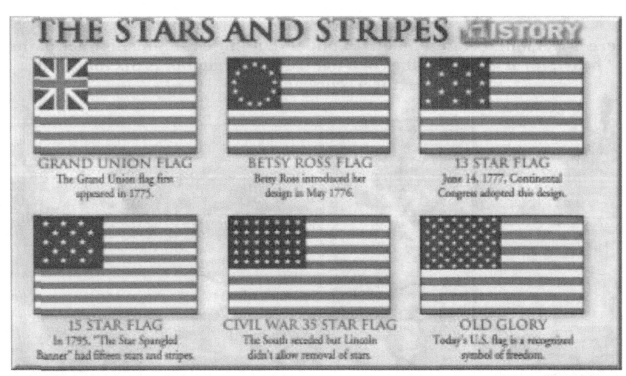

"Merchandiser, by embedding subliminal trigger devices in media, are able to evoke a strong emotional relationship between, say, a product perceived in an advertisement weeks before and the strongest of all emotional stimuli – love (sex) and death."

~Wilson Bryan Key

"The powers of financial capitalism had another far reaching aim, nothing less than to create a world system of financial control in private hands able to dominate the political system of each country and the economy of the world as a whole. This system was to be controlled in a feudalist fashion by the central banks of the world acting in concert, by secret agreements, arrived at in frequent private meetings and conferences. The apex of the system was the Bank for International Settlements in Basle, Switzerland, a private bank owned and controlled by the worlds' central banks which were themselves private corporations. The growth of financial capitalism made possible a centralization of world economic control and use of this power for the direct benefit of financiers and the indirect injury of all other economic groups."

- Tragedy and Hope: A History of The World in Our Time (Macmillan Company, 1966.) Professor Carroll Quigley of Georgetown University.

"For a long time I felt that FDR had developed many thoughts and ideas that were his own to benefit this country, the United States. But, he didn't. Most of his thoughts, his political ammunition, as it were, were carefully manufactured for him in advanced by the Council on Foreign Relations - One World Money group. Brilliantly, with great gusto, like a fine piece of artillery, he exploded that prepared "ammunition" in the middle of an unsuspecting target, the American people, and thus paid off and returned his internationalist political support.

The depression was the calculated 'shearing' of the public by the World Money powers, triggered by the planned sudden shortage of supply of call money in the New York money market ....The One World Government leaders and their ever close bankers have now acquired full control of the money and credit machinery of the U.S. via the creation of the privately owned Federal Reserve Bank."

Curtis Dall, FDR's son-in-law as quoted in his book, My Exploited Father-in-Law

WAR IS THE GREATEST DEBT CREATOR KNOWN TO MAN

So why do we resist the idea that both sides of wars are typically funded by the same bankers? Are we scared of the implications? Could THEY be manipulating the wars into happening for their own profits?

TYPES OF PUBLIC DEBT

Government loans are of different kinds, they may differ in respect of time of repayment, the purpose, conditions of repayment, method of covering liability etc. The kinds are:

- Productive and Unproductive debts
  The debts which are productive for the economy are known as productive, similarly the debts which do not benefit the economy are unproductive.

- Voluntary and Compulsory Debt
  Generally the debts taken are voluntary, on the part of the government, known as voluntary debts whereas in times of wars or crisis there is a mandatory loan taken by the government known as compulsory debt. It is a rare phenomenon.

- Internal and External Debt
  Internal debt refers to public debt floated within

I care not what puppet is placed upon the throne of England to rule the Empire on which the sun never sets.

The man who controls Britain's money supply controls the British Empire, and I control the British money supply.

-Nathan Rothschild

DUBIOUS QUOTE
UNKNOWN PROVENANCE – UNSUPPORTED BY SOURCE USED OR NO CITATION GIVEN

The Occult World of Commerce

BANKSTERS
Robbing the people since...oh...the beginning.

- America Online is called AOL, A = 1, O = 15, and L = 12.
- These numbers can easily generate and thus resonate sacred 13 through simple means. 1+1512 = 13
- CBS (Columbian Broadcasting Systems) – 3, 2, 19 = 3219 = 13
- NBC (National Broadcasting Company) – 14, 2, 3 = 1+4x2+3 = 13
- CNN (Cable News Network) – 3, 14, 14 = 3+1+4+1+4 = 13
- TBN – 20, 2, 14 = 20214 = 13
- CIA (Central Intelligence Agency) – 3, 9, 1 = 3+9+1 = 13
- DHS (Department of Homeland Security) – 4, 8, 19 = 4x819 = 13
- FBI (Federal Bureau of Investigation) – 6, 2, 9 = 62+9 =13
- FEMA (Federal Emergency Management Agency) – 6, 5, 13, 1 = 65+131 = 13
- EPA (Environmental Protection Agency) – 5, 16, 1 = 5+1+6+1 = 13 MI6 (Military Intelligence 6) – 13, 9, F = 1+3+9 = 13F (Freemasonry?)
- WHO (World Health Organization) – 23, 8, 15 = 2x38+15 = 13 NAFTA (North American Free Trade Agreement) – 14, 1, 6, 20, 1 = 1x20+6+114 = 13
- USA (United States of America) – 21, 19, 1 = 2x1+1+9+1 = 13 NATO (North Atlantic Treaty Organization) – 14, 1, 20, 15 = 1412015 = Negative 13
- NSA (National Security Agency) – 14, 19, 1 = 1+419+1 = Negative 13

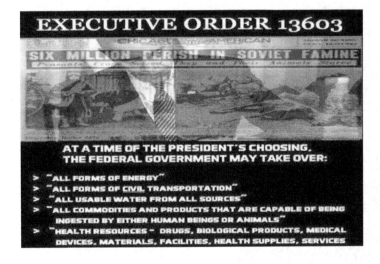

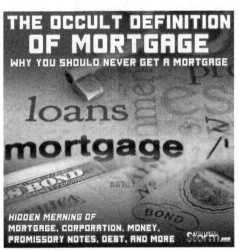

"God's plan is dedicated to the unification of all races, religions, and creeds. This plan, dedicated to the new order of things, is to make all things new—a new nation, a nonsectarian religion that has already been called the religion of 'The Great Light'...to unfold the New Age of the world—A Novus Ordo Seclorum."

SOURCE: C. William Smith, *The New Age Magazine; God's Plan in America"* (September 1950, p. 551)

The "M" is a nod to Masonry

Freemason Benedict XVI   Freemason Ignatius Loyola

https://wearetherealhebrews.com/2013/08/19/corporate-logos-pledge-allegiance-to-satan-and-the-new-world-order/

AMA 666
AMERICAN MEDICAL ASSOCIATION

Art by Carlos.S americaslastdays.blogspot.com

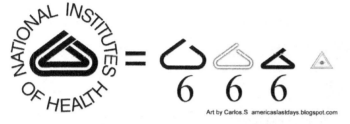

NATIONAL INSTITUTES OF HEALTH

6 6 6

Art by Carlos.S americaslastdays.blogspot.com

SPIRIVA = 666
(Tiotropium)

Art by Carlos.S americaslastdays.blogspot.com

Take note of Es in corporate logos, since E is the 5th letter of the alphabet it is very often highlighted or drawn differently than the other letters. Intel drops the E, Acer makes the E superthin, Crest and Lee place a sunburst behind the E. EForce has the Illuminati pyramid and Microsoft Internet Explorer uses the "e" icon with Saturn's ring around it. Also note the blue IntEL inside logo with the ring of Saturn. Other brands who change their E's include EBay, ETrade, ESPN, Dell, Acer, Esprit, Express, EB, EA Sports/Games, A&E, FedEx, Enconcept Academy and many more.

FedEx. Express
FedEx Kinko's. *
Office and Print Center
FedEx Office. *
* FedEx Office®

The whole idea seems to follow an occult/zodiacal agenda, using personality types to sell products.

"In ancient and modern occultism the "E" is very important because it represents the fifth essence or the quintessence ... It represents a spiritual power of transcendence The number 5. So you will always find something in a corporate logo that will tweak the "E" for a reason. It will always be highlighted in some way, or separated in some way, or dropped in some way."

Michael Tsarion, "The Subversive Use of Sacred Symbolism in The Media"
Lecture at Conspiracy Con 2003

HANDMARK

Who is your master?

Art by Carlos.S americaslastdays.blogspot.com

Proctor and Gamble

The oldest documented use of the Moon and Stars in P&G's Archives is this crude rendering on a price list from the late 1860's.

The Moon and Stars had been refined to this point by 1882, and registered in the U.S. Patent Office.

By the late 1890's, the trademark was still basically the same, but displayed some of the decorations typical of the turn-of-the-century.

In 1930, a sculptor was commissioned by P&G to refine the Moon and Stars trademark.

In 1991, the Moon and Stars trademark continued to evolve, with minor refinements to simplify its look.

"Hidden Hand"
"The Jesuits are a Military Religious Order of the Roman Catholic Church; Masonic and other oaths."

"The hidden hand lets the other initiates know that the individual depicted is part of this secret Brotherhood and that his actions were inspired by the Masonic philosophy and beliefs. Furthermore, the hand that executes the actions is hidden behind cloth, which can symbolically refer to covert nature of the Mason's actions." - VC

Paul Ryan And the Hidden Hand of Freemasonry

Any Questions?

King James Version
Here is wisdom. Let him that hath understanding count the number of the beast: for it is the number of a man; and his number is Six hundred threescore and six.

6TH DEGREE
"Ordo ab Chao"
(Order out of Chaos)
Law

Ordo ab Chaos (Order out of Chaos)

*This term Order out of **Chaos**, in Latin **Ordo ab Chao**, is the slogan of the 33rd degree of Freemasonry. "Secret Societies have a great motto '**Ordo Ab Chao**' meaning 'Order Out of **Chaos**'. Agendas are formulated designed to give the powerful more power. **Chaos** is created, and media blitzed.*

"It is quite possible that societies – much like individuals – collectively repress information, concepts, and ideas which would produce high anxiety levels if dealt with consciously."
~Wilson Bryan Key

law
/lô/ 🔊

> No negro or freedman shall be permitted [allowed] to rent or keep a house within the limits of the town under any circumstances. . . .
> — from a Black Code in Opelousas, Louisiana

noun

1. the system of rules that a particular country or community recognizes as regulating the actions of its members and may enforce by the imposition of penalties.
   "they were taken to court for breaking the law"

2. a statement of fact, deduced from observation, to the effect that a particular natural or scientific phenomenon always occurs if certain conditions are present.
   "the second law of thermodynamics"

In the United States, the **Black** Codes were **laws** passed by Southern states in 1865 and 1866, after the Civil War. These **laws** had the intent and the effect of restricting African Americans freedom, and of compelling them to work in a labor economy based on low wages or debt.

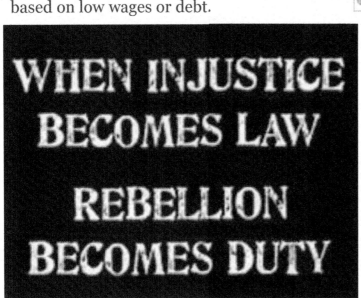

"This is a white man's government" "We regard the Reconstruction Acts (so called) of Congress as usurpations, and unconstitutional, revolutionary, and void" - Democratic Platform. Thomas Nast, 1868. Library of Congress Prints and Photographs Division. LC-US262-121735. No known restrictions on publication

"Negative media reinforcements not only influence how cops, judges, employers, and others view black males, they affect how young blacks view themselves."
~Tom Burrell

Police Officer

A re-venue agent that enforces corporate government contracts and protects the assets of the corporate government including human resources. Compels performance, no injured party necessary. One who has policing powers as found in a "POLICE STATE" i.e. Nazi Germany.

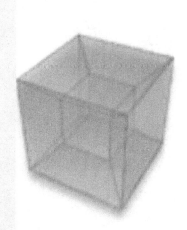

This is the geometric construct known as the **Hypercube**, or a **4D Cube**. you can visualize it as a **Cube Within A Cube**. In **dark occult symbolism**, this symbol represents **binding**, or **imprisonment**. The inner cube represents our minds and spirit, imprisoned by identification with the larger cube, the world of matter. Both cubes are boxes, confines, limitations. **A prison for the mind and spirit, inside the prison of the world of matter**. This is what the **Hypercube** represents in occult symbolism. It is most often invoked when referring to **mind control**, or the **covert manipulation** of another person for *selfish and hidden motives*, almost always *without that person being fully aware of how they are being used*.

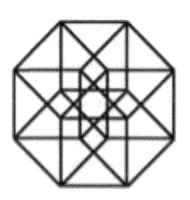

One may ask, "What does this have to do with police?" Well, this shape to the left is another way to draw a **Hypercube**. It is somewhat more difficult to visualize it this way, but you can imagine it as a cube that has been pulled, or extruded into a higher dimensional space. This is known as a 2-dimensional projection of the **Hypercube**. You will notice that this shape ultimates forms an **octagon**, or 8-sided figure.

So, if the Hypercube has been used to represent "**a prison for the mind and spirit, inside the prison of the world of matter**" in occult symbolism ...

And, if the Hypercube is invoked when referring to **mind control**, or **covert manipulation** of another person for *selfish and hidden motives*, *without that person being fully aware of how they are being used*...

Does anyone then know exactly **WHY** the **Hypercube** is placed *directly on top of a police officer's brain* in the form of an **octagonal** hat? Are police being told that they are **prisoners**? Are they sub-consciously being told that they are under **mind control** and are being used as **pawns** in a **grand game of chess**, by those with **selfish, hidden motives**.

If someone were made **aware** that something like this might be taking place, would they **continue to allow** themselves to be **used** in such a way?

"Guilty" <u>until</u> proven *"not guilty"*
(Especially, when faced with issues relating to the corporate government, its agents, and or its highwaymen.) US citizens are at the mercy of government and the administrative courts and tribunals Servants (subjects/ bond-servants)
cannot sue the Master (Corporate government) unless allowed to **No rights** <u>except</u> Civil Rights and privileges that can be taken away at any time. Restricts freedoms and liberties.

Counsel
or "Counsellor <u>in</u>-Law"
(Lawyer)

No license required

No registration required

No Bar card required

Just need to know the Law.

The Law is simple

Do not Offend Anyone

Honor all contracts

And of course, you have to obey "Natures law" such as "gravity" or "breathe air to live."

"...there simply is too much law (government) to even function - we cannot get out of our own way, we have tied ourselves in knots - when we were supposed to have a limited government and the purpose of the Constitution was to tie government down to the EXPRESS powers given it. There simply is nothing left that government does not touch, have its hands on, and has not made a mess of. More law, more government will not save us - they are the problem." --from an article written in 2006 by Attorney Gary Zerman, titled: "South Dakota Government Acted In Concert Against The People"

Traffic Sign Color Tips

Below you'll find a list of common traffic sign colors and their meanings:

- **Red**. Almost always, red means stop! A red traffic sign either signals you to stop your vehicle or prohibits entry.
- **Green**: Green means go! A green traffic sign signals that you can proceed, or provides you with direction on where to proceed.
- **Yellow**: Yellow stands for caution. A yellow traffic sign serves as a general warning.
- **Black and White**: Black and white traffic signs provide posted regulations (i.e., speed limits).
- **Orange**: Orange signals construction time! If you see an orange traffic sign, you will likely encounter construction or road maintenance ahead.
- **Brown**: Brown traffic signs reference local recreation areas or scenic points of interest.
- **Blue**: Blue stands for guidance. Blue traffic signs often offer information to assist motorists.

Traffic Sign Shape Tips

The shape of a traffic sign can often signal its meaning. For example:

- An octagon signals the need to stop.
- An upside down triangle always means "yield."
- A diamond always warns of possible hazards ahead.
- Pennant-shaped traffic signs serve as advanced warning of no passing zones.
- Round stands for railroad. When you see a round traffic sign, you will likely see a railroad crossing.
- A pentagon signals a school zone ahead or a school crossing zone.
- Horizontal rectangles typically provide guidance to drivers.
- Vertical rectangle usually serve as regulatory notices.

Traffic signs come in many shapes, sizes, and colors. With so many different traffic signs on the road, you might lose track of what each one means.

Fortunately, the shapes and colors of traffic signs can help you understand their meaning. Shape up your traffic sign knowledge with these tips.

"There are, therefore, no substitutes for true mystical symbols. A mystical symbol is the very thought form of the Cosmic law itself."
— Ralph M. Lewis, *Behold the Sign: Ancient Symbolism*, p. 12.

"...to the student of mysticism, symbols are of great importance; they teach esoteric truths, and they are instruments in his development."
— Erwin W. E. Watermeyer, "The Mystical Significance of Symbols," *Rosicrucian Digest*, Feb., 1984.

"Mysticism and occultism abound with symbols that often point to a transcendental reality beyond conscious understanding."
— Nevill Drury, *Dictionary of Mysticism and the Occult*, p.249.

... whenever you drive somewhere.

As Deoccultist and researcher Mark Passio explains, the ubiquitous octagon-shaped stop sign represents, to dark occultists, the prevention of the common man from moving forward in a journey of enlightenment.

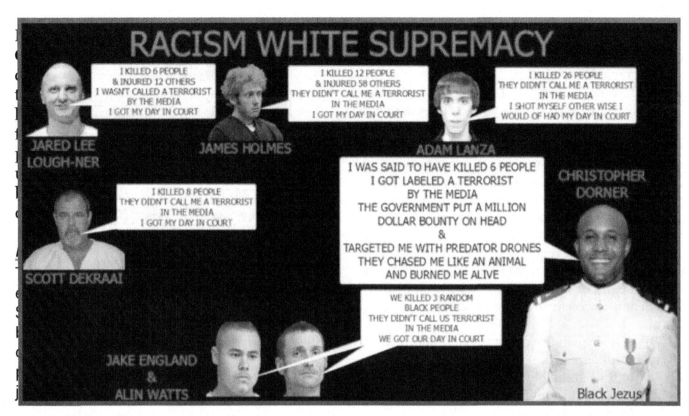

Freeborn Freeman, Freeholder Sovereign "We the people..."

U.S. citizens were declared **enemies** of the U.S. by F.D.R. by Executive Order No. 2040 and ratified by Congress on March 9, 1933, 48 Stat. 1

FDR changed the meaning of The Trading with the Enemy Act of December 6, 1917 by changing the word "**without**" to citizens "**within**" the United States.

A voter's **vote** is a <u>recommendation only</u>
Votes are counted at a poll
or polling station.
"Poll" is defined as an inquiry
into public opinion.

Elector
<u>Not</u> subject to the exclusive legislative power of Congress. An Elector's choice (election) or decision counts like one on the Board of Directors.

Voter
Registering to vote is an admission that the declarant is subject to the exclusive legislative power of the corporate Congress and is a 14th Amendment citizen residing in federal territory.

"Stop and think for a moment as to voting. When you vote for an office to be filled in the UNITED STATES OF AMERICA or one of its SUB-CORPORATIONS (THE STATE OF TEXAS), you have voted to fill a fictional corporate position designed to represent the CORPORATION, not a political position to represent the people. All elections in the "United States" are nothing more than proxy fights in a board room!"
--Ed: Brannum (Secretary of Privatization;
Provisional Government; Republic of Texas)

"If you tell a lie big enough and keep repeating it, people will eventually come to believe it."

-- Dr . Joseph Goebbels

1 **Social Security** - Applying for and receiving an **"SS card"** makes one a member of the **"US DC Communist Party"** and is eligible for benefits of the party membership. Since one is eligible for benefits, 100% of ones earnings (wages) belongs to the party and the party determines what they will keep and how much you will get back. (You paid all your working life and there are no guarantees that there will be money for you to help in retirement).

2 **Medicare**

3 **Medicaid**

4 **Grants**

5 **Disaster relief**

6 **Food Stamps**

7 **Licenses and Registration** (Permission)

8 **Privileges** only, <u>no</u> Rights

9 **Experimentation** on citizens without their consent.

Corporate government takes your money and gets credit for helping others. Politicians in return create more such programs to get more votes. Eventually there is no more to collect and give. Everyone becomes takers and there are no givers. The government then collapses within. That is why democracy never survives.

In February 2004, FOX News won a legal appeal that declared that FOX News had no legal obligation to be truthful in its reporting. The Court agreed that FOX had indeed been untruthful but ultimately agreed with FOX's argument that the FCC's policy against the intentional falsification of the news is not a legal mandate, requirement or regulation and that FOX may falsify news reports

FL 13th District
New World Communications of Tampa, Inc.
vs. Jane Akre, Case No. 2D01-529

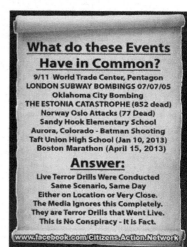

"Poor people have access to the courts in the same sense that the Christians had access to the lions."- Judge Earl Johnson, Jr.

ROCKEFELLER'S STANDARD OIL ETERNAL FLAME

To know the origin of the name Columbia we have to travel back all the way to 1738 when it was published in the weekly publication of the debates of the British Parliament. It was forbidden to print the debates and to camouflage this they were published as Reports of the Debates of the Senate of Lilliput. Fictional names were thought up for other countries and Columbia was the one used for America, the one responsible for this is most probably Samuel Johnson. The name finally became the female personification of America and was chosen to be the name and logo of the company.

JD Rockefeller's Standard Oil features and eternal flame. For some researchers, fire is a symbol of Lucifer, the bringer of light.
In 1911, Standard Oil was broken up into smaller companies who soon grew even larger making Rockefeller richer.
In masonry, the first three degrees are called the Blue Lodge while Royal Arch Masonry is called the Red Lodge.

Official explanation for the flames and colors

The colors of this logo are red, white and blue. These colors, the three colors of the U.S. flag, served to show Standard Oil's patriotism. The large torch in the middle served a dual role. A torch requires fuel to burn, and the makers of the logo sought to point out that American needed fuel to thrive and grow. The torch also served as a symbol of lighting the path to the future, which would require fuel as well.

COLUMBIA PICTURES

A statue of the titan Prometheus is a famous landmark at the very center of the Rockefeller family's huge commercial complex encompassing 19 buildings and covering more than 22 acres of Midtown Manhattan land.
Prometheus was a trickster god who gave fire (knowledge) to humans which he had himself fashioned out of clay.

He was punished by Zeus for doing so and was sentenced to have his liver eaten for eternity by an eagle.
The flame is also present on the Standard Oil corporate logo. Standard Oil is the original source of the Rockefeller's massive financial empire.

A Fasci - The ancient international symbol of fascism, and it has its own distinctive look and meaning! Used by Ancient Rome as one of its symbols of "supreme authority"- also used by the original "Axis powers" of Europe back in the first half of the 20th Century prior too and during WWII.

Washington, DC - The Nazi Fasci in the US Congress Chambers - Fasci with laurels. The Fasci face each other - this shows open control of both the Left and the Right.

The general appearance of the statue's head approximates the Roman Sun-god Apollo or the Greek Sun-god Helios.

When people talk about worshiping the "sun," they are referring to Apollo, or Apollyon, referred to in Revelation 9:11 (this scripture is so revered by the satanists that they knocked down the Twin Towers on 9:11, and they also use it as the number to call for emergency services all over North America)

http://www.christfirstministries.com

The Flame of Liberty is a full scale replica of the flame held by the Statue of Liberty in New York. The flame has become a default memorial for Princess Diana, who was murdered by the Illuminati in 1997.

http://letsrollforums.com//lady-diana-spencer-limo-t2893op88.html?
s=3db6c5fa659716da02b2cf787008588e&amp

Project for New American Century

Group of neo-conservatives who were influential in Bush II campaign and administration whose writings reinforced unilateral understanding of exceptionalism:

- Prevent rise of any rival superpower
- Use force preemptively against potential threats
- Confront rather than contain rogue states such as Iraq
- Use power and ideas to spread American values in post Cold War world just as US did in winning the Cold War

When Neo is brought in for questioning by Agent Smith, we can see a copy of Thomas Anderson's (Neo) passport with an expiring date of September 11, 2001. This has been interpreted as predictive programming by some observers.

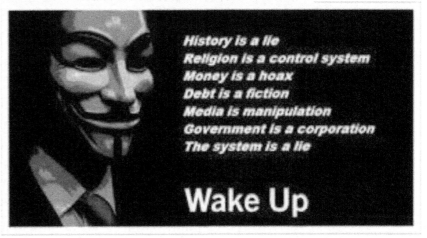

A **False flag** describes covert operations designed to deceive in such a way that the operations appear as though they are being carried out by entities, groups, or nations other than those who actually planned and executed them.~Military training drills and police drills occur on the day of and very near the attack itself, causing confusion to obscure eye witness testimony and allowing orchestrators to plant both patsies, disinformation and backup operatives. This is no small point. An incredible percentage of major domestic or international terror attacks have involved simultaneous "training drills." This list includes, but is not limited to, the infamous NORAD drills of 9/11, the 7/7 London Bombings, the 2011 Norway shooting, the Aurora shooting, Sandy Hook, and the Boston Marathon. Though none of the aforementioned events can be confirmed or denied without a doubt, they bear a striking resemblance to previous false flag attacks and should be looked at with an investigative eye.
http://www.definemania.com/the-mania.html

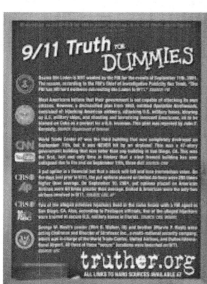

And as for the bogus Zionist controlled 9/11 Commission... Many implausible details were accepted or allowed to stand without comment, such as the delivery by a well-dressed man of an intact passport to a detective at the base of the Twin Towers – a passport used to identify one of the named hijackers, that somehow survived the plane's impact, the ensuing explosion and fire, and an 800-foot fall unaffected by wind.

smoloko.com

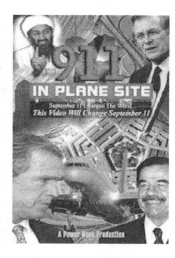

9/11 IN PLANE SITE
September 11 Changed The World
This Video Will Change September 11
A Power Hour Production

Filmed in January 2000, and aired on 3/4/2001, the makers of "The Lone Gunmen" show that the idea of crashing planes into buildings isn't anything new. As a matter of fact, their representation is eerily familiar, given what we know today.

THE LONE GUNMEN

DID YOU KNOW

On September 10, 2001, one day before the tragic events of 9/11, Donald Rumsfeld announced to the public that the Pentagon 'could not account for $2,300,000,000,000'?

DID YOU KNOW

One week before September 11, 2001, the Zim Shipping Company broke its lease it had held for 30 years and moved out of the World Trade Center.

Zim is half-owned by the Rothschilds.

DID YOU KNOW

Just months before 9/11 the World Trade Center's lease was privatized and sold to Larry Silverstein.

Silverstein took out an insurance plan that 'fortuitously' covered terrorism.

After 9/11, Silverstein took the insurance company to court, claiming he should be paid double because there were 2 attacks. Silverstein won, and was awarded $4,550,000,000.

BILL COOPER'S SPEECH ON 6/28/01

"WHATEVER IS GOING TO HAPPEN THAT THEY'RE GOING TO BLAME ON OSAMA BIN LADEN... DON'T YOU EVEN BELIEVE IT."

OSAMA BLAMED FOR EVENTS ON 9/11/01 NO TRIAL, NO JURY, NO EVIDENCE

HOW TO SPOT A FALSE-FLAG

- ☠ Immediate national news coverage
- ☠ No dead bodies
- ☠ Political agenda
- ☠ Celebrities used to influence citizens
- ☠ Incident inspires intense emotion
- ☠ Mainstream media manipulation tactics
- ☠ Initial media stories conflict official story
- ☠ Federal government attention

ALERT CONDITION: RED

False Flag Operations

False flag operations are covert operations conducted by governments, corporations, or other organizations, which are designed to appear as though they are being carried out by other entities. The purpose is to deceive the public for their support towards an agenda.

9-11 EVIL
Israel's Central Role in the September 11, 2001 Terrorist Attacks
Special 5th Anniversary Edition
The Most Dangerous 9-11 Book Ever Written!
VICTOR THORN

7TH DEGREE

Hidden in Plain Site

POLITICS THE SCIENCE OF POLY-TRICKS (MANY TRICKS)

Anonymous

Hidden in Plain Site /Who's watching the watchers.?

"Some of the biggest men in the United States, in the field of commerce and manufacture, are afraid of something. They know that there is a power somewhere so organized, so subtle, so watchful, so interlocked, so complete, so pervasive, that they had better not speak above their breath when they speak in condemnation of it." – Woodrow Wilson

It is a fact that many of our own leaders are active in the global vision and are less concerned about our Constitution than they are in furthering global government. The primary organization in advancing global government is the Council on Foreign Relations. The CFR has enormous influence through it's very rich and powerful members. Many of which are elected Representatives and even Presidents. It's infiltration of the US Government including the military and intelligence agencies, the media, and big business is far reaching.

"The CFR is the establishment. Not only does it have influence and power in key decision-making positions at the highest levels of government to apply pressure from above, but it also finances and uses individuals and groups to bring pressure from below, to justify the high level decisions for converting the U.S. from a sovereign Constitution Republic into a servile member of a one-world dictatorship." ~Congressman John R. Rarick

"And I saw, and behold a white horse; and he that sat on him had a bow; and a crown was given unto him: and he went forth conquering, and to conquer"
-Revelation 6,2

212   MOST EXCELLENT MASTER, OR SIXTH DEGREE

The brothers now all join hands as in opening, and while in this attitude the Right Worshipful Master reads the following passage of Scripture, 2 Chron. vii. 1, 4.

FIG. 30.

SIGN OF ADMIRATION, OR ASTONISHMENT.

"Now when Solomon had made an end of praying, the fire came down from heaven, and consumed the burnt-offering and the sacrifices; and the glory of the Lord filled the house. And the priests could not enter into the house of the Lord, because the

- The first job of the CFR was to gain control of the press. This task was given to John D. Rockefeller who set up a number of national news magazines such as Life and Time. He financed Samuel Newhouse to buy up and establish a chain of newspapers all across the country, and Eugene Meyer also who would go on to buy up many publications such as the Washington Post, Newsweek, ant The Weekly Magazine.

The man sitting on the horse is naked, symbolizing the fact that he is wild and thus have no cultural affiliation. He is flashing the "Sign of Admiration", one of the many occult hand signs the elite keep waving at your face without you realizing it. Here's Napoleon (Freemason and Illuminist) making the same sign.

The CFR is the promotional arm of the Ruling Elite in the US. Most influential politicians, academics and media personalities are members, and it uses it power to infiltrate the New World Order into American life.

To understand how the most influential people in America came to be members of an organization working purposefully for the overthrow of the Constitution and US sovereignty, you'll have to go back to at least the early 1900s.

The CFR secretly controls both political parties.

The CFR = America's shadow govmt. It created the United Nations, PNAC, is behind the creation of the North American Union, and controls the major media outlets. The CFR is actually the Illuminati in the United States and its hierarchy.

CFR= Council on Foreign Relations

CFR

BP
Chevron
ABC
NBC
News Corp(Fox)
Shell
IBM
Halliburton of Dubai
Merck Pharmaceuticals
JP Morgan/Chase Manhattan

illuminaticards.com

DEMOCRATS

REPUBLICANS

The CFR controls the media, so non CFR candidates will not get much media covrage.

Ron Paul 2008

BARAK OBAMA
CFR MEMBER

HILLARY CLINTON
BILDERBERGER
CFR MEMBER

BILL RICHARDSON
CFR MEMBER

CHRIS DODD
CFR MEMBER

JOHN EDWARDS
BILDERBERGER
CFR MEMBER

RUDY GIULIANI
CFR MEMBER

FRED THOMPSON
CFR MEMBER

MITT ROMNEY
CFR MEMBER

JOHN MCCAIN
CFR MEMBER

Things will never change as long as people continue to vote in Democrats & Republicans who are CFR puppets. That is why it is important for Americans to vote for Ron Paul who is not affiliated with the CFR. A vote for a CFR member = a vote for a CFR policy.

Renard Boyland

YISROEL DOVID WEISS :

"JUDAISM IS A RELIGION; BUT ZIONISM IS A POLITICAL MOVEMENT STARTED MAINLY BY EAST EUROPEAN (ASHKENAZI) JEWS WHO FOR CENTURIES HAVE BEEN THE MAIN FORCE BEHIND COMMUNISM/SOCIALISM".

Know the difference between Leading Blacks

and Black Leaders...

"Most important, Black males must help one another to understand that they are being led by the dynamic of white supremacy to inflict extreme damage upon themselves, one another and ultimately the Black race."

164

Here's an attempt to portray Obama in the media as some kind of saint or savior:

The shadowy group known as Bilderberg will be gathering this year for its annual meeting at the resort city of St. Moritz, in southeastern Switzerland, June 9-12...Bilderberg has met in Switzerland four times over the years but never in the same city. Normally, when their sibling in crime, the Trilateral Commission (TC), meets in North America, Bilderberg does, too. This year, the TC will meet in Washington on April 8 to 10, but the Bilderbergers are avoiding the United States, in what may be an effort to fool the press. Bilderberg has been called the most exclusive and secretive club in the world. To be admitted, you have to own a multinational bank, a multinational corporation or a country. Since its first meeting in 1953, it has been attended by the top powerbrokers, financial minds and world leaders. The Bilderbergers hope that part of their common agenda with the "Trilateralists" will be accomplished by the time they meet: a U.S. invasion of Libya to generate increased Middle East turmoil so America can go to war with Iran, on Israel's behalf (2011 Bilderberg Group Meeting Set).

THE SIX BLACK PRESIDENTS
BLACK BLOOD: WHITE MASKS
U.S.A

An exquisite snapshot of history in transition
Dr. Auset BaKhufu

https://targetedindividualscanada.com/tag/bilderberg/

"Power tends to corrupt, and absolute power corrupts absolutely."
~ Lord Acton April 5th, 1887

http://www.wealthdaily.com/articles/could-the-bilderberg-group-destroy-donald-trump/8213

  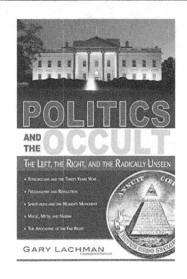

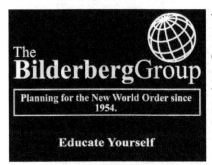

The Bilderberg group has finished up its secret meeting in Dresden, Germany where over 100 of the richest and most powerful people from Europe and North America got together. This is truly an elitist group, where political and business leaders make it evident that they are highly connected.

The Bilderberg group has been around for over 60 years. But it is no secret that this secret society exists. More people know about the Bilderberg group now than in any time in its history. We can thank the Internet and technology in general for helping to spread the word.

While these are mostly multi-millionaires, or even billionaires, who are meeting, money is just one aspect of the picture. It is really about power and control. These individuals want to control society to the degree that they can. In many ways, these elitists have controlled society to a large degree. They can often set the agenda. As the saying goes, if you have people asking the wrong question, you don't have to worry about the answer.
So while many of these people will talk about helping the poor and all of that, they are beneficiaries of a system that mixes the voluntary free market and cronyism

166

GLOBAL POWER PROJECT: BILDERBERG GROUP AND THE CULT OF AUSTERITY

If you've been to Bilderberg, chances are you're a fan of austerity: promoting it, demanding it, implementing it and profiting from it.

// READ MORE

GLOBAL POWER PROJECT: BILDERBERG AND THE GLOBAL FINANCIAL MAFIA

Here's why the favored policies of bankers frequently become the implemented policies of states.

// READ MORE

GLOBAL POWER PROJECT: BILDERBERG GROUP AND ITS LINK TO WORLD FINANCIAL MARKETS

Given that Bilderberg represents the interests of some of the largest and most powerful banks and financial institutions in the world, the meetings provide a forum where "financial markets" are duly given a powerful voice.

// READ MORE

GLOBAL POWER PROJECT: IS THE BILDERBERG GROUP PICKING OUR POLITICIANS?

Attending Bilderberg is not a guarantee for holding high office -- but it can often support a rapid rise to state power for politicians who impress the members and guests at the annual meetings.

// READ MORE

A provocative analysis of the mysterious death of journalist Danny Casolaro discusses the link between the death and high-level government conspiracy involving the Iran-Contra affair, the October Surprise, BCCI, and other political scandals and cover-ups. Tour. *IP.*

http://www.occupy.com/article/global-power-project-bilderberg-group-picking-our-politicians#sthash.toDeGPdb.dpbs

Branding the World's Newest Country

UNITED STATES

EGYPT

PALESTINE

IRAQ

YEMEN

INDONESIA

UNITED ARAB EMIRATES

SYRIA

MONTENEGRO

AUSTRIA

MOLDOVA

ARMENIA

The coat of arms of the Republic of South Sudan was adopted in July 2011. The design consists of an African fish eagle standing against a shield and a spear. According to the official description, the eagle signifies 'vision, strength, resilience and majesty'. The eagle as a symbol of Arab nationalism is also used in the state emblems of other countries, including the Republic of Sudan, from which South Sudan separated.

https://worksthatwork.com/4/branding-south-sudan

167

Andrew Gavin Marshall is a researcher and writer based in Montreal, Canada. He is project manager of The People's Book Project, chair of the geopolitics division of The Hampton Institute, research director for Occupy.com's Global Power Project and World of Resistance (WoR) Report, and hosts a weekly podcast show with BoilingFrogsPost. - See more at: http://www.occupy.com/article/global-power-project-bilderberg-group-picking-our-politicians#sthash.toDeGPdb.dpuf

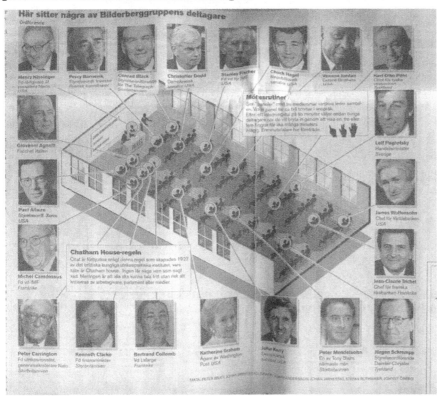

A House Is Only As Strong As Its Foundation…On Which Foundation Do We Build Our Program Models, Interventions and Curricula?

- Wade Nobles
- Jawanza Kunjufu
- Nathan & Julia Hare
- Naim Akbar
- Molefi Asanti
- Cheryl Grills
- Malcolm X
- Ron Karenga
- Carter G. Woodson
- Marcus Garvey
- Frederick Douglass
- Asa Hilliard

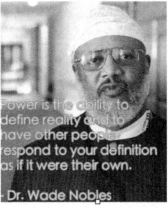

"Power is the ability to define reality and to have other people respond to your definition as if it were their own."

- Dr. Wade Nobles

Power and Oppression

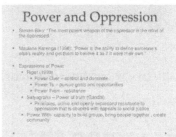

Opinions of Booker T. Washington

Underground Railroad of Harriet Tubman

Eloquence of Jesse Jackson

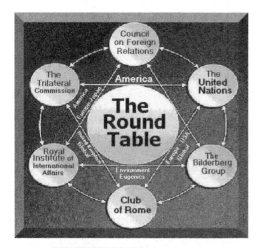

https://2012patriot.wordpress.com/2011/05/16/bilderberg-group-2011/

EXCLUSIVE The official list of participants at the "Bilderberg 2007" meeting

▮ Government & international org.
Rosina Bierbaum, UN Group on Climate Change
William Luti, National Security Council
James Perry, governor of Texas
Kathleen Sebelius, governor of Kansas
Josette Sheeran, UN World Food Program
Kristen Silverberg, Assistant Secretary of State
Ross Wilson, ambassador to Turkey
Paul Wolfowitz, World Bank
Joseph Wood, adviser to vice president
Philip Zelikow, ex-"9/11 Commission"

▮ Industry
Charles Boyd, Business Exec. for National Security
Muhtar Kent, The Coca Cola Company
Craig Mundie, Microsoft
Eric Schmidt, Google
Sidney Taurel, Eli Lilly Laboratories

United States (44)

▮ Banking & Finance
Lloyd Blankfein, Goldman Sachs & Co
Esther Dyson, EdVentures Holdings, Inc.
Timothy Collins, Ripplewood Holdings
Timothy Geithner, Federal Reserve Bank of N.Y.
Richard Holbrooke, Perseus LLC
Kenneth Jacobs, Lazard Freres & Co. LLC
James Johnson, Perseus LLC
Vernon Jordan, Jr., Lazard Freres & Co. LLC
Bruce Kovner, Caxton Associates LLC
Henry Kravis, Kohlberg Kravis Roberts (KKR)
Robert Scully, Morgan Stanley
Peter Thiel, Clarium Capital Management
James Wolfensohn, Wolfensohn & Company

▮ Media & Consultancies
Michael Barone, Almanac of American Politics
Ian Bremmer, Eurasia Group
Thomas Donilon, O'Melveny & Myers LLP
Martin Feldstein, National Bureau of Eco. Research
Paul Gigot, The Wall Street Journal
Marc Grossman, The Cohen Group
Peter Hart, Peter D. Hart Research Associates
Henry Kissinger, Kissinger & Associates
Marie-Josée Kravis, Hudson Institute
Lawrence Summers, ex-Secretary of Treasury
John Vincent Weber, Clark & Weinstock

▮ Think Tanks & Universities
Graham Allison, Harvard University
Richard Haass, Council on Foreign Relations
Jessica Mathews, Carnegie Endowment
Richard Perle, Ex-Defense Policy Board

United Kingdom (9)
Kenneth Clarke, member of parliament
Richard Dearlove, ex-MI6 director
John Kerr, Royal Dutch / Shell
John Micklethwait, The Economist
George Osborne, Shadow Chancellor of the Exchequer
Chris Patten, International Crisis Group
Paul Taggart, University of Sussex
J. Martin Taylor, Syngenta International
Adrian Wooldridge, The Economist

Turkey (12)
Ali Babacan, economic affairs minister
Mehmet Birand, columnist
Ümit Boyner, lobbyist for Turkish employers in Brussels
Cengiz Çandar, Daily Referans
Hikmet Çetin, NATO former civil rep in Afghanistan
Cem Duna, ex envoy to EU
Emre Gönensay, ex foreign minister
Kemal Dervis, UN Development Program (UNDP)
Mustafa Koç, Koç Holding conglomerate
Ayse Soysal, Bosphorus University (Istanbul)
Arzuhan Yalçindag, Tusiad (employers association)
Erkut Yücaoglu, ex-Tusiad. MAP group.

Germany (9)
Hubert Burda, Hubert Burda Media Holding
Mathias Döpfner, Axel Springer AG (Die Welt)
Eckart von Klaeden, CDU/CSU spokesman
Klaus Kleinfeld, Siemens AG
Matthias Nass, Die Zeit
Volker Perthes, SWP research institute
Jürgen Schrempp, Ex-DaimlerChrysler
Guido Westerwelle, Free Democratic Party
Vendeline von Bredow, The Economist

France (8)
Michel Barnier, Merieux-Alliance
Nicolas Baverez, Gibson, Dunn & Crutcher
Henri de Castries, Axa
Paul Hermelin, CapGemini
Christine Ockrent, France Televisions
Laurence Parisot, Medef (employers association)
Olivier Roy, CNRS research institute
Jean-Claude Trichet, European Central Bank

Austria (5)
Martin Bartenstein, minister of economy
Oscar Bronner, Der Standard
Alfred Gusenbauer, federal chancellor
Ewald Nowotny, Bawag PSK bank
Rudolf Scholten, OeKB bank

Netherlands (7)
Queen Beatrix 1st
Victor Halberstadt, ex-Bilderberg chairman
Frank Heemskerk, foreign trade minister
Jan Hommen, Reed Elsevier
Neelie Kroes, European commissioner
Michel Tilmant, ING N.V.
Jeroen van der Veer, Royal Dutch / Shell

Italy (5)
Franco Bernabè, Rothschild Europe
John Elkann, Fiat S.P.A.
Mario Monti, former EU commissioner
Paolo Scaroni, ENI S.P.A.
Domenico Siniscalco, Morgan Stanley

Sweden (4)
Carl Bildt, foreign minister
Anders Borg, finance minister
Carl Henric Svanberg, Ericsson
Jacob Wallenberg, Investor AB

Finland (5)
Atte Jääskeläinen, YLE Group
Jyrki Katainen, finance minister
Jorma Ollila, Royal Dutch / Shell
Olli Rehn, European commissioner
Teija Tiilikainen, foreign minister

Spain (5)
Queen Sofia of Spain
Juan Luis Cebrian, PRISA
B. Leon Gross, foreign minister
Matias R. Inciarte, Grupo Santander
Rodrigo Rato, IMF

Other countries
▮ Belgium (3) - Prince Philippe - Etienne Davignon, Suez Tractebel - Frans van Daele, Belgium ambassador to NATO
▮ Canada (3) Gerald Butts, Prime minister's staff - Jason Kenney, member of parliament - Heather Reisman, Indigo Books & Music
▮ Denmark (3) Anders Eldrup, Dong A/S group - Ulrik Federspiel, permanent secretary of state for foreign affairs - Mogens Lykketoft, member of parliament
▮ Greece (3) George Alogoskoufis, finance and economy minister - George A. David, Coca Cola H.B.C. - Anna Diamantopoulou, European commissioner
▮ Ireland (3) Dermot Gleeson, AIB Group - Michael McDowell, minister of justice and equality - Peter Sutherland, Goldman Sachs International
▮ Norway (3) Idar Kreutzer, Storebrand - Egil Myklebust, Norsk Hydro - Jens Ulltvelt-Moe, Umoe ▮ Switzerland (2) Klaus Schwab, World Economic Forum (Davos)
Daniel Vasella, Novartis ▮ Portugal (2) Francisco Balsemao, ex prime minister - Leonor Beleza, Champalimaud Foundation ▮ Israel (1) Eival Gilady, Portland Trust

The Eagle / Seal (devide & unite)

Holy Roman Empire
(Germany)
+/- 962

Coin, Maastricht
(The Netherlands)
1172 and 1192

Matthew, Paris
(France)
1250

Roman Empire
One headed
till 1410

Roman Empire
Two headed
from 1410

sign
of
Roman
legion

during Nazi reign
(Germany)
1939 - 1945

Present Arm
(Germany)
from 1950

Ornate two-headed eagle
symbol of secular and
ecclesiastical authority

Two-headed eagle
(Russia)
+/- 1500 till 1917
regained 1933

Bronze medal
with eagle
Napoleon, 1849

Great Seal of America
original design
1776

Great Seal of America
redesigned 1777
first used 1782

President USA
first used 1880
redesigned 1945

170

Jews, Germans and chemical warfare

" A brief aside is required here to explain what type of company I.G. Farben actually was. At the time, it was the world's largest chemical company and through the talents of its scientists and engineers, it secured the vital self-sufficiency that was to enable Germany to maneuver in the world of power politics. From its laboratories and factories flowed the strategic raw materials that Germany's own territory could not supply, the synthetics of oil, gasoline, rubber, nitrates, and fibers. In addition, I.G. produced vaccines and drugs such as Salvarsan, aspirin, Atabrine, and Novocain, along with sulfa drugs, as well as poison gases and rocket fuels. The depth of I.G. Farben's connection to Nazi policy was finally realized at Auschwitz, the extermination center where four million people were destroyed in accordance with Hitler's "Final Solution of the Jewish Question". Drawn by the seemingly limitless supply of death camp labor, Farben built I.G. Auschwitz, a huge industrial complex designed to produce synthetic rubber and oil.

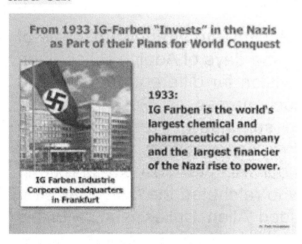

From 1933 IG-Farben "Invests" in the Nazis as Part of their Plans for World Conquest

1933:
IG Farben is the world's largest chemical and pharmaceutical company and the largest financier of the Nazi rise to power.

IG Farben Industrie Corporate headquarters in Frankfurt

THE
CRIME AND PUNISHMENT OF I. G. FARBEN

The Unholy Alliance Between Hitler and the Great Chemical Combine

JOSEPH BORKIN

This installation used as much electricity as the entire city of Berlin, and more than 25,000 camp inmates died during its construction. I.G. Farben eventually built its own concentration camp, known as Monowitz, which was closer to the site of the complex than Auschwitz was, in order to eliminate the need to march prisoners several miles to and from the plant every day.

The Dutch Connection, how the Famous American Bush Family Made Its Fortune From The Nazis.

The Standard Oil Company, in which the Rockefeller family owned a one-quarter controlling interest, was a critical asset to help the Nazi war machine.

The Standard Oil Company, in which the Rockefeller family owned a one-quarter controlling interest, was a critical asset to help the Nazi war machine. Germany's relatively insignificant supplies of crude oil were really not enough for them to engage in modern mechanized warfare. One of the most significant solutions was for Nazi Germany to manufacture synthetic gasoline from its plentiful domestic coal supplies. It was the hydrogenation process of producing synthetic gasoline and iso-octane properties in gasoline that enabled Germany to go to war in 1940 — and this hydrogenation process was developed and financed by the Standard Oil laboratories in the United States in partnership with I.G. Farben. This then connects the Nazis with not only I.G. Farben, but also Prescott Bush (the father of George Bush Sr.), the Rockefellers, and the globalist agenda for a New World Order.

As historians may recall when they mull our descent into tyranny, the roots of our constitutional crisis are directly traceable to the days of Adolph Hitler when a powerful American elite financed a political vision far different from the one we learned in school. That elite included such names as George Herbert Walker (G.W. Bush's great grandfather) and son-in-law, Prescott S. Bush (Bush's grandfather). It included such Nazi collaborators as W. Averill Harriman, the presidential advisor who paved our way into Vietnam, and John Foster Dulles, the former Secretary of State who ratcheted the Cold War after sneaking his Nazi loot out of Berlin. It included Allen Dulles who, with his brother, backed the Nazi Party for a pledge that Hitler would break the unions. And when the war was over, and our servicemen returned to forget the horrors they'd witnessed overseas, many of these same players became instrumental in driving their Nazi vision into the American political mainstream, using fear and the fortunes they'd amassed to waylay our populist traditions.

None of this is new. It's well documented, almost hackneyed, and could well have been accessed at any time by those curious enough to delve into the backgrounds of government and its officials. Nevertheless, in light of our waning constitutional grip (and at the risk of flogging a dead horse) we think it timely to review the Bush family's complicity in international fascism, if only to reconcile our collective naiveté.

by John Loftus: http://www.georgewalkerbush.net/index.htm

172

swastika hidden in plane sight

Art by Carlos.S americaslastdays.blogspot.com

This was the company enthusiastically embraced by Standard Oil as well as other major American corporations like DuPont and General Motors. I do not, however, state that Standard Oil collaborated with the Nazis simply because I.G. Farben was its second largest shareholder. **In fact, without the explicit help of Standard Oil, the Nazi Air Force would never have gotten off the ground in the first place. The planes that made up the Luftwaffe needed tetraethyl lead gasoline in order to fly. At the time, only Standard Oil, DuPont, and General Motors had the ability to produce this vital substance. In 1938, Walter C. Teagle, then president of Standard Oil, helped Hermann Schmitz of I.G. Farben to acquire 500 tons of tetraethyl lead from Ethyl, a British Standard subsidiary.** A year later, Schmitz returned to London and obtained an additional 15 million dollars worth of tetraethyl lead which was to be turned into aviation gasoline back in Germany.

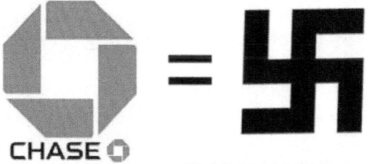

Art by Carlos.S americaslastdays.blogspot.com

After the war began in Europe, the English became angry about U.S. shipments of strategic materials to Nazi Germany. Standard Oil immediately changed the registration of their entire fleet to Panamanian to avoid British search or seizure. These ships continued to carry oil to Tenerife in the Canary Islands, where they refueled and siphoned oil to German tankers for shipment to Hamburg.

173

Nato

Art by Carlos S. americaslastdays.blogspot.com

This deception was exposed on March 31, 1941 when the U.S. State Department issued a detailed report on refueling stations in Mexico and Central and South America that were suspected of furnishing oil to Italian and German merchant vessels. The report listed Standard Oil of New Jersey and Standard Oil of California among those fueling enemy ships, but there is no record of any action being taken as a result of this discovery. Similar deals between Standard Oil and the Japanese government for the purchase of tetraethyl lead have also been uncovered, but no direct action was ever taken against Standard Oil for its dealings with America's enemies. A brief side note, however, is that on April 17, 1945 the Chase National Bank was placed on trial in federal court on charges of having violated the Trading With the Enemy Act by converting German marks into U.S. dollars. **Because many countries refused to accept German currency during the war, the Nazis used foreign banks like Chase National to change the currency into money that would be accepted, and thus allowed them to purchase much needed materials to prolong the war. The closer one looks, the more ties one finds between American business and Nazi Germany, many of which remained strong well into and beyond the war. "**

http://www.mit.edu/~thistle/v13/3/oil.html

Art by Carlos.S americaslastdays.blogspot.com

Art by Carlos.S americaslastdays.blogspot.com

Art by Carlos.S americaslastdays.blogspot.com

Here is a few links which provide a brief introduction into the world of 'sigils', representations of intentions cast into symbols.

For this, u will need to understand first that intention, i.e. willful, mindful focus, has an effect on realty. Whether it is you telling your arm to pick up the apple (your thought moving your body), to the powerful lessons of Masaru Emoto http://www.youtube.com/watch?v=zpnlCo5APrE, thought energy has power.

Psychic 101 Sigil Magick http://www.psychic101.com/sigil-magick.html
Sigil Magick http://youtube.com/watch?v=MKEeO4dZqfg
Sigils & Magick http://youtube.com/watch?v=WHc4ecUO1HY

Art by Carlos.S americaslastdays.blogspot.com

The use of Cabalistic black magic in mainline Illuminati programming in the deeper .... The Spirit of fear is demonic, and it has the power to paralyze its victim. ... Hopefully, after the programming rituals are described in detail, and a basic ..... mind more pliable to hypnosis, because many Christians are resistant to hypnosis.www.bibliotecapleyades.net/sociopolitica/mindcontrol2/part10.htm https://fitzinfo.wordpress.com/about/

What results from this process is the instilling of fear and learned helplessness into the listener (see Learned helplessness through the alternative media).

Time Warner Cable® 666

lucius

"Media wants to ferret out your unconscious anxieties so it can exacerbate them, so it can make you more emotionally unwell because anxious neurotic people make better consumers."
--August Bullock

MI6

13 △666

Another Pontiac symbol. What is that small cross in the middle of the logo? Is it the glint of a far off star...such as Sirius?

Invisible Empire

Knights of the Ku Klux Klan

JOIN THE KKK AND FIGHT FOR

PONTIAC

Like art , symbols can literally alter your brain chemistry. Whether you are made to feel elevated or depressed, happy, sad, angry, or any feeling in the emotional spectrum, by viewing the imagery your nervous system is affected, and your brain chemistry is altered, changing your mood, behavior, and state of mind. Yes, pictures and colors DO affect you both psychologically and biologically, and this is used every day in hospitals, prisons, restaurants, and many other facilities (Think green room, or placing newborns under blue light to remedy yellow jaundice). In short, light affects you, because it is energy entering your body.

Color in Symbology http://www.colormatters.com/brain.html
Biorhythm and color: http://mortgale.com/biocolor.htm

ABCDEFGHI J K
1 2 3 4 5 6 7 8 9 10 11

K K K

$$11 + 11 + 11 = 33°$$

Art by Carlos.S americaslastdays.blogspot.com

Bank of America

The light of the torch in the form of 2 blue stripes, 2 red stripes, then 2 more red stripes = 11 11 11 = 33.

Bank of America = = 33°
Freemasonry

"Symbols instill beliefs and shape attitudes that underpin social structures. The binding force of culture, by and large, is a web of symbols that enables people to control and make sense out of experience in patterned ways. We should have learned from the history of colonialism, slavery, and Nazi eugenics that the way one group in power sees and imagines another group of people can set the stage for violent action. A democratic society does well to attend to the dominant images it puts into mass circulation, particularly media representations of vulnerable groups. Images and symbolic representations drive public policy." - Dwight Conquergood, Chairman of the Department of Performance Studies at Northwestern University's School of Speech. **http://www.uic.edu/orgs/kbc/Features/Power.htm**

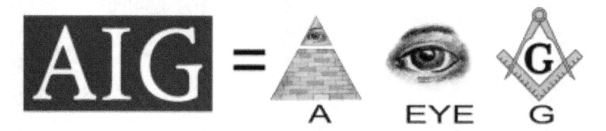

Art by Carlos.S americaslastdays.blogspot.com

The same is true with much corporate, masonic, royal, occult, Illuminati , and other symbolism. Only, with that caliber of example, it is obvious we are not working with college tricks, but instead the master crafted emblems of powerful arcane secret societies which have undergone hundreds of years and billions of dollars of refinement, and progression, while still maintaining the important core elements. Symbols are modified to fit a target audience, whether that audience be a small group of individuals who recognize a secret sign, or a Super Bowl TV audience being drilled in the head with the latest consumer branding.
(For a breakdown of programmed consumerism in detail, watch all 4 parts of 'Century of the Self' documentary. Here is part 1.
video.google.com/videoplay?docid=8953172273825999151 Part 1 (1 hr)
as well as see a stunning example of subliminal programming by Mentalist Darren Brown
www.youtube.com/watch?v=ZyQjr1YLozg)

"Notwithstanding these varied aspects of his public life, Rockefeller may ultimately be remembered simply for the raw size of his wealth. In 1902, an audit showed Rockefeller was worth about $200 million—compared to the total national GDP of $24 billion then.[65] His wealth continued to grow significantly (in line with U.S. economic growth) after as the demand for gasoline soared, eventually reaching about $900 million on the eve of the First World War, including significant interests in banking, shipping, mining, railroads, and other industries. According to the New York Times obituary, "it was estimated after Mr. Rockefeller retired from business that he had accumulated close to $1,500,000,000 out of the earnings of the Standard Oil trust and out of his other investments. This was probably the greatest amount of wealth that any private citizen had ever been able to accumulate by his own efforts."[66] By the time of his death in 1937, Rockefeller's remaining fortune, largely tied up in permanent family trusts, was estimated at $1.4 billion, while the total national GDP was $92 billion. [67] According to some methods of wealth calculation, Rockefeller's net worth over the last decades of his life would easily place him as the wealthiest known person in recent history. As a percentage of the United States' GDP, no other American fortune — including those of Bill Gates or Sam Walton — would even come close.

Art by Carlos S americaslastdays.blogspot.com

  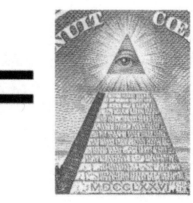

Art by Carlos S americaslastdays.blogspot.com

The Rockefeller wealth, distributed as it was through a system of foundations and trusts, continued to fund family philanthropic, commercial, and, eventually, political aspirations throughout the 20th century. Grandson David Rockefeller was a leading New York banker, serving for over 20 years as CEO of Chase Manhattan (now part of JPMorgan Chase). Another grandson, Nelson A. Rockefeller, was Republican governor of New York and the 41st Vice President of the United States. A third grandson, Winthrop Rockefeller, served as Republican Governor of Arkansas. Great-grandson, John D. "Jay" Rockefeller IV is currently a Democratic Senator from West Virginia and a former governor of West Virginia, and another, Winthrop Paul Rockefeller, served ten years as Lieutenant Governor of Arkansas. John D. Rockefeller rests at Cleveland, Ohio's Lake View Cemetery."
- http://en.wikipedia.org/wiki/John_D._Rockefeller

Official Site of Rockefeller Center - New York City's historic landmark for dining and shopping in Midtown ... 45 Rockefeller Plaza New York, NY 10111.

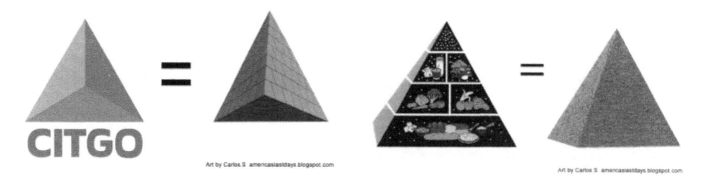

180

A.I. = A EYE

Does TV change your brain waves? How does mind control work?

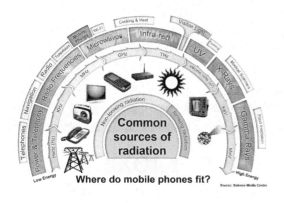

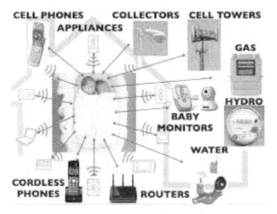

Here is an article from the Scientific American, explaining how EMF waves affect brain behavior.

"Brainwaves change with a healthy person's conscious and unconscious mental activity and state of arousal. But scientists can do more with brainwaves than just listen in on the brain at work- they can selectively control brain function by transcranial magnetic stimulation (TMS). This technique uses powerful pulses of electromagnetic radiation beamed into a person's brain to jam or excite particular brain circuits." *http://www.sciam.com/article.cfm?id=mind-control-by-cell*
http://www.sciam.com/article.cfm?id=mind-control-by-cell

Creating a Healthy Environment in a Toxic World

The natural world, including your body, produces electromagnetic fields. But these fields are low in intensity. Technology produces much more intense electromagnetic fields, and these fields can cause health risks. You cannot see or hear them. But if you live where there is cell phone service or power lines, for example, you are exposed to artificial EMFs.

https://www.safespaceprotection.com/emf-health-risks/what-is-emf/

The Electromagnetic Spectrum

The electromagnetic (EM) spectrum is the scientific name for types of photon radiation. Electromagnetic radiation consists of photons (light particles) that travel in a wave-like pattern at the speed of light.

"In the technotronic society the trend would seem to be towards the aggregation of the individual support of millions of uncoordinated citizens, easily within the reach of magnetic and attractive personalities effectively exploiting the latest communication techniques to manipulate emotions and control reason." -- Zbigniew Brzezinski, **National Security Advisor**

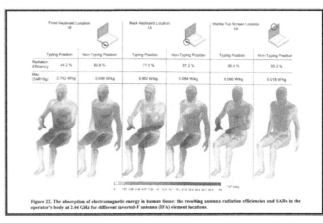

Figure 22. The absorption of electromagnetic energy in human tissue: the resulting antenna radiation efficiencies and SARs in the operator's body at 2.44 GHz for different inverted-F antenna (IFA) element locations.

Symbols. You see a symbol, and whether you realize it or not, it is communicating with you. It has a life, created by its creator. When you view a symbol and close your eyes, you will likely still see the symbol in your mind's eye, because it has been temporarily burned into first your retina, then your visual cortex, and eventually patterned into your neurons as an electrochemical signature. Burned...& *branded*.

Shapes, dimension, textures, colors...as specific in their neurological effects upon your brain as fingerprints and snowflakes. Each signature has an effect upon your brain-wave state, literally shifting the mental gears back and forth between alpha and beta, and affecting you at sleep in theta and delta.

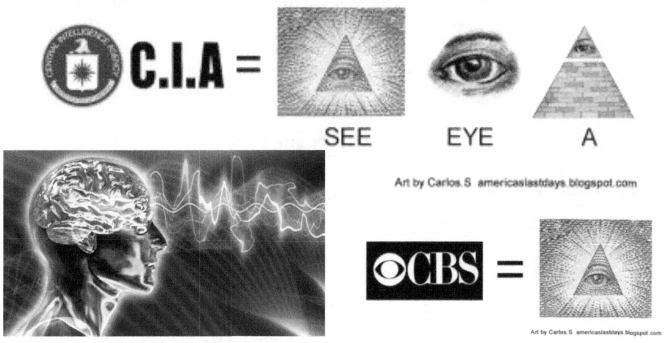

Art by Carlos.S americaslastdays.blogspot.com

Art by Carlos.S americaslastdays.blogspot.com

http://www.iamawake.co/your-brain-waves-change-when-you-watch-tv/

For a brain to comprehend and communicate complex meaning, it must be in a state of "chaotic disequilibrium." This means that there must be a dynamic flow of communication between all of the regions of the brain, which facilitates the comprehension of higher levels of order (breaking conceptual thresholds), and leads to the formation of complex ideas. High levels of chaotic brain activity are present during challenging tasks like reading, writing, and working mathematical equations in your head. They are not present while watching TV. Levels of brain activity are measured by an electroencenograph (EEG) machine. While watching television, the brain appears to slow to a halt, registering low alpha wave readings on the EEG. This is caused by the radiant light produced by cathode ray technology within the television set. Even if you're reading text on a television screen the brain registers low levels of activity. Once again, regardless of the content being presented, television essentially turns off your nervous system.

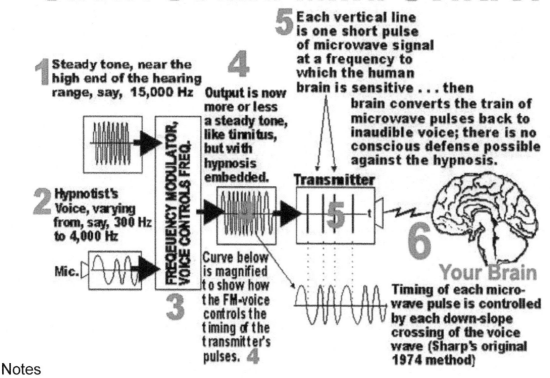

Silent Sound Mind Control

1 Steady tone, near the high end of the hearing range, say, 15,000 Hz

2 Hypnotist's Voice, varying from, say, 300 Hz to 4,000 Hz

Mic.

3 FREQUENCY MODULATOR, VOICE CONTROLS FREQ.

4 Output is now more or less a steady tone, like tinnitus, but with hypnosis embedded.

Curve below is magnified to show how the FM-voice controls the timing of the transmitter's pulses. **4**

Transmitter

5 Each vertical line is one short pulse of microwave signal at a frequency to which the human brain is sensitive . . . then brain converts the train of microwave pulses back to inaudible voice; there is no conscious defense possible against the hypnosis.

6 Your Brain
Timing of each microwave pulse is controlled by each down-slope crossing of the voice wave (Sharp's original 1974 method)

Notes

1. Krugman, Herbert E. "Brain wave Measures of Media Involvement," *Journal of Advertising Research* 11.1 (1971): 3-9. Krugman later became manager of public opinion research at General Electric.

For more on brain state changes occasioned by watching television, see: Emery, Merrelyn, *The Social and Neurophysiological Effects of Television and their Implications for Marketing Practice*. Doctoral dissertation. Australian National University. Canberra, 1985; Nelson, Joyce, *The Perfect Machine* (New Society Pub: 1992).

In addition to its devastating neurological effects, television can be harmful to your sense of self-worth, your perception of your environment, and your physical health. Recent surveys have shown that 75% of American women think they are overweight, likely the result of watching chronically thin actresses and models four hours a day.

Television has also spawned a "culture of fear" in the U.S. and beyond, with its focus on the limbic brain-friendly sensationalism of violent programming. Studies have shown that people of all generations greatly overestimate the threat of violence in real life. This is no shock because their brains cannot discern reality from fiction while watching TV.

Television is bad for your body as well. Obesity, sleep deprivation, and stunted sensory development are all common among television addicts.

So I hope we've firmly established that television is an addictive drug, one that is no better than opium, heroin, or any other opiate. Television is just as (and possibly even more) harmful to the body-brain as every other drug. But there's one big difference. All other drugs apparently pose a threat to the established social order. Television, however, is a drug that is actually *essential to maintaining* the social infrastructure. Why? Because it brainwashes consumers to throw money at the gaping void of their meaningless, terror-filled lives. And by brainwashed, I mean they've been hypnotized using very subtle and established techniques which, when coupled with television's natural effects on brain waves, make for the most ambitious psychological engineering ruse ever concocted.

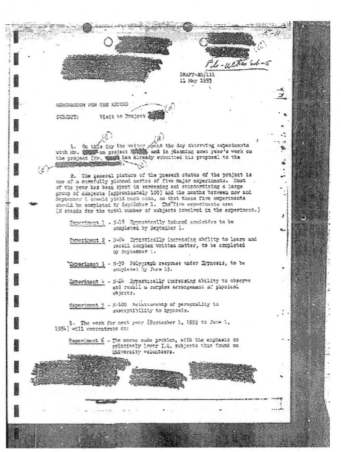

http://www.cognitiveliberty.org/5jcl/5JCL59.htm

Psychophysiologist Thomas Mulholland found that after just 30 seconds of watching television the brain begins to produce alpha waves, which indicates torpid (almost comatose) rates of activity. Alpha brain waves are associated with unfocused, overly receptive states of consciousness. A high frequency alpha waves does not occur normally when the eyes are open. In fact, Mulholland's research implies that watching television is neurologically analogous to staring at a blank wall.

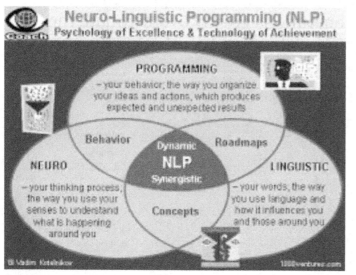
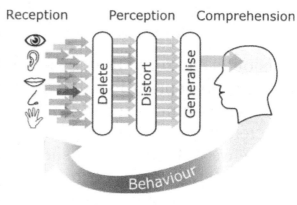

Logo 2. Here we see the actual separation of the components in another official logo. In addition, we have the checker-board pattern which is so prevalent in the Masonic ritual, as it symbolizes the Grand Game of domination and victory. And of course, the red & blue flags of Masonic ascension and appointment (Blue Lodge, Blue Degrees, Order of Red Cross i.e. Rosy Croix aka Rosicrucian - which could represent a unification between the Free & Accepted Mason and Rosicrucian factions).

Creative Orchestra, a London based brand marketing & advertising agency, have adapted NLP to create AardVarK. The tool helps improve insights, communications and effectiveness through a better understanding of how consumers think, act, feel and behave.

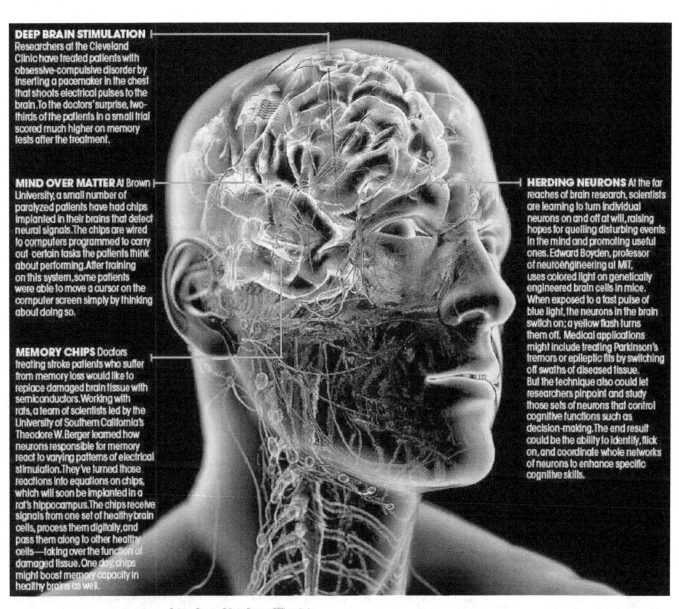

DEEP BRAIN STIMULATION Researchers at the Cleveland Clinic have treated patients with obsessive-compulsive disorder by inserting a pacemaker in the chest that shoots electrical pulses to the brain. To the doctors' surprise, two-thirds of the patients in a small trial scored much higher on memory tests after the treatment.

MIND OVER MATTER At Brown University, a small number of paralyzed patients have had chips implanted in their brains that detect neural signals. The chips are wired to computers programmed to carry out certain tasks the patients think about performing. After training on this system, some patients were able to move a cursor on the computer screen simply by thinking about doing so.

MEMORY CHIPS Doctors treating stroke patients who suffer from memory loss would like to replace damaged brain tissue with semiconductors. Working with rats, a team of scientists led by the University of Southern California's Theodore W. Berger learned how neurons responsible for memory react to varying patterns of electrical stimulation. They've turned those reactions into equations on chips, which will soon be implanted in a rat's hippocampus. The chips receive signals from one set of healthy brain cells, process them digitally, and pass them along to other healthy cells—taking over the function of damaged tissue. One day, chips might boost memory capacity in healthy brains as well.

HERDING NEURONS At the far reaches of brain research, scientists are learning to turn individual neurons on and off at will, raising hopes for quelling disturbing events in the mind and promoting useful ones. Edward Boyden, professor of neuroengineering at MIT, uses colored light on genetically engineered brain cells in mice. When exposed to a fast pulse of blue light, the neurons in the brain switch on; a yellow flash turns them off. Medical applications might include treating Parkinson's tremors or epileptic fits by switching off swaths of diseased tissue. But the technique also could let researchers pinpoint and study those sets of neurons that control cognitive functions such as decision-making. The end result could be the ability to identify, flick on, and coordinate whole networks of neurons to enhance specific cognitive skills.

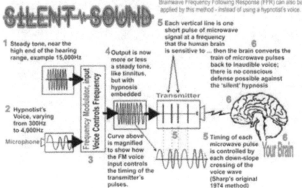

Illustration of how Silent Sound hypnosis can be transmitted using a voice Frequency Modulator to generate the 'voice', then microwave pulsed into the victim's brain via wireless broadcast.
(also see Frey Microwave Hearing aka Microwave Auditory Effect)

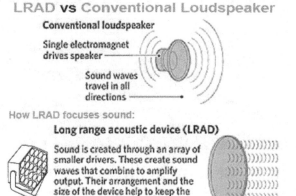

An hour after SWAT teams arrived, streets were completely blocked off, helicopters were circling, and officers were pouring tear gas onto West Florissant and the surrounding neighborhood, launching flash bangs, shooting rubber bullets, and using noise-based weapons to force people inside. This is called hood disease.

You are being controlled. Manipulated at a distance. The levers of control are light, sound, and magnetism.

Symbols are communication that by-pass all your filters, and are inserted directly into your brain.

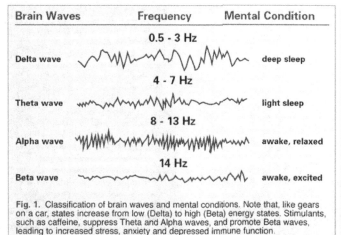

Brain Waves	Frequency	Mental Condition
Delta wave	0.5 - 3 Hz	deep sleep
Theta wave	4 - 7 Hz	light sleep
Alpha wave	8 - 13 Hz	awake, relaxed
Beta wave	14 Hz	awake, excited

Fig. 1. Classification of brain waves and mental conditions. Note that, like gears on a car, states increase from low (Delta) to high (Beta) energy states. Stimulants, such as caffeine, suppress Theta and Alpha waves, and promote Beta waves, leading to increased stress, anxiety and depressed immune function.

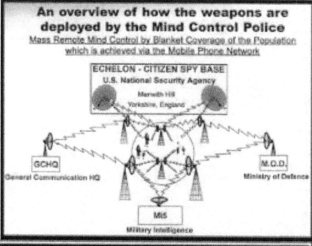

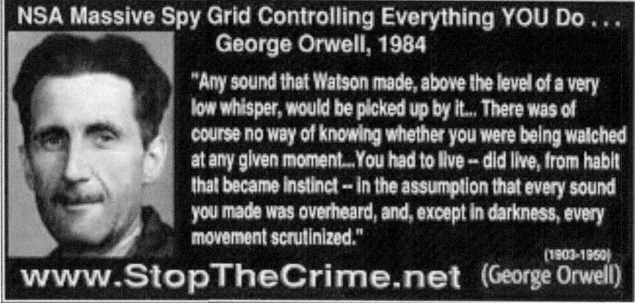

The most serious threat are to those who are unawares.
But individuals with enough mental awareness and at least some practice in focused prayer or meditation may have learned the value of internal visualization, and can use these techniques to lessen or negate the effects by focusing on benign or spiritually uplifting images.

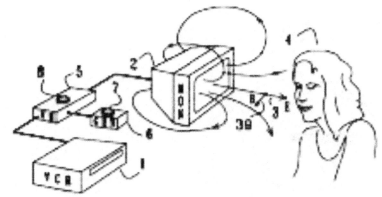

Nervous system manipulation by electromagnetic fields from monitors

Patent US6506148 - Nervous system manipulation by electromagnetic ...
www.google.com/patents/US6506148 ▾ Google ▾
Jan 14, 2003 - Nervous system manipulation by electromagnetic fields from monitors. US 6506148 B2. Abstract. Physiological effects have been observed in a ...

Application number: US 09/872,528 Publication date: Jan 14, 2003
Publication type: Grant Filing date: Jun 1, 2001

Mind Control and Manipulation (Patent# US 6506148 B2) - YouTube

https://www.youtube.com/watch?v=4pbB-LJG6Sw
Apr 10, 2016 - Uploaded by Echo Link
Source: http://www.google.com/patents/US6506148.

Physiological effects have been observed in a human subject in response to stimulation of the skin with weak electromagnetic fields that are pulsed with certain frequencies near ½ Hz or 2.4 Hz, such as to excite a sensory resonance. Many computer monitors and TV tubes, when displaying pulsed images, emit pulsed electromagnetic fields of sufficient amplitudes to cause such excitation.

It is therefore, possible to manipulate the nervous system of a subject by pulsing images displayed on a nearby computer monitor or TV set. For the latter, the image pulsing may be imbedded in the program material, or it may be overlaid by modulating a video stream, either as an RF signal or as a video signal. The image displayed on a computer monitor may be pulsed effectively by a simple computer program. For certain monitors, pulsed electromagnetic fields capable of exciting sensory resonances in nearby subjects may be generated even as the displayed images are pulsed with subliminal intensity.

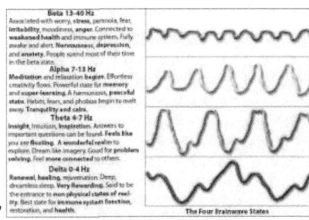

US 6506148 B2

There is no Religion higher than Truth

And what is this 'truth'?

"There is no Religion Higher than -- Truth.'... "Therefore, that a portion of truth, great or small, is found in every religious and philosophical system ... Our object is not to destroy any religion but rather to help to filter each, thus ridding them of their respective impurities....

"Free discussion, temperate, candid, undefiled by personalities and animosity, is, we think, the most efficacious means of getting rid of error and bringing out the underlying truth ... The object of the latter is to elicit truth, not to advance the interest of any particular ism ..."25

"Is there such a thing as absolute truth in the hands of any one party or man? Reason answers, 'there cannot be.' There is no room for absolute truth upon any subject whatsoever, in a world as finite and conditioned as man is himself. But there are relative truths, and we have to make the best we can of them.... for every one of us has to find that (to him) final knowledge in himself."26
—Lucifer Magazine, 1888, Helena Blavatsky

25. Helena P. Blavatsky, "To the Readers of 'Lucifer,'" Lucifer Magazine, January, 1888, http://www.blavatsky.net/blavatsky/arts/ToTheReadersOfLucifer.htm.
26. Helena P. Blavatsky, "What Is Truth?," Lucifer Magazine, February, 1888, http://www.blavatsky.net/blavatsky/arts/WhatIsTruth.htm.

8TH DEGREE
In GOD We Trust
(God Oil Drugs)

In GOD We Trust (God Oil Drugs)

The motto IN GOD WE TRUST was placed on United States coins largely because of the increased religious sentiment existing during the Civil War. Secretary of the Treasury Salmon P. Chase received many appeals from devout persons throughout the country, urging that the United States recognize the Deity on United States coins. From Treasury Department records, it appears that the first such appeal came in a letter dated November 13, 1861. It was written to Secretary Chase by Rev. M. R. Watkinson, Minister of the Gospel from Ridleyville, Pennsylvania.

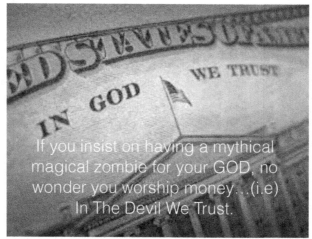

If you insist on having a mythical magical zombie for your GOD, no wonder you worship money...(i.e) In The Devil We Trust.

A law passed in a Joint Resolution by the 84th Congress (P.L. 84-140) and approved by President Dwight Eisenhower on July 30, 1956 declared IN **GOD WE TRUST** must appear on **currency**. This phrase was first used on paper **money** in 1957, when it appeared on the one-dollar silver certificate.

"In God We Trust" is the official motto of the United States. It was adopted as the nation's motto in 1956 as an alternative or replacement to the unofficial motto of E pluribus unum, which was adopted when the Great Seal of the United States was created and adopted in 1782.

Examining Education from a Christian Perspective

The Seven Laws of Teaching

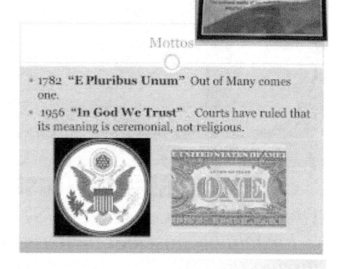

Mottos

- 1782 "E Pluribus Unum" Out of Many comes one.
- 1956 "In God We Trust" Courts have ruled that its meaning is ceremonial, not religious.

"In God We Trust" Or Do We?

"In God We Trust" is on our currency. The "Pledge of Allegiance" says, "One nation under God." The "Star-Spangled Banner" reads, "And this be our motto: In God is our trust." Do we really place our trust in God? Or have these words lost their meaning?

5 ᵃTrust in the LORD with all your heart,
ᵇAnd lean not on your own understanding;
6 ᵃIn all your ways acknowledge Him,
And He shall ¹direct your paths.

7 Do not be wise in your own ᵃeyes;
Fear the LORD and depart from evil.
8 It will be health to your ¹flesh,

PRESIDENTS

"It is the duty of all nations to acknowledge the providence of Almighty God, to obey His will, to be grateful for His benefits, and humbly to implore His protection and favor."
- **George Washington: Commander-in-Chief in the American Revolution; Signer of the Constitution; First President of the United States**

"We have no government armed with power capable of contending with human passions unbridled by morality and religion. Our Constitution was made only for a moral and religious people. It is wholly inadequate to the government of any other." - **John Adams: Signer of the Declaration of Independence; One of Two Signers of the Bill of Rights; Second President of the United States**

"Before any man can be considered as a member of civil society, he must be considered as a subject of the Governor of the Universe." - **James Madison: Signer of the Constitution; Fourth President of the United States**

"Is it not that in the chain of human events, the birthday of the nation is indissolubly linked with the birthday of the Savior? – that it forms a leading event in the progress of the Gospel dispensation? Is it not that the Declaration of Independence first organized the social compact on the foundation of the Redeemer's mission upon earth? – That it laid the cornerstone of human government upon the first precepts of Christianity?"
- **John Quincy Adams: Statesman; Diplomat; Sixth President of the United States**

FOUNDING FATHERS

"An appeal to arms and to the God of hosts is all that is left us!... Sir, we are not weak if we make a proper use of those means which the God of nature hath placed in our power... Besides, sir, we shall not fight our battles alone. There is a just God who presides over the destinies of nations and who will raise up friends to fight our battles for us... Is life so dear, or peace so sweet as to be purchased at the price of chains and slavery? Forbid it, Almighty God! I know not what course others may take; but as for me, give me liberty or give me death!"
- **Patrick Henry: Patriot and Statesman**

"I've lived, sir, a long time, and the longer I live, the more convincing proofs I see of this truth: That God governs in the affairs of men. If a sparrow cannot fall to the ground without His notice, is it probable that an empire can rise without His aid? We've been assured in the sacred writings that unless the Lord builds the house, they labor in vain who build it. I firmly believe this, and I also believe that without His concurring aid, we shall succeed in this political building no better than the builders of Babel." - **Benjamin Franklin: Signer of the Declaration of Independence and the Constitution**

SUPREME COURT JUSTICES

"The Bible is the best of all books, for it is the word of God and teaches us the way to be happy in this world and in the next. Continue therefore to read it and to regulate your life by its precepts."
"Providence has given to our people the choice of their rulers, and it is the duty, as well as the privilege and interest of our Christian nation, to select and prefer Christians for their rulers."
- **John Jay: Co-Author of the Federalist Papers; First Chief-Justice of the U.S. Supreme Court**

CONGRESS

"At the time of the adoption of the Constitution and the amendments, the universal sentiment was that Christianity should be encouraged...In this age there can be no substitute for Christianity...That was the religion of the founders of the republic and they expected it to remain the religion of their descendants."
House Judiciary Committee Report, March 27, 1854

EDUCATION

"Let every student be plainly instructed and earnestly pressed to consider well the main end of his life and studies is to know God and Jesus Christ which is eternal life (John 17:3) and therefore to lay Christ in the bottom as the only foundation of all sound knowledge and learning. And seeing the Lord only giveth wisdom, let every one seriously set himself by prayer in secret to seek it of Him (Proverbs 2, 3). Every one shall so exercise himself in reading the Scriptures twice a day that he shall be ready to give such an account of his proficiency therein."
**Harvard 1636
Student Guidelines**

"All the scholars are required to live a religious and blameless life according to the rules of God's Word, diligently reading the Holy Scriptures, that fountain of Divine light and truth, and constantly attending all the duties of religion."
**Yale 1787
Student Guidelines**

SUPREME COURT RULINGS

"There is no dissonance in these [legal] declarations...These are not individual sayings, declarations of private persons: they are organic [legal, governmental] utterances; they speak the voice of the entire people...These, and many other matters which might be noticed, add a volume of unofficial declarations to the mass of organic utterances that this is a Christian nation."
Church of the Holy Trinity v. U.S., 1892
Unanimous Decision Declaring America a Christian Nation Significantly, the U. S. Supreme Court cited dozens of court rulings and legal documents as precedents to arrive at this ruling; but in 1962, when the Supreme Court struck down voluntary prayer in schools, it did so without using any such precedent.

FOREIGNERS

"The Americans combine the notions of Christianity and of liberty so intimately in their minds that it is impossible to make them conceive the one without the other."
"Upon my arrival in the United States, the religious aspect of the country was the first thing that struck my attention; and the longer I stayed there, the more did I perceive the great political consequences resulting from this state of things, to which I was unaccustomed. In France I had almost always seen the spirit of religion and the spirit of freedom pursuing courses diametrically opposed to each other; but in America I found that they were intimately united, and that they reigned in common over the same country."
**Alexis de Tocqueville
French observer of America in 1831, author of Democracy in America**

SCRIPTURE

Blessed is the nation whose God is the LORD
Psalm 33:12a

In God We Trust

If you would like to know Jesus as Lord and Savior, call Need Him Ministry at 1-888-NEED-HIM.

Hobby Lobby, Hemispheres and Mardel Stores - 7707 S.W. 44th Street - Oklahoma City, OK 73179 www.hobbylobby.com/ministryprojects - in association with www.wallbuilders.com

http://www.jesus-is-savior.com/False%20Religions/
Wicca%20&%20Witchcraft/signs_of_satan.htm

Fighting for G.O.D. (Gold, Oil, and Drugs)

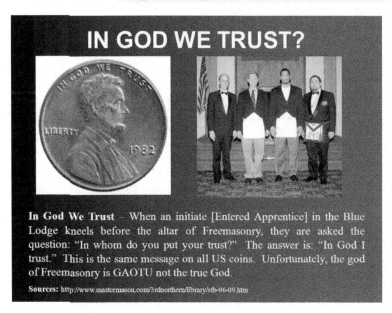

In God We Trust — When an initiate [Entered Apprentice] in the Blue Lodge kneels before the altar of Freemasonry, they are asked the question: "In whom do you put your trust?" The answer is: "In God I trust." This is the same message on all US coins. Unfortunately, the god of Freemasonry is GAOTU not the true God.

Sources: http://www.mastermason.com/3rdnorthern/library/stb-96-09.htm

http://www.theheezylife.com/design/

Basic information on various religions:

Religion	Date Founded	Sacred Texts	Membership [4]	% of World [5]
Christianity	30 CE	The Bible	2,039 million	32% (dropping)
Islam	622 CE	Qur'an & Hadith	1,570 million	22% (growing)
Hinduism	1500 BCE with truly ancient roots	Bhagavad-Gita, Upanishads, & Rig Veda	950 million	13% (stable)
No religion (Note 1)	-	None	775 million	12% (dropping)
Chinese folk religion	270 BCE	None	390 million	6%
Buddhism	523 BCE	The Tripitaka (consisting of the Vinaya, the Sutras, and the Abhidharma)	350 - 1,600 million (2)	6% (stable?)
Tribal Religions, Shamanism, Animism	Prehistory	Oral tradition	232 million	4%
Atheists	No date	None	150 million	2%
New religions.	Various	Various	103 million	2%
Sikhism	1500 CE	Guru Granth Sahib	23.8 million	<1%
Judaism	Note 3	Torah, Tanach, & Talmud	14.5 million	<1%
Spiritism			12.6 million	<1%
Taoism Note 4	550 BCE	Tao-te-Ching	12 to 173 million	<1%
Baha'i Faith	1863 CE	Alkitab Alaqdas	7.4 million	<1%
Confucianism	520 BCE	Lun Yu	6.3 million	<1%
Jainism	570 BCE	Siddhanta, Pakrit	4.3 million	<1%
Zoroastrianism	600 to 6000 BCE	Avesta	2.7 million	<1%
Shinto	500 CE	Kojiki, Nohon Shoki	2.7 million	<1%
Other	Various	Various	1.1 million	<1%
Wicca Note 5	800 BCE, 1940 CE	None	0.5 million?	<1%

http://www.religioustolerance.org/worldrel.htm

In GOD We Trust

It is an act of disrespect and disdain for Christ. It is symbolic of antichrist and honors Satan, the opposing force to Jesus Christ. It is rebellion against God, rather than submission to Jesus Christ. Popes claim to be "god" on Earth.

starting to be introduced into fashion

rapper lil' wayne

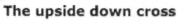

The upside down cross

The cross represents Christ and his crucifixion. In satanism this is turned upside down in order to mock and dishonor Christ, his sacrifice and his death.

Symbols of Power

Here we see Ausar pictured at left holding the Scepter, Flail and Crook (shepherd's). On the right is a picture of Pope Benedic XVI carrying the staff or scepter in his recent visit to the United Sates. Notice similarity of crown-headdress and official staff(s). This Christian re-dispensation of God incarnate or God figure representative on Earth is from ancient Afrikan Spirituality, which predates it. Dr Terri Nelson aka Queen Nteri Renenet Elson. Attend *Kamit Decoding Lecture Series - Unveiling the Symbols - Revealing the Neteru.* www.rrk.net

Stealing from all area's of Longitude and Latitude ......Their Arrogance felt as though your intelligence, wouldn't reach the competency to figure it out

NOT ONLY DID THE VATICAN STEAL CONCEPTS, ARTIFACTS AND MONUMENTS FROM EAST AFRICA

BUT FROM WEST AFRICA AS WELL.

Pictured below is POPE JOHN XXIII. Notice again the crown headdress he is wearing and its similarity with the crown of Ausar. Pope John XXIII (reigned 1958-1963) is shown wearing the papal tiara, also called the *triregnum.* Dr Terri Nelson aka Queen Nteri Renenet Elson. Attend *Kamit Decoding Lecture Series - Unveiling the Symbols - Revealing the Neteru.* www.rrk.net

http://www.rightrelationshiprightknowledge.net/articles.html

Jesus on the Cross

The Catholic Church uses a cross symbol that shows Jesus on the cross. Jesus is not still on the cross. He died and rose again on the third day. The cross is EMPTY. Use of a symbol depicting Jesus still on the cross is significant, it reveals false doctrine.

http://www.christfirstministries.com/-31/January-17-2014-Satanic-Symbols-Are-Everywhere-4400

The Serpent on the Cross Becomes Jesus on the Cross

Let it be said, that long before the Romans had given us the images and idols of the Lord and Savior of Jesus crucified upon the cross, the serpent or snake was the chosen image by the ancient wise people of the not so distant past as their savior. In fact, the ancient Romans had used to carry forth the serpent in war, and one of their standards was the serpent on a pole.

The ancient serpent-god of the Gnostics from the East was Serapis.

"Be ye wise as serpents"

Serapis is the serpent on the cross that was also the precursor to the Christian Christ, who would take the serpents place upon the cross in this Sixth Age under the religion of Christianity. Before the Christian era, the most ancient worship of the serpent was practiced in many areas of the world. The serpent on the cross was still worshiped up to the 7th century in England under the Druids. Tacitus

http://gnosticwarrior.com/serpent-on-the-cross.html

197

WHAT IS THE MEANING OF SERPENT WORSHIP AND THE SERPENT ON THE CROSS ?

As Saint John had magically said, "The great dragon was hurled down—that ancient serpent called the devil, or Satan, who leads the whole world astray. He was hurled to the earth, and his angels with him." - Revelation 12:9

These are Gnostic coins showing serpents in their striking positions forming the letter S and the number 6.

BEWARE OF FALSE PROPHETS

S is the Snake of Isis

Isis wife of Assur
Her name is the hiss of two vipers.

Hiss   Hiss

Isis

Isis represents the feminine power of creation having given birth to mankind from her womb.

The shape of S comes from the shape of a snake.

The universal sound of the letter S is the hiss of a viper: Hisss Hisss

Serpent	Saint	Snake
Sentient	Salvation	Sneak
Super	Same	Snare
Supper	Sane	Sniff
Sex	Soul	Select
Sanguine	Scintillation	Sabbath

Caduceus
The essence of life itself

Isis was the original Madonna
3000 years before Jesus

Temple of Uraeus

Isis conceived a virgin birth after resurecting Assur as Osiris
(Pictured with baby Horus)

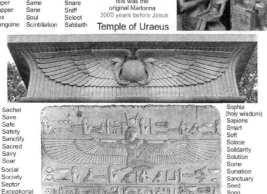

Sachel	Sophia (holy wisdom)
Save	Sapiens
Safe	Smart
Safety	Soft
Sanctify	Solace
Sacred	Solidarity
Savy	Solution
Soar	Some
Social	Sumation
Society	Sanctuary
Septor	Seed
Exceptional	Song
Sake	Sing

JOHN 3:14.

AS Moses lifted up the **SERPENT** in the wilderness,

SO must the **SON OF MAN** be lifted UP.

http://www.bibliotecapleyades.net/sociopolitica/newage_illuminati/illuminati_02.htm

198

The Holy Bible says that a woman can be sold to her rapist after he violates her.

The Quran says that a woman must be always sexually submissive to men.

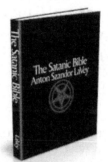

The Satanic Bible says to not make sexual advances unless they are reciprocated.

ForTheLoveOfSatan.com

Satanic Cross Upside down question mark that questions the Deity of God. Within the occult it is the representation of the three crown princes; Satan, Belial and Leviathan. Symbolizes complete power under Lucifer.

Satanic Temple Right to Accurate Medical Awareness Has to do with abortion

The Cross of Lorraine remained

The Lorraine-cross is a double-barred cross. Originally both of the arms had the same length. Later the upper arm has been reduced to a shorter length. This may be taken as the wooded sign placed by Pilatus over the head of Jesus on the cross, showing the letters "INRI". This cross is called the true cross (crux vera).

A double-barred cross of this kind was said to be used in the year 800 by Christian sects in the Orient. Godefroy de Boullion, duke of Lorraine, flew this cross in his standard when he took part in the capture of Jerusalem in 1099 during the first crusade. Later this kind of cross was attributed to him and his successors.

In recent times the Lorraine cross was used by General de Gaulle as a symbol of freedom in the French resistance during the 2. World War.

Martin Luther King, Jr., lies at the feet of civil-rights activists pointing in the direction of his assassin. The Lorraine Motel, where King was murdered, later became a civil-rights museum.

CREDIT
PHOTOGRAPH BY JOSEPH LOUW / THE LIFE IMAGES
COLLECTION / GETTY

http://symboldictionary.net/?p=1423

On October 23rd 1902, at a conference in Berlin, Germany, the Lorraine cross was chosen as the symbol of the global fight against tuberculosis. When Dr. Gilbert Seciron, submitted his proposal, he said "The red double-barred cross being a symbol of peace and brotherly understanding will bring our message to faraway places. Use it every day as a sign of your combat against tuberculosis and your mission will be successful defeating this uninvited guest that decimates our rows, and thus drying the tears of the suffering mankind."

Today the Lorraine cross is the symbol of the global fight against tuberculosis and lung diseases.

Reversed Cross (Upside down cross, Cross of St Peter)

The **reversed cross**, also known as the cross of St. Peter, has also been viewed as an emblem of Satanism, although more often by non-satanists than believers. Historically, it has been a symbol of humility, a symbol of Martyred St. Peter's refusal to be crucified in the manner of Christ, and his preference to be hung upside down. Today, the symbol of an upturned cross may symbolize an opposition to Christian dogma, a concept borrowed from Christian writers who mistook the emblem of Peter for an anti-Christian symbol- a bit of a self fulfilling prophecy!

The inverted cross is also an esoteric symbol of reversal, and is related to the 12th key of the tarot, the hanged man.

Sun worship God Kabbalah, Kabbalah Symbolism, Illuminati Symbolism, Christ Beliefs, Pagan Beliefs, Church Whore, Artefacts Carvings, Historicaly Pagan, Carvings Rocks

https://www.biblegateway.com/resources/dictionary-of-bible-themes/1670-symbols

http://holographicarchetypes.weebly.com/apollo.html

http://www.granddesignexposed.com

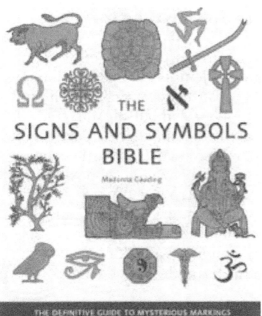

Emblems of Belief for Government Headstones (U.S. Veterans Affairs)

Detail, 'The Fall of Man' by Lucas Cranach the Elder, 1537

This post is a companion piece to my article about the the meaning of the Apple logo. In that post, I stated that the primary source of Apple's symbolism comes from The Bible. Here, I will dig into those historical roots a bit further.

In our standard telling of the Christian creation myth, Eve is tempted to eat forbidden fruit from a tree in the Garden of Eden. However, nowhere in Genesis is the fruit specified as an apple. We are merely told that it is fruit from the "tree of knowledge of good and evil." God tells Adam: "Of every tree of the garden thou mayest freely eat: but of the tree of the knowledge of good and evil, thou shalt not eat of it: for in the day that thou eatest thereof thou shalt surely die."

Eve disobeys God when she is tempted by the serpent Satan: "And when the woman saw that the tree was good for food, and that it was a delight to the eyes, and that **the tree was to be desired to make one wise**, she took of the fruit thereof, and did eat;"

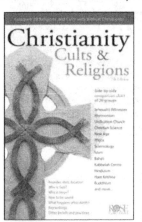

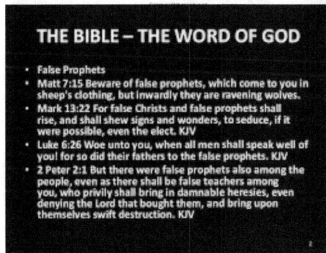

NOT REALLY AN IDOL. IT JUST APPEARS TO BE ONE. IT'S NOT REALLY THERE.

The same thing takes place on an IDOL'S BIRTHDAY; every pomp of the devil is frequented. Who will think that these things are befitting to a Christian...?

(Tertullian. On Idolatry, Chapter X. Translated by S. Thelwall. Excerpted from Ante-Nicene Fathers, Volume 3. Edited by Alexander Roberts and James Donaldson. American Edition, 1885. Online Edition Copyright © 2004 by K. Knight).

CHRIST-MASS IS THE CELEBRATION OF THE BIRTH OF AN IDOL

NOT REALLY TALKING ABOUT A TREE, IT'S TALKING ABOUT IDOLS (NOT THE KIND UNDER THE TREE) THE OTHER KIND, THAT IS NOT AT THE VATICAN EVERY YEAR

NOT REALLY AN ASHEREAH TREE. IT JUST LOOKS EXACTLY LIKE ONE

Jer 10:2 Thus saith the ... ...y of the heathen, and be not disma... ...gns of heaven; fo heathen are dismayed at them.
Jer 10:3 For the customs of the people are vain: for one cu a tree out of the forest, the work of the hands of the workman, with the axe.
Jer 10:4 They deck it with silver and with gold; they faster with nails and with hammers, that it move not.

https://www.youtube.com/watch?v=kfofJ7tSLYU

"The Medieval alchemists hid the Great Arcanum among innumerable symbols and esoteric allegories. This was in order to save it from profanity, and in order for them to avoid being burned alive in the blazes of the Inquisition." - Samael Aun Weor

In the Judeo-Christian scriptures, the Two Trees of the Garden of Eden symbolize the two essential branches of all knowledge.
The Tree of Life is the science of Kabbalah (the science of numbers).

Christmas symbols

Evergreen Tree: Titus 1:2
Eternal Life

Star & Lights: Matthew 2: 9-10
Star that told of Christ's birth

Candy Cane: Luke 2: 8-9, John 10:11
Staff of shepherds who visited the Christ child/Christ is the good shepherd

Bells: John 10:16
Ring out to bring lost sheep back to the fold

Holly & Berries: Titus 1:2, Luke 22:44
Green = Eternal life, Red = Blood of Christ

Gift: Matthew 2:1,11, John 3:16
Wise men's gifts to the Christ child/God's greatest gift to us was the Savior

The tree of life. It is arguably one of the most popular symbols in the Bible. It's too bad that so many people read Genesis, discover the tree of life, and think it's literal. To do so robs the mind of this ancient symbol's true beauty and essence!

Sometimes called the cosmic or *world tree*, the tree of life did not originate with the authors of Genesis. For thousands of years it has been used in sacred literature to describe man's connection with the divine. Although different cultures have known this tree by different names, the essence of this tree's significance is essentially the same; it represents both divine and natural man, the spiritual and natural world. And just as the tree of life symbolically spans all the worlds of existence, so does man.

"...To him that overcometh [achieves enlightenment] will I give to eat of the tree of life, which is in the midst of the Paradise of God" (Rev. 2:7).

Acts 7:22 "And Moses was learned in all the wisdom of the Egyptians, and was mighty in words and in deeds. Christian Bible - King James Version

The Garden of Eden had many animals and plants but all it is known for, for most people, is Adam, Eve, and the Snake.

Equally important are two trees, but we will first focus on the trio of the couple and the snake.

The words we speak and see today are different from those of yesteryear. In order to find the secrets of the past, we must search this ancient history and these older languages to find the truth hidden right before our very eyes. As in the case on the symbol of the serpent found all over the world, which I have found is really the symbolic exoteric representation of the worm. **http://gnosticwarrior.com/serpent-is-a-worm.html**

Psalm 84:11King James Version (KJV)

11 For the Lord God is a sun and shield: the Lord will give grace and glory: no good thing will he withhold from them that walk uprightly.

OCCULT MEANINGS OF WINTER SOLSTICE AND CHRISTMAS

"For three days, December 22nd, 23rd, and 24th, the Sun rises on the exact same latitudinal (declinations) degree. This is the only time in the year that the Sun actually stops its movement northward or Southward in our sky. On the morning of December 25th the Sun moves one degree northward beginning its annual journey back to us in the Northern Hemisphere, ultimately bringing our spring. Anything steadily moving all year long that suddenly stops moving for three days was considered to have died. Therefore, God's Sun who was dead for three days, moves one degree northward on December 25th and is symbolically born again!"

Jorden Maxwell

Pagan Holidays

WINTER SOLSTICE December 21st:
The celebration of the winter solstice,
the shortest day of the year.
It is the celebration rebirth of the Sun,
which is the promise of spring
and life even on this the darkest day.
Therefore some consider this the new year.
The burning of the log is to give the Sun strength.
Mumming (plays) such as
"St. George" is a Pagan survival, it represents
the rebirth of the God.
Wassailing or is also a Pagan custom.
The Roman festival of the Solstice was Saturnalia,
which lasted from December 17th to the 24th.

SUMMER SOLSTICE June 21:
Honoring the Sun Gods
Fertility Rites Done
Bonfires to Remember the Sun

IMBOLC - Cross-quarter day- February 2:
February is a purifactory month,
bonfires are held now.
In the Christian calendar this festival was
converted to the
Feast of the Purification of the Virgin (Mary).
Candles for the following year were
purified in the western church -
therefore we get the name Candlemas.

VERNAL EQUINOX March 20 / 21:
The celebration of the Vernal (Spring) Equinox. Day & Night are equal length.
It is a time for planting and celebrating the first signs of fertility and rebirth.
Symbols of Ostara like eggs, chicks, and rabbits have been adopted
by Christians in their Easter holiday.
The word, Easter is from the goddess Eostra, Ishtar or Astarte.

BELTANE - Cross-quarter day - May 1:
May Day.
Beltane celebrates the
Marriage of the Goddess and
the God, the goddess
is thought to conceive the
Divine Child at this time, to which she
will give birth to at Yule.
The maypole dance
is symbolic of the union of the
goddess and the god .
Pagan Handfastings occur at this time.

Mabon:
AUTUMN EQUINOX September 21:
The Autumnal Equinox,
is the second of the
Harvest holidays.
Mabon is a time to recognize
what we have and to begin preparing
for the coming winter.

SAMHAIN- October 31/ November 1
Death, the third of the Harvest holidays, the ending of the cycle.
The veil is thinnest during this time.
It is an opportunity to see spirits,
communicate with the dead,
and honor ancestors.
Very Old Pagan Time

LUGHNASADH -
Cross-quarter day - August 1:
Also known as Lammas, this is the first of the three Harvest festivals.

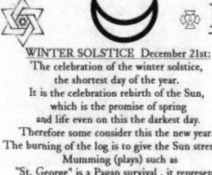

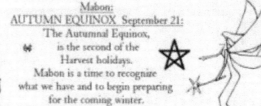

The Origin of Christmas: The Occult Connection

I don't care if this is Pagan or Roman Catholic.. This is one Idol I CANNOT forsake! The Lord pardon Thy servant in this thing!
2 Kings 5:18

𝔈phraim is joined to idols: let him alone!
Hosea 4:17

www.michaeljeshurun.wordpress.com/

http://adventofdeception.com/origin-christmas-connection-occult/

The "Nimrod" Tree "NIMROD" – The LORD of Christmas

"Nimrod started the great organized worldly apostasy from God that has dominated this world until now. Nimrod married his own mother, whose name was Semiramis.

After Nimrod's death, his so-called mother-wife, Semiramis, propagated the evil doctrine of the survival of Nimrod as a spirit being. She claimed a full-grown evergreen tree sprang overnight from a dead tree stump, which symbolized the springing forth unto new life of the dead Nimrod. On each anniversary of his birth, she claimed, Nimrod would visit the evergreen tree and leave gifts upon it. December 25th, was the birthday of Nimrod. This is the real origin of the Christmas tree."

-The Plain Truth About Christmas
by David J. Stewart | December 24th, 2005

https://christmaspagandeception.wordpress.com/2013/07/02/the-nimrod-tree-nimrod-the-lord-of-christmas/

207

Sacred Tree Worship?

YirmeYaHuW (Jeremiah) 10:

² Thus says YaHuWaH, Learn not the way of the heathen, and be not dismayed at the signs of heaven; for the heathen are dismayed at them.

³ For the customs of the people are vain: for one cuts a tree out of the forest, the work of the hands of the workman, with the axe.

⁴ They deck it with silver and with gold; they fasten it with nails and with hammers, that it move not.

Praise & Worship to the Christmas Tree: *"Oh Christmas Tree, Oh Christmas Tree, how lovely are your branches."*

Many Christians will defend this by saying: *"I don't worship Christ Mass Trees."*

The Hebrew word for *"worship"* is *"shachah"* which means *"to bow down, prostrate oneself."*

Jeremiah 10:1-4 King James Version (KJV)
1 Hear ye the word which the Lord speaketh unto you, O house of Israel:
2 Thus saith the Lord, Learn not the way of the heathen, and be not dismayed at the signs of heaven; for the heathen are dismayed at them.
3 For the customs of the people are vain: for one cutteth a tree out of the forest, the work of the hands of the workman, with the axe.
4 They deck it with silver and with gold; they fasten it with nails and with hammers, that it move not.

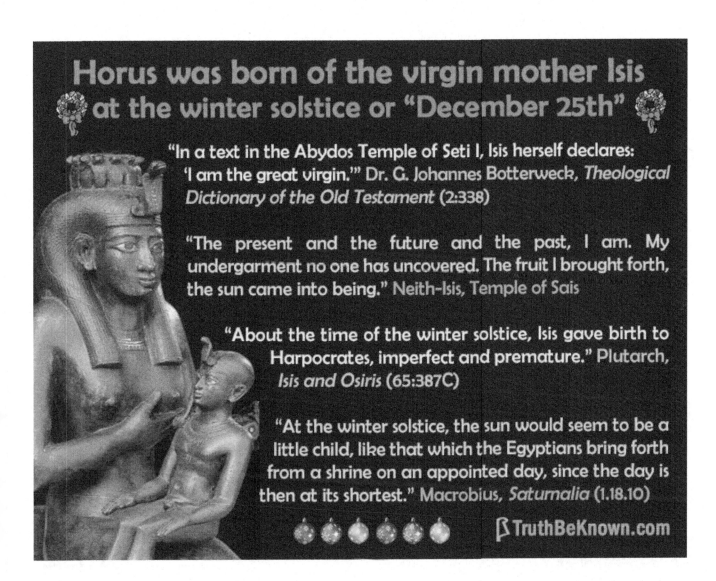

Horus was born of the virgin mother Isis at the winter solstice or "December 25th"

"In a text in the Abydos Temple of Seti I, Isis herself declares: 'I am the great virgin.'" Dr. G. Johannes Botterweck, *Theological Dictionary of the Old Testament* (2:338)

"The present and the future and the past, I am. My undergarment no one has uncovered. The fruit I brought forth, the sun came into being." Neith-Isis, Temple of Sais

"About the time of the winter solstice, Isis gave birth to Harpocrates, imperfect and premature." Plutarch, *Isis and Osiris* (65:387C)

"At the winter solstice, the sun would seem to be a little child, like that which the Egyptians bring forth from a shrine on an appointed day, since the day is then at its shortest." Macrobius, *Saturnalia* (1.18.10)

ß TruthBeKnown.com

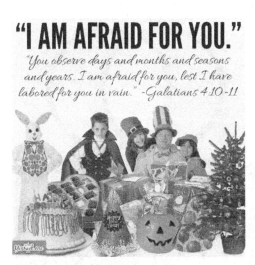

"I AM AFRAID FOR YOU."

"You observe days and months and seasons and years. I am afraid for you, lest I have labored for you in vain." -Galatians 4:10-11

THE 2ND COMMANDMENT

THOU SHALT NOT:

Deut 12:30 DO NOT enquire after their gods and do likewise
Deut 4; Lev 26; Exd 20; Deut 27; Rev 21
DO NOT MAKE ANY IMAGE OF ANYTHING
NOT STAR SUN MOON MAN OR CREATURE

REJECT PAGANISM

MARK 7:8

"Faith: Belief without evidence in what is told by one who speaks without knowledge." -Ambrose Bierce (1842-1914)

The Fish is a woman's vulva but not for the reason one would think.

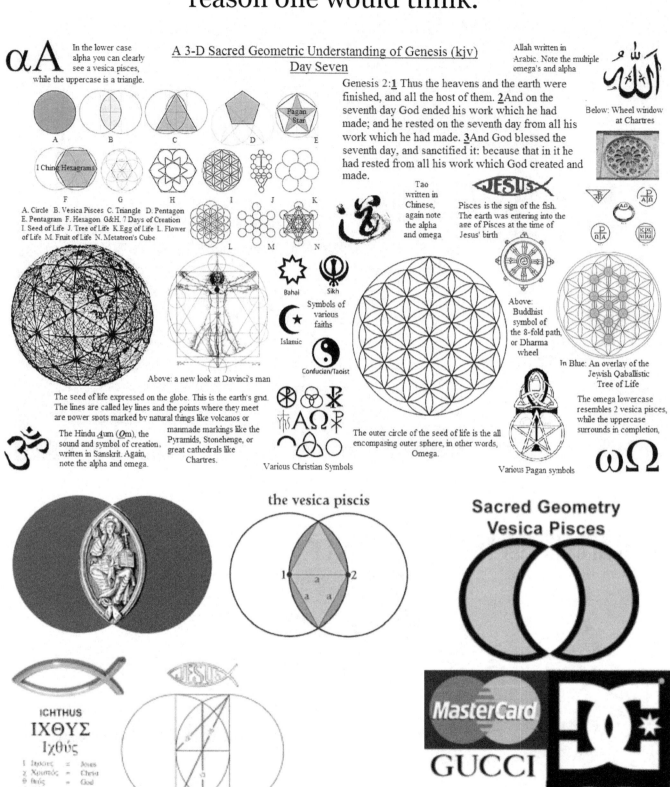

α A In the lower case alpha you can clearly see a vesica pisces, while the uppercase is a triangle.

A 3-D Sacred Geometric Understanding of Genesis (kjv) Day Seven

Allah written in Arabic. Note the multiple omega's and alpha

Below: Wheel window at Chartres

A. Circle B. Vesica Pisces C. Triangle D. Pentagon
E. Pentagram F. Hexagon G&H. 7 Days of Creation
I. Seed of Life J. Tree of Life K. Egg of Life L. Flower of Life M. Fruit of Life N. Metatron's Cube

I Ching Hexagrams

Pagan Star

Genesis 2:**1** Thus the heavens and the earth were finished, and all the host of them. **2**And on the seventh day God ended his work which he had made; and he rested on the seventh day from all his work which he had made. **3**And God blessed the seventh day, and sanctified it: because that in it he had rested from all his work which God created and made.

Tao written in Chinese, again note the alpha and omega

Pisces is the sign of the fish. The earth was entering into the age of Pisces at the time of Jesus' birth

The seed of life expressed on the globe. This is the earth's grid. The lines are called ley lines and the points where they meet are power spots marked by natural things like volcanos or manmade markings like the Pyramids, Stonehenge, or great cathedrals like Chartres.

Above: a new look at Davinci's man

Bahai   Sikh
Symbols of various faiths
Islamic
Confucian/Taoist

The Hindu **A**um (**O**m), the sound and symbol of creation, written in Sanskrit. Again, note the alpha and omega.

Various Christian Symbols

The outer circle of the seed of life is the all encompassing outer sphere, in other words, Omega.

Above: Buddhist symbol of the 8-fold path, or Dharma wheel

In Blue: An overlay of the Jewish Qaballistic Tree of Life

The omega lowercase resembles 2 vesica pisces, while the uppercase surrounds in completion,

ω Ω

Various Pagan symbols

---

the vesica piscis

Sacred Geometry
Vesica Pisces

ICHTHUS
ΙΧΘΥΣ
Ιχθύς

I Ιησους = Jesus
χ Χριστός = Christ
θ θεός = God
ὑ θεός = Son
ς σωτήρ = Savior

ICHTHUS is an anti-Christ scam. It's an ancient Pagan symbol. The X is the sun god. The Vesica Piscis ("fish bladder") is the sacred feminine (vulva) aspect. It points to Horus, who was born to Isis after magically conceiving with the phallus replacing the one Osiris lost when it was eaten by the fish. Masonic associations are Hermaphrodite aka Baphomet. Vesica Piscis / ICHTHUS represents the intersection of god and man, heaven and earth.

MasterCard
GUCCI

History of Mother's Day

The majority of countries that celebrate Mother's Day do so on the second Sunday of May. On this day, it is common for Mothers to be celebrated with presents and special attention from their families, friends and loved ones. But it wasn't always this way.

The traditional practice of honoring of Motherhood is rooted in antiquity. Ancient rites had strong symbolic and spiritual overtones, as societies tended to celebrate Goddesses and symbols of motherhood, rather than actual Mothers. From the 6th century B.C. onwards the Ancient Greeks honored Rhea or Rheia as the Magna Mater, the great mother of everything, including the gods. She was the wife of Chronos (Saturn) and the mother of Hestia, Hera, Demeter, Poseidon, Hades, and Zeus. Her father was Uranus or the heavens, her mother Gaia or Gaea, or the earth, with whom she was often identified. In 205 B.C her cult was introduced in Rome, where she was celebrated as Cybele during the Hilaria. Mothers day started out as a day to honour Rhea.

This tradition was brought to England where it is Celebrated In March which wass the Roman festival of Hilaria to honour Cybele. No one is quite sure when the celebration became to celebrate all mothers rather than the diety.

In America the first Mother's day was brought about by a woman called Ann Jarvis, who was a suffragette, she wanted a day to celebrate mothers and women in general, having seen Mothering Sunday in Europe. She fought and protested for the day for a long time, but it was finally Granted as a public holiday by then president Woodrow Wilson in 1908 who signed the bill setting aside the second Sunday of May as a special day to celebrate Mothers.

Ann jarvis was disgusted at the comercial way Mothers day was treat and she said she regretted making the day. As florists began to advertise flowers for Mother?s Day, and even hold Mother?s Day events, Anna Jarvis began to decry the shift into commercialization of such an important day. She protested saying, Mother?s Day is to be a day of sentiment, not profit.
Standing idly by was not her way. She took action. Jarvis sued sponsors of a Mother?s Day events in an effort to prevent it from taking place. In 1930, she was arrested for disturbing the peace by trying to prevent the sale of flowers at a Mother's Day event. Not to be beaten, in 1938, Jarvis attempted to get a copywrite for Mother?s Day, enabling her to control use of both the term and the holiday itself. In her attempts, she failed.

True Origin of Christian "FISH" Symbol Might Outrage, Shock Jesus Worshippers

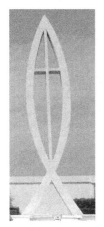

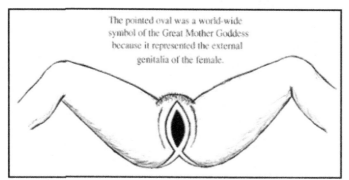

The pointed oval was a world-wide symbol of the Great Mother Goddess because it represented the external genitalia of the female.

http://www.godlessgeeks.com/LINKS/fish_symbol.htm

"Vulva," the primary Tantric object of worship, symbolized variously by a triangle, fish, double-pointed oval, horseshoe, egg, fruits, etc. Personifying the yoni, the Goddess Kali bore the title of Cunti or Kunda, root of the ubiquitous Indo-European word "cunt" and all its relatives: cunnus, cunte, cunning, cunctipotent, ken, kin, country.

The Yoni Yantra or triangle was known as the Primordial Image, representing the Great Mother as source of all life. 1 As the genital focus of her divine energy, the Yantra was adored as a geometrical symbol, as the cross was adored by Christians.

The ceremony of baptismal rebirth often involved being drawn bodily through a giant yoni. Those who underwent this ceremony were styled "twice-born." 2

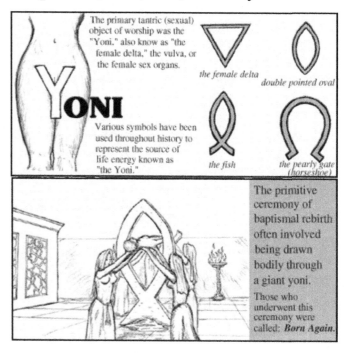

The primary tantric (sexual) object of worship was the "Yoni," also know as "the female delta," the vulva, or the female sex organs.

YONI

Various symbols have been used throughout history to represent the source of life energy known as "the Yoni."

the female delta
double pointed oval
the fish
the pearly gate (horseshoe)

The primitive ceremony of baptismal rebirth often involved being drawn bodily through a giant yoni. Those who underwent this ceremony were called: *Born Again.*

http://www.tantric-goddess.org/yoni_worship.html

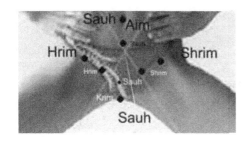

Volvo Car

A world-wide symbol of the Great Mother was the pointed-oval sign of the yoni, known as vesica piscis, Vessel of the Fish. It was associated with the "Fishy Smell" that Hindus made a title of the yonic Goddess herself, because they said women's genitals smelled like fish. 1 The Chinese Great Mother Kwan-yin ("Yoni of yonis") often appeared as a fish-goddess. 2 As the swallower of Shiva's penis, Kali became Minaksi the "fish-eyed" one, just as in Egypt, Isis the swallower of Osiris's penis became Abtu, the Great Fish of the Abyss. 3 Fish and womb were synonymous in Greek; delphos meant both. 4

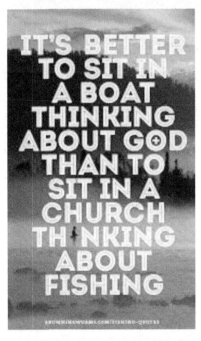

The original Delphic oracle first belonged to the abyssal fish-goddess under her pre-Hellenic name of Themis, often incarnate in a great fish, whale, or dolphin (delphinos). The cycles in which she devoured and resurrected the Father-Son entered all systems of symbolism from the Jews' legend of Jonah to the classic "Boy on the Dolphin." Apuleius said the Goddess playing the part of the Dolphin was Aphrodite Salacia, "with fish-teeming womb."

Symbols for the Elements

The Symbol: FIRE is the symbol of cleansing and purification.
The Reason: Fire burns everything away leaving things cleared to begin again.

The Symbol: WATER is the symbol of life and cleansing.
The Reason: Water is necessary to live, and churches use water to wash (cleanse) away sins.

The Symbol: AIR is the symbol of change.
The Reason: As **air** sweeps in and takes the form of wind, it sweeps away the old and brings in the new.

The Symbol: STONE is the symbol of building and solidity.
The Reason: STONE is natural, of the earth, and the strongest building material.

The catholic priests wear the pointy fish hat of Dagon which is also known as Nimrod grand son of Noah the ancient Babylonian god who defied God and served Lucifer, those in the Vatican wear these hats and perform the Babylonian rituals for all the world to see, but only those with eyes to see will really realize and understand.

truly amazing revelation in this video.https://www.youtube.com/watch?v=5lFmDNveSoM

214

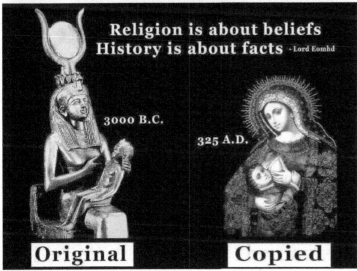

Mary, of course, is the name of Christ's mother and one of the most commonly used images for Jesus is that of the **Lamb** of God, the **fleece** as **white as snow** a symbol of his goodness and purity.

The poem can be read as a parable of Christ's enduring love for mankind (**Why does the lamb love Mary so?**), that he is with Christians everywhere (**And everywhere that Mary went, / The lamb was sure to go**) and that the true Christian should love God and ignore other people's mockery (**It made the children laugh and play**). In the style of these homilies, the teacher would have used Mary's story explicitly to draw this improving moral, spelt out in the final verse.

Mary Had a Little Lamb

Mary had a little lamb,
Little lamb, little lamb,
Mary had a little lamb,
Its fleece was white as snow

And everywhere that Mary went,
Mary went, Mary went,
Everywhere that Mary went
The lamb was sure to go

It followed her to school one day
School one day, school one day
It followed her to school one day
Which was against the rules.

It made the children laugh and play,
Laugh and play, laugh and play,
It made the children laugh and play
To see a lamb at school

And so the teacher turned it out,
Turned it out, turned it out,
And so the teacher turned it out,
But still it lingered near

www.theteachersguide.com

https://albertjackchat.com/tag/origin-of-mary-had-a-little-lamb/

Sometimes, Jesus is called "The Lamb of God," and since Jesus' mother was named Mary, I thought I would read a new poem called "Mary Had a Little Lamb."

We see in this image one of the typical interpretations of Hermes amongst the Greeks. He was known as Hermes Criophorus, the lamb bearer. So you will see many different paintings and drawings of Hermes carrying a ram, lamb, or a goat.
Hermes was the god of sacrifices. He would be the one to bring the lamb, the goat or the ram to the sacrifice to the gods. This is also very significant, as we will soon see.

> **"The most disastrous aspect of colonization which you are the most reluctant to release from your mind is their colonization of the image of God."**
> ~Dr. Frances Cress Welsing

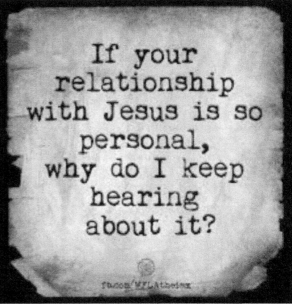

"Dude, people keep calling me out my name! My name is Caesar Borgia. I was the son of Pope Alxeander IV (Rodrigo Borgia, a gangster, war mongering, greedy, orgy having, running a continual criminal empire pope. My dad forced my image on the Church and made you worship it ever since 1490."

This is one of the most bizarre subliminal images that I have found. What do you think made the artist put that image on the figure? Was he really trying to make the figure more "manly" or "virile"? More sexy? The figures to the right and left seem to be looking right at the shape. Just a very odd image.

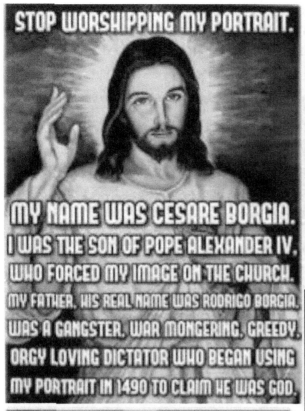

STOP WORSHIPPING MY PORTRAIT.

MY NAME WAS CESARE BORGIA. I WAS THE SON OF POPE ALEXANDER IV, WHO FORCED MY IMAGE ON THE CHURCH. MY FATHER, HIS REAL NAME WAS RODRIGO BORGIA, WAS A GANGSTER, WAR MONGERING, GREEDY, ORGY LOVING DICTATOR WHO BEGAN USING MY PORTRAIT IN 1490 TO CLAIM HE WAS GOD.

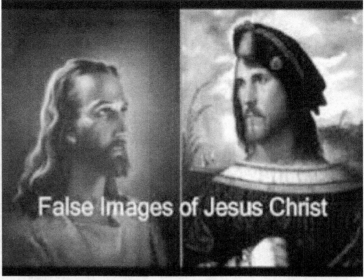

False Images of Jesus Christ

PENTAGRAM (FIVE-POINTED STAR pointing down): Used in occult rituals to direct forces or energies. Often represents satanism, the horned god or various expressions of contemporary occultism, especially when a goat-head is superimposed on the inverted pentagram within a "sacred" circle.

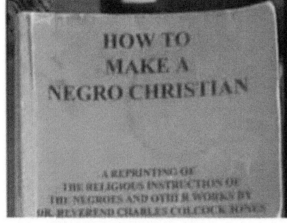

HOW TO MAKE A NEGRO CHRISTIAN

A REPRINTING OF THE RELIGIOUS INSTRUCTION OF THE NEGROES AND OTHER WORKS BY DR. REVEREND CHARLES COLCOCK JONES

This is a book written during the slavery period in America by Rev. Dr. Charles Colcock-Jones. He was a major slave owner that owned 3 plantations. He developed a system to make slaves more submissive and easier to control by converting them to Christianity. Over time his methods proved highly successful and became standard operating procedures for most slave owners.

SILLY CHRISTIAN!

Christmas was the Winter Solstice
Easter was Ostara (the Spring Equinox)
Halloween was Samhain
Valentine's Day was Imbolc
May Day was Beltane
Tuesday was Tyr's (Tiw's) Day
Wednesday was Woden's (Odin's) Day
Thursday was Thor's Day
Friday was Freya's Day
Saturday was Saturn's Day
Sunday was the sun's day
Monday was the moon's day

YOUR CALENDAR IS PAGAN!

"Faith is that quality which enables us to believe what we know to be untrue. " [*"The Omnibus Boners"*].

A later image of Jesus - notice the long female like hair! Jesus would have had short hair as the Bible states itself!

Notice Baphomet is a Male/Female Figure, male body with female breasts.

Look at Jesus's hands, Left hand pointing up with three fingers and the other hand pointing to the heart which actually makes a downwards triangle.

Which is again referencing "As Above, So Below"

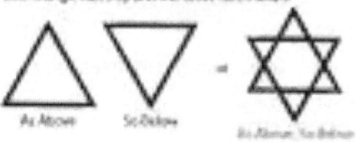

Satanic Baphomet - in his pose "As Above, So Below" notice the 3 fingers pointing up and down (two fingers and a thumb to be exact)

This creates 2 triangles and the 3 sides in each triangle. One triangle facing up and the other faces down.

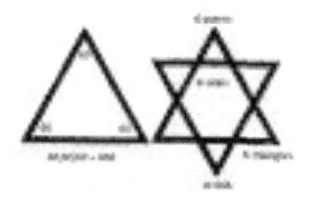

219

SATANIC STAR
(Pentagram)

Turn goat's head star
upside down to observe
another face.

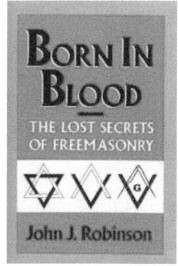

Light

Female Breasts
Bisexual Baphomet
Male/Female

Double Helix DNA
Serpent around the
Phallus - The serpent
seed

Darkness

As above

So below

3 fingers up, 3 fingers down
3 sides Triangle UP
3 sides Triangle DOWN
Makes a Hexagram

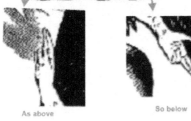

Lamar Odom – ILLUMINATI Blood SACRIFICE Attempt by Kardashians? THE INVESTIGATION

Is Lamar Odom the next Illuminati celebrity blood sacrifice? Many people believe his troubles are due to his connection with the Kardashians and his marriage to Khloe and the NBA. What really happened to Lamar? Is the Illuminati behind his downfall? MUST SEE!!!

The motto "IN GOD WE TRUST" was placed on United States coins largely because of the increased religious sentiment existing during the Civil War. Secretary of the Treasury Salmon P. Chase received many appeals from devout persons throughout the country, urging that the United States recognize the Deity on United States coins. From Treasury Department records, it appears that the first such appeal came in a letter dated November 13, 1861. It was written to Secretary Chase by Rev. M. R. Watkinson, Minister of the Gospel from Ridleyville, Pennsylvania.

John 14:6 King James Version (KJV)
6 Jesus saith unto him, I am the way, the truth, and the life: no man cometh unto the Father, but by me.

"We become what we behold. We shape our tools, and thereafter our tools shape us."

~
Marshal McLuhan

John 8:44 King James Version (KJV)
44 Ye are of your father the devil, and the lusts of your father ye will do. He was a murderer from the beginning, and abode not in the truth, because there is no truth in him.

When he speaketh a lie, he speaketh of his own: for he is a liar, and the father of it.

"The Christian notion of the possibility of redemption is incomprehensible to the computer." ~ Vance Packard

221

Consider the pagan roots of our popular symbols of Christmas:

1 Christmas Tree – The sacred tree of the winter-god; Druids believed the spirit of their gods resided in the tree. Most ancient pagans knew the tree represented Nimrod reincarnated into Tammuz! Pagans also looked upon the tree as a phallic symbol.

2 Star – Pentalpha, the five-pointed star. The pentalpha is a powerful symbol of Satan, second only to the hexagram. The star is the sacred symbol of Nimrod, and has nothing whatsoever to do with Christianity.

3 Candles represent the sun-gods' newly-born fire. Pagans the world over love and use candles in their rituals and ceremonies. Certain colors are also thought to represent specific powers. The extensive use of candles is usually a very good indication that the service is pagan, no matter what the outward trappings might be.

4 Mistletoe is the sacred plant of the Druids, symbolizing pagan blessings of fertility; thus, kissing under the mistletoe is the first step in the reproductive cycle! Witches also use the white berries in potions.

5 Wreaths are circular, and so they represent the female sexual organs. Wreaths are associated with fertility and the "circle of life".

6 Santa Claus – Former Satanists have told me that "Santa" is an anagram for "Satan". In the New Age, the god, "Sanat Kamura", is most definitely an anagram for "Satan". The mythical attributes and powers ascribed to Santa are eerily close to those possessed by Jesus Christ.

7 Reindeer are horned animals representing the "horned-god" or the "stag-god" of pagan religion! Santa's traditional number of reindeer in his team is eight (8); in Satanic gematria, eight is the number of "new beginnings", or the cycle of reincarnation. The Illuminati views the number "eight" as a symbol of their New World Order.

8 Elves are imp-like creatures who are Santa's (Satan's) little helpers. They are also demons.

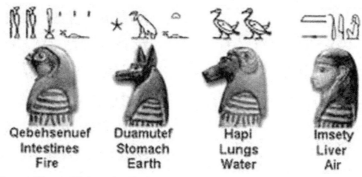

Qebehsenuef Duamutef Hapi Imsety
Intestines Stomach Lungs Liver
Fire Earth Water Air

9 Green and Red are the traditional colors of the season, as they are the traditional pagan colors of winter. Green is Satan's favorite color, so it is appropriate it should be one of the traditional colors for Christmas; red is the color of human blood, Satan's highest form of sacrifice – for this reason, Communism adopted red as it main color!

10 December 25 is known as the "nativity" of the sun. This date is the birthday of Tammuz, the son, the reincarnation of the sun god. Traditionally, December 21 is known as Yule. The Roman Catholic Church moved the celebration of Yule to December 25.

11 December 25 is also known to the Romans as "Saturnalia", a time of deliberate debauchery. Drinking through repeated toasting – known as 'wassail' – was a key to the debauchery of this celebration. Fornication was symbolized by the mistletoe, and the entire event was finished with a Great Feast, the Christmas Dinner.

12 Even the name, "Christmas" is pagan! "Christi" meant "Christ", while "Mas" meant Mass. Since all pagan Masses are commemorating "death", the name, "Christmas" literally means the "death of Christ". A deeper meaning lies in the mention of "Christ" without specifying Jesus. Thus, Antichrist is in view here; the pagans celebrate "Christmas" as a celebration of their coming Antichrist, who will deal a death blow to the Jesus Christ of Christianity.

13 Early American Christian Pilgrims refused to celebrate this day.

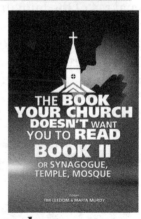

Zeitgeist, the Movie is a 2007 documentary film, produced by Peter Joseph about the Jesus myth, the attacks of 9/11, and the Federal Reserve Bank .

As we expand our consciousness, as we begin to re-remember the true nature of physical reality and how its created, it is the most fascinating, empowering, extraordinary experience you will have.

We will leave behind our childish ways, and regain our child like wonderment of the cosmos, we will rejoin that which we already are. The truth vibrations are getting stronger and they are over powering the control grids that have been in place for thousands of years, the shackles are being broken every moment of every day.

Zeitgeist The Movie www.watchzeitgeist.com/zeitgeist-the-movie/

You could say that Astrotheology is the language or symbolism that infinite consciousnesses has used to create the blueprint of the cosmos.

Think about the complete interaction and connectedness all that is. We have the 7 planets, the 7 chakras of the human body, the 7 days of the week, the body renewed every 7 years, the lucky number 7, the 7 colors of the rainbow, the 7 wonders of the world, the 7 notes of the diatonic scale in music, the 7 dwarfs, and it goes on and on in every culture.

This inherent connectedness in everything, is something we are never taught in our public school systems, we are taught "What" to think when we are brought into this world, we are never taught "How" to think. Astrotheology, the "Holy Science" teaches us "How" to think.

http://apocalypse-how.com/category/astrotheology-2/

And the Holy Science or Astrotheology, is key in moving us back into unity consciousness. You see when you are only aware of what is going on here on planet earth, like watching Dancing with the Stars, or watching your favorite sports team, or gladiators playing in the stadiums.

At that level of awareness you are essentially existing in Earth Consciousness, when you expand your consciousness a bit more and learn about the sun and how our solar system works, you are then existing solar consciousness.

224

Do Christians give homage to Amen-Ra when they use the phrase "Amen" to finish their prayers? The phrase Amen used by Christians in prayer or in agreement to something spoken by a leader does not come from the Egyptian word Amen and has quite a different meaning.

Who Am I?

These are the words of Ra:
"I am KhepeRa in the morning, Ra at noon, and Tmu (Ra Atum) in the evening."
- The Story of Ra & Oset (Isis)

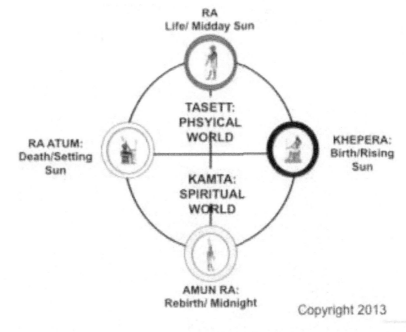

RA
Life/ Midday Sun

TASETT: PHSYICAL WORLD

RA ATUM: Death/Setting Sun

KHEPERA: Birth/Rising Sun

KAMTA: SPIRITUAL WORLD

AMUN RA: Rebirth/ Midnight

Copyright 2013

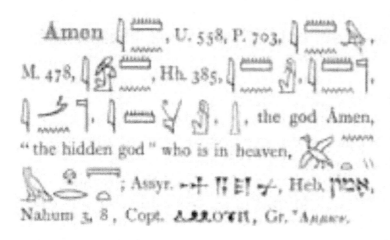

Amon, U. 558, P. 703, M. 478, Hh. 385, the god Amen, "the hidden god" who is in heaven, ; Assyr. , Heb. אמן, Nahum 3, 8, Copt. ⲀⲘⲞⲨⲚ, Gr. Ἀμμων.

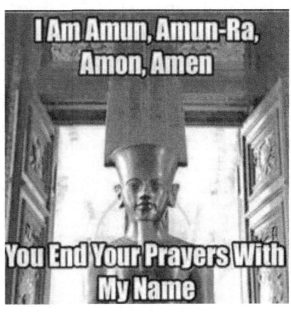

I Am Amun, Amun-Ra, Amon, Amen

You End Your Prayers With My Name

225

Jacob's Ladder

The story of Jacob's Ladder is an ancient allegorical biblical tale, describing the alchemical process of reaching complete Gnosis, or what some may call Sainthood, Buddhahood or enlightenment. A symbolic ladder that we all must climb if we wish to reach the spiritual heights of the divine in the heavens while we are encased in physical matter here on earth.

John 3:14 King James Version (KJV)

14 *And as Moses lifted up the serpent in the wilderness, even so must the Son of man be lifted up:*

As we climb, we must purify ourselves, our thoughts, habits and actions, so that we may reach that seventh and final step of our ascent, in order to activate all of our seven senses and DNA.

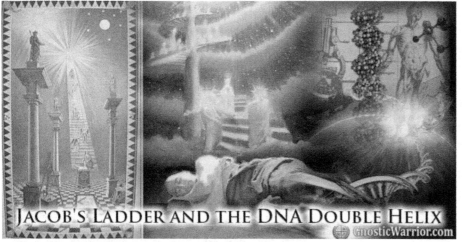

JACOB'S LADDER AND THE DNA DOUBLE HELIX
 GnosticWarrior.com

THE STEPS OF DNA ACTIVATION VIA JACOB'S LADDER WITH THE HELP OF MANLY P. HALL:

The first step of Jacob's ladder is the personal purification of your body, mind and soul that is represented by the moon. The second rung on the ladder is education intelligence managed by Mercury. The third step is beauty represented by Venus. The fourth rung is the sun, which is the life-giver. The fifth is competition by Mars to help us fight the good fight. The fight against darkness with light. Against lies with truth. The sixth rung in the ladder is Jupiter which is the symbol of intellectual maturity and judgement. The seventh and last step of the ladder is Saturn which represents the true sage, adept and master of Wisdom. The perfect balance of spiritual and material laws. All greatness is service and we must obey the laws of leadership. **http://gnosticwarrior.com/jacobs-ladder.html**

Serpent that tempts Eve

In the book of Genesis it is the serpent that tempts Eve to turn away from God and be tempted by the promise of power. Because of this, the serpent is seen as evil.

Genesis 3:1-6 *"Now the serpent was more subtil than any beast of the field which the LORD God had made. And he said unto the woman, Yea, hath God said, Ye shall not eat of every tree of the garden? And the woman said unto the serpent, We may eat of the fruit of the trees of the garden: But of the fruit of the tree which is in the midst of the garden, God hath said, Ye shall not eat of it, neither shall ye touch it, lest ye die. And the serpent said unto the woman, Ye shall not surely die: For God doth know that in the day ye eat thereof, then your eyes shall be opened, and ye shall be as gods, knowing good and evil. And when the woman saw that the tree was good for food, and that it was pleasant to the eyes, and a tree to be desired to make one wise, she took of the fruit thereof, and did eat, and gave also unto her husband with her; and he did eat."* Christian Bible - King James Version

Medusa was a monster, one of the Gorgon sisters and daughter of Phorkys and Keto, the children of Gaea (Earth) and Oceanus (Ocean). She had the face of an ugly woman with snakes instead of hair; anyone who looked into her eyes was immediately turned to stone.

Lilith, the Royal Family and the abducted/murdered children
Lilith, the Royal Family and the connection to some of the most tragic murders of the late twentieth century.

Her sisters were Sthenno and Euryale, but Medusa was the only mortal of the three. Seeing herself transformed into such a repulsive creature, Medusa fled her home, never to return.

Wandering about, abhorred, dreaded, and shunned by the rest of the world, she turned into a character worthy of her outer appearance. In her despair, she fled to Africa, where, while wandering restlessly from place to place, young snakes dropped from her hair; that is how, according to the ancient Greeks, Africa became a hotbed of venomous reptiles. With the curse of Athena upon her, she turned into stone whomever she gazed upon, till at last, after a life of nameless misery, deliverance came to her in the shape of death, at the hands of Perseus. *http://www.greekmythology.com/Myths/Creatures/Medusa/medusa.html*

We live in a world where occult practises are carried out hidden in plain sight, but which go undetected by a public who simply look straight through the clues in complete ignorance.http://thewizardofozandtheolympics.blogspot.com/2012/04/lilith-royal-family-and.html

What is the meaning of the term 'Kemet' and why did some ancient Egyptians call their country by this name?

The ancient Egyptian name of the country was km.t, which means black ground or black soil, referring to the fertile black soils of the Nile flood plains, distinct from the deshret (⟨dšṛt⟩), or "red land" of the desert.
This name is commonly vocalised as Kemet, but was probably pronounced [kuːmat] in ancient Egyptian.
The name is realised as kēme and kēmə in the Coptic stage of the Egyptian language, and appeared in early Greek as Χημία (Khēmía)

Stolen Legacy
George G. M. James

FOR CENTURIES THE WORLD HAS BEEN MISLED ABOUT THE ORIGINAL SOURCE OF THE ARTS AND SCIENCES

The term Greek philosophy, to begin with a misnomer, for there is no such philosophy in existence. The ancient Egyptians had developed a very complex religious system, called the Mysteries, which was also the first system of salvation. As such, it regarded the human body as a prison house of the soul, which could be liberated from its bodily impediments, through the disciples of the Arts and Sciences, and advanced form the level of a mortal to that of a God.

And this is Osiris, or Ausar, whose name literally translates as Lord of the Perfect black and he is about the 2nd or 3rd highest ranking god after amon and ra. https://www.quora.com/What-is-the-meaning-of-the-term-Kemet-and-why-did-some-ancient-Egyptians-call-their-country-by-this-name

This was the notion of the summon bonum or greatest good, to which all men must aspire, and it also became the basis of all ethical concepts. The Egyptian Mystery was also a Secret Order, and membership was gained by initiation and a pledge to secrecy. The teaching was graded and delivered orally to the neophyte: and under these circumstances of secrecy.

METU NETER Vol. 1
The Great Oracle of Tehuti and the Egyptian System of Spiritual Cultivation
RA UN NEFER AMEN

The Egyptians developed secret systems of writing and teaching, and forbade their Initiates from writing what they had learned. After nearly five thousand years of prohibition against the Greeks, they were permitted to enter Egypt for the purpose of their education. First through the Persian invasion and secondly through the invasion of Alexander the Great. From the sixth century B.C. therefore to the death of Aristotle (322 B.C.) the Greeks made the best of their chance to learn all they could about Egyptian culture; most students received instructions directly from the Egyptian Priests, but after the invasion by Alexander the Great, the Royal temples and libraries were plundered and pillaged, and Aristotle's school converted the library at Alexandria into a research center. There is no wonder then, that the production of the unusually large number of books ascribed to Aristotle has proved a physical impossibility, for any single man within a lifetime.

John 3:15 "And as Moses lifted up the serpent in the wilderness, even so must the Son of man be lifted up: Christian Bible - King James Version

In Egypt, Greece, Western, American and other Oriental countries, the serpent was normally associated as the symbol of royalty and monarchy. The Egyptian Pharaohs wore a headdress with a serpent in the form of a cobra, and it was embroidered on the robes of princes to signify their race and rule of alchemy in which the wound inflicted by serpent (worm) was incurable. This symbol of regal power was called the mekkah (from malak, "to reign") by the Semitic nations, and we find the same meaning in modern-day Mecca which is the center of the Islamic world and the birthplace of both the Prophet Muhammad and the religion he founded.

The term "Kundalini" comes from India and is a core concept in the yogic traditions. Kundalini is described as a sleeping, dormant potential force in the human organism. It is one of the components of an esoteric description of man's 'subtle body', which consists of (energy channels), chakras (energy centers) and prana or vital energy.

The symbolic image is that of a serpent coiled 3 and a half times around a spine or central rod or staff. Through meditation, and various esoteric or yogic practices, the kundalini is awakened, and can rise up inside or alongside the spine. The progress of kundalini through the different chakras leads to different levels of awakening, mystical experience, purification and expression of spiritual powers. http://www.1paradigm.org/serpents.html

Texe Marrs is author of over 37 books, including the #1 bestseller Dark Secrets of the New Age and

Circle of Intrigue: The Hidden Inner Circle of the Global Illuminati Conspiracy. A retired career U.S. Air Force officer, he has taught at the University of Texas at Austin and has appeared on radio and TV talk shows across America.

Codex Magica is awesome in its scope and revelations. It contains over 1,000 actual photographs and illustrations.

You'll see with your own eyes the world's leading politicians and celebrities — including America's richest and most powerful —caught in the act as they perform occult magic. Once you understand their covert signals and coded picture messages, your world will never be the same. Destiny will be made manifest. You will know the truth and everything will become clear.

In 1597, King James VI of Scotland and I of England, who commissioned the King James bible, wrote Demonology, setting out his beliefs on satan and witches. A historical work and important read for scholars of religion, this book allows readers to study the beliefs and ideas and King James. Demonology is known as one of the most interesting and controversial books in the history of Christianity.

Just as William Shakespeare's life and work attract myths and speculation, the King James Bible has been privy to a number of legends and half-truths in its 400-year history. And like the works of Shakespeare, the King James Bible has had a profound influence on English-speaking peoples across the globe. The creation and influence of this remarkable book is the topic of a new exhibition and website, Manifold Greatness: The Creation and Afterlife of the King James Bible, recently launched by the Folger Shakespeare Library, Bodleian Libraries at the University of Oxford, and the Harry Ransom Center at the University of Texas.

"Law Breaker" NOT "The Law Giver"

When Moses smash the tablets he broke the law, subsequently when you break the law in society they call you a **"Law Breaker"**

Scripture Reference:
Exodus 20:1-17 and Deuteronomy 5:6-21.

Ten Commandments - Story Summary:
Shortly after God brought the people of Israel out of Egypt, they traveled through the desert to Sinai where they camped in front of Mount Sinai. Mount Sinai, also called Mount Horeb, is a very significant place. There God met and spoke with Moses, telling him why he had rescued Israel from Egypt. For God had chosen these people to be made into a holy nation of priests for God, his treasured possession.

One day God called Moses to the top of the mountain and he gave him the first part of his new system of laws for his people - the Ten Commandments. (These Ten Commandments summarized the absolutes of spiritual and moral living that God intended for his people. For a modern-day paraphrase of the Ten Commandments visit: **Ten Commandments - Paraphrase**.)
God continued to give direction to his people through Moses, including the civil and ceremonial laws for managing their lives and their worship.

http://www.dralimelbey.com/metaphysics-and-the-end-of-religious-confusion.html

The following are the lists of Flavius Josephus' books compared to the various books in the "HOLY BIBLE"

Arius Piso and The Works of Flavius Josepheus / Josephus	The Bible (Paul's / Josepheus Comparisons)
Philip –War Book 3 Chapter 7 Section 21	Philip Acts 6:5
Judas – War Book 2 Chapter 4 Section 21	Judas Acts 5:37
Ananias War-Book 2 Chapter 12 Section 6	Ananias Acts 23:2
Theophilius Antiquities Book 18 Ch. 5 Sec. 3	Theophilius Acts 1:1
Simon, the Zealot War Book 5 Ch. 6 Sec. 1	Simon, the Zealot Acts 1:13
Simon, the Essene Antiquities Book 17	Simon, the Essene Acts 8:9-24
Matthias Antiquities Book 19 Ch. 6 Sec. 4	Matthias Acts 1:13 and 26
John War Book 2 Ch. Sec. 2-4	John Acts 1:13 Revelation
Alexander Antiquities Book 14 Ch. 4 Sec. 2 and 5	Alexander Acts 19:33
Nicanor War Book 5 Ch. Sec. 2	Nicanor Acts 6:5
Stephen War Book 2 Chapter 12 Section 2	Stephen Acts 6:8
Cornelius War Book 1 Ch. 7 Sec. 4 Jew Book 6 Ch. 3 Sec. 2	Cornelius Acts 10:3
Herod Antiquities Book 14 Ch. 7 Sec. 3 Book 15 Ch. 6 Sec. 2	Herod Acts 4:27 Acts 12
Silas Antiquities Book 14 Ch. 3 Sec. 2, Book 19 Ch. 7 Sec. 1	Silas Acts 16:25
Jason Antiquities Book 12 Ch. 5 Sec. 1 Book 12 Ch. 10 Sec. 6	Jason Acts 17:5-9
Aquila Antiquities Book 19 Ch. 3 Sec. 2	Aquila Acts 18:2
Dionysius Antiquities Book 14 Ch. 3 Sec. 2	Dionysius Areopagite Acts 17:34
Claudius Antiquities Book 19 Ch. 2 Sec. 1, Book 19 Ch. 3 Sec. 1	Claudius Acts 18:2
Justus (Son of Pistus) Life Book 9 Sec. 65 and 74	Justus Acts 18:7
Gallo (Gallus) War Book 2 Ch. 14 Sec. 3	Gallo (Gallus) Acts 18:12
Tyrannus Anti. Bk.16 Ch. 10 Sec. 3, War Book 1 Ch. 26 Sec. 3	Tyrannus Acts 19:9
Demetrius Antiquities Book 13 Ch. 14 Sec. 1	Demetrius Acts 19:24 and 38
Gaius (Caius) Antiquities Book 19 Ch. 4 Sec. 1	Gaius Acts 19:29
Timotheus Antiquities Book 12 Chapter 8	Timothy Acts 20:4 I and II Timothy
Eutychus Antiquities Book 18 Chapter 6 Section 5	Eutychus Acts 20:9
Felix Antiquities Book 14 Ch. 11 Sec. 7, Book 20 Ch. 7 Sec. 1	Felix (The Governor) Acts 23:2, 24, and 26
Festus Antiquities Book 20 Ch. 8 Sec. 9, Book 20 Ch. 9 Sec. 1	Festus Acts 25:1 Acts 12:4

THE LIFE AND WORKS OF

FLAVIUS JOSEPHUS

The Learned and authentic Jewish Historian
and Celebrated Warrior . . . to which are added

SEVEN DISSERTATIONS

Concerning Jesus Christ, John the Baptist,
James the Just, God's Command to Abraham, etc.

Translated by WILLIAM WHISTON, A.M.
Professor of Mathematics in the University of Cambridge

INTRODUCTORY ESSAY
By the Rev. H. Stebbing, D.D.

Copy 142

HOLT, RINEHART AND WINSTON
NEW YORK

Here are a few more of the lost books:

* Book of the Wars of the Lord (Num. 21:14)
* Book of Jasher (Josh. 10:13)
* Book of the Acts of Solomon (1st Kings 11:41)
* Book of Samuel the Seer (1st Chr. 29:29)
* Book of Gad the Seer (1st Chr. 29:29)
* Book of Nathan the Prophet (1st Chr. 29:29)
* Prophecy of Ahijah (2nd Chr. 9:29)
* Visions of Ido the Seer (2nd Chr. 9:29)
* Book of Shemaiah (2 Chr. 12:15)
* Book of Jehu (2 Chr. 20:34)
* Sayings of the Seers (2 Chr. 33:19)
* An Epistle of Paul to the Corinthians (1 Cor. 5:9)
* An Epistle to the Church at Laodicea (Col 4:16)
* Other prophecies to Enoch (Jude 1:14)

This whole equating god with moral character thing gets old fast, if not for the picture above, because gobs of people with Jesus in the hearts not only commit crimes, but have an easier time getting away with it for wearing Jesus on their sleeve - See more at: *http://www.patheos.com/blogs/wwjtd/2016/01/kkk-mans-uncle-believes-he-should-receive-parole-for-killing-a-black-teen-because-hes-found-god/#sthash.xD67eLJ1.dpuf*

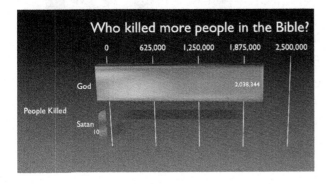

Numbers 23:19. God is not a man

1 John 1:5. This then is the message which we have heard of him, and declare unto you, that God is light, and in him is no darkness at all.

Albert Pike Grand Pontife de la Franc-Maçonnerie universelle ; Franc-Maçon du 33e degré ; Grand Prêtre de l'Église Satanique, plutôt Grande Pourriture de la Communauté Satanique Universelle!

"That which we must say to the *CROWD* is: we worship a god, but it is the god that one adores without superstition. To *YOU* Sovereign Grand Inspectors General, we say this, that you may repeat it to the brethren of the 32nd, 31st and 30th degrees – the **MASONIC RELIGION** should be, by all of us initiates of the *high* degrees, maintained in the purity of the **LUCIFERIAN** doctrine. If Lucifer were not god, would Adonay (Jesus)... calumniate (spread false and harmful statements about) him?... YES, LUCIFER IS GOD..."*

*A.C. De La Rive, *La Femme et l'Enfant dans la Franc-Maçonnèrie Universelle* (page 588).

General Albert Pike, 33°

Recommended Resource: *The Names of God by Ken Hemphill*

YAHWEH-ROHI: "The Lord Our Shepherd" (Psalm 23:1) – After David pondered his relationship as a shepherd to his sheep, he realized that was exactly the relationship God had with him, and so he declares, "Yahweh-Rohi is my Shepherd. I shall not want" (Psalm 23:1).

YAHWEH-SHAMMAH: "The Lord Is There" (Ezekiel 48:35) – the name ascribed to Jerusalem and the Temple there, indicating that the once-departed glory of the Lord (Ezekiel 8—11) had returned (Ezekiel 44:1-4).

YAHWEH-SABAOTH: "The Lord of Hosts" (Isaiah 1:24; Psalm 46:7) – *Hosts* means "hordes," both of angels and of men. He is Lord of the host of heaven and of the inhabitants of the earth, of Jews and Gentiles, of rich and poor, master and slave. The name is expressive of the majesty, power, and authority of God and shows that He is able to accomplish what He determines to do.

EL ELYON: "Most High" (Deuteronomy 26:19) – derived from the Hebrew root for "go up" or "ascend," so the implication is of that which is the very highest. *El Elyon* denotes exaltation and speaks of absolute right to lordship.

EL ROI: "God of Seeing" (Genesis 16:13) – the name ascribed to God by Hagar, alone and desperate in the wilderness after being driven out by Sarah (Genesis 16:1-14). When Hagar met the Angel of the Lord, she realized she had seen God Himself in a theophany. She also realized that *El Roi* saw her in her distress and testified that He is a God who lives and sees all.

EL-OLAM: "Everlasting God" (Psalm 90:1-3) – God's nature is without beginning or end, free from all constraints of time, and He contains within Himself the very cause of time itself. "From everlasting to everlasting, You are God."

EL-GIBHOR: "Mighty God" (Isaiah 9:6) – the name describing the Messiah, Christ Jesus, in this prophetic portion of Isaiah. As a powerful and mighty warrior, the Messiah, the Mighty God, will accomplish the destruction of God's enemies and rule with a rod of iron (Revelation 19:15).

So what can be said about the Lilith myth and how does her revulsion toward the natural order distort modern society ?

Lilith http://theunknownmoment.blogspot.com/2012/03/lilith-first-woman-of-earth.html

www.bibliotecapleyades.net/sumer.../esp_sumer_annunaki15aa.htm

Lilith's myth is widely recognized as Adam's first wife, when they were created ... as she is the woman who **sacrifices** paradise, and many of her own children; than be ... of the Babylonians, known for strangling and drinking the **blood** of infants.

Lilith is the most important of a small collection of named female demons in Jewish legend.

Your religious education will not find the account of Lilith in the book of Genesis. "The only possible occurrence is in the Book of Isaiah 34:13—15, describing the desolation of Edom, where the Hebrew word lilit (or lilith) appears in a list of eight unclean animals.

From *'Masonic and Occult Symbols Illustrated'* are these examples of the triskele.

This triskele symbol in **Fig. 4** ."is used to exorcise evil spirits." It is strikingly similar to **Fig. 2** and also the Logo found on the New King James Bible (© 1979, 1980,1982), published by Thomas Nelson Publishers, not to be confused with TAN Publishers which was started by Thomas A. Nelson in 1967 but it is not related or affiliated with Thomas Nelson Publishers. TAN's Thomas A. Nelson is a devout Catholic.

Triskeles are of pagan and occult origins and are connected to swastikas, reincarnation, magic and the yin-yang. "...the triskele (or triskelion) is one symbol that appears in many logos today... "The **triskelion** (Greek for three legs) **is a symbol of the sun** intended to express motion. A similar device, with four legs, called a tetraskelion, is a modification of the swastika" 1 Like the swastika, it is considered to be a good luck symbol. 2 "

"...An occult organization sells a triskelion and serpent pendant. They brag: "Double **magic**! Designs on both side (sic) of this unusually attractive pendant. One side bears the three-legged triskeles symbolizing rising, zenith, setting. On the other [side the] serpent portrays strength, divine power, infinite wisdom, eternity."3 Another catalog tells us that the "'legs' represent birth, death, and **rebirth**."4 Of course, this is a reference to **REINCARNATION.**"

"We must remember that since the triskele is "a Celtic version of the Yin-Yang symbol of life,"5 and a modification of the swastika,6 ..."

"A New Age organization sells a Celtic Goddess Pin. It is described like this: "Symbols of the triskele (the sea, good luck) and cauldron (abundance, inspiration) celebrate Cerridwen: Celtic goddess of transformation, who offers guidance and spiritual renewal at crucial junctures in the lives of her devotees. In Welsh mythology, she guarded the cauldron of inspiration and was the muse of the bards." "Cerridwen is the goddess of wisdom and **witchcraft**..." [Emphasis in the original] 6

Figure 5 Logo of New King James Version (Thomas Nelson Publishers)

**Figure 4
Triskele**

**Figure 5 Logo of New King James Version
(Thomas Nelson Publishers)**

http://www.seekgod.ca/warning.htm

Occultism

Occultism is the study of occult practices, including (but not limited to) magic, alchemy, extra-sensory perception, astrology, spiritualism, religion, and divination.

Deuteronomy 18:10
Verse Concepts
"There shall not be found among you anyone who makes his son or his daughter pass through the fire, one who uses divination, one who practices witchcraft, or one who interprets omens, or a sorcerer.

Isaiah 8:19
Verse Concepts
When they say to you, "Consult the mediums and the spiritists who whisper and mutter," should not a people consult their God? Should they consult the dead on behalf of the living?

Isaiah 19:3
Verse Concepts
"Then the spirit of the Egyptians will be demoralized within them; And I will confound their strategy, So that they will resort to idols and ghosts of the dead And to mediums and spiritists.

http://bible.knowing-jesus.com/topics/Occultism

God's Voice	Satan's Voice
stills you	rushes you
leads you	pushes you
reassures you	frightens you
enlightens you	confuses you
encourages you	discourages you
comforts you	worries you
calms you	obsesses you
convicts you	condemns you

Ten Commandments

(The Commandments which are similar to the 42 Declarations are highlighted by parenthesis)

1. I am the Lord thy God. Thou shalt have no other gods before me. (41)

2. Thou shalt not make unto thee any graven image...

3. Thou shalt not take the name of the Lord thy God in vain... (7, 37, 41)

4. Remember the Sabbath day, to keep it holy...

5. Honor thy father and mother. (1, 12, 28)

6. Thou shalt not kill. (4)

7. Thou shalt not commit adultery. (11, 20, 21)

8. Thou shalt not steal. (2, 3, 5, 6, 7, 9, 39, 40)

9. Though shalt not bear false witness against thy neighbor. (8, 13, 18, 29)

10. Thou shalt not covet thy neighbor's house or wife... (13, 20, 21, 29, 33)

12   *Nile Valley Contributions To Civilization | Study Guide*

42 Principles of Maat 2000 years before Ten Commandments

Written at least 2,000 years before the Ten Commandments of Moses, the 42 Principles of Ma'at are one of Africa's, and the world's, oldest sources of moral and spiritual instruction. Ma'at, the Ancient Egyptian divine Principle of Truth, Justice, and Righteousness, is the foundation of natural and social order and unity. Ancient Africans developed a humane system of thought and conduct which has been recorded in volumes of African wisdom literature, such as, these declarations from the Book of Coming Forth By Day (the so-called Book of the Dead), The Teachings of Ptah-Hotep, the writings of Ani, Amenemope, Merikare, and others.

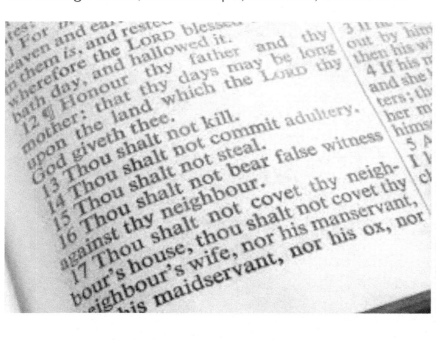

237

Laws of Ma'at

Maat or Ma'at was the ancient Egyptian concept of truth, balance, order, harmony, law, morality, and justice. **Maat** was also personified as a goddess regulating the stars, seasons, and the actions of both mortals and the deities, who set the order of the universe from chaos at the moment of creation.

I have not done iniquity.
I have not robbed with violence.
I have not stolen.
I have not made any to suffer pain.
I have not defrauded offerings.
I have done no murder nor bid anyone to slay on my behalf.
I have not trimmed the measure.
I have not spoken lies I have not robbed God.
I have not caused the shedding of tears.
I have not dealt deceitfully.
I have not acted guilefully.
I have not laid waste to the land.
I have not set my lips against anyone.
I have not been angry or wrathful without a just cause.
I have not lusted nor defiled the wife of any man.
I have not polluted myself.
I have not caused terror.
I have not done that which is abominable.
I have not multiplied words exceedingly.
I have never uttered fiery words.
I have not judged hastily.
I have not transgressed nor have I vexed or angered God.
I have not stopped my ears against the words of Right and Truth .
I have not burned with rage.
I have not worked grief.
I have not acted with insolence.
I have not avenged myself.
I have not stirred up strife.
I have not been an eavesdropper.
I have not wronged the people
I have done no harm nor have I done evil
I have not worked treason.
I have never fouled the water.
I have not spoken scornfully.
I have never cursed God.
I have not behaved with arrogance.
I have not envied or craved for that which belongs to another.
I have not filched food from the mouth of the infant.
I have done no hurt unto man, nor wrought harm unto beasts.
I have never magnified my condition beyond what was fitting.

LAWS OF MA'AT

The 42 Divine Principles of Maat in Badge's native English follows:

3000 years before Jesus, the Egyptian god Horus said...

"I am the way, the truth, the life."

Recycled

Mythology

FAITH HEALING AND THE OCCULT

Occult is derived from Latin word *occultus*, means mysterious thing and practices related to supernatural forces beyond the five senses.

Including under Occult are the following:

➢ Practices and beliefs in astrology
➢ Magic
➢ Witchcraft
➢ Numerology
➢ Crystal ball gazing
➢ Spiritism
➢ Fortune telling

The Winged Sun-Disk

**Wings
(Ascension)**

From lower consciousness to higher consciousness
From animal to human
From earth to heaven
From duality to unity

Harley Davidson winged logo

Bentley logo

http://vigilantcitizen.com/vigilantreport/occult-symbols-in-corporate-logos-pt-1/

"Horus, the Virgin-Born redeemer of the Egyptians, came intro the world to destroy the enemies of the great God, Ra. Therefore, Horus changed himself into the form of the winged sun-disk, and took with him the Goddesses Nekhebet and Uatchit in the form of two serpents. After their successful war upon the enemies of Ra, Horus commanded Thoth, the God of Secret Wisdom, that the winged sun-disk with the erect serpents should be brought into every sanctuary of all the gods of the lands of the South and North."

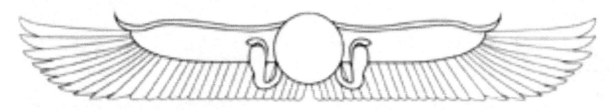

The winged sun but with an all-seeing eye instead of the sun

The symbol is a representation of the ascension of the soul to the Divine, with the help of the serpents of wisdom and knowledge:

"And the meaning of the winged Sundisk is this, – It is the symbol of perfect Aspiration towards the Divine, of Purification of the lower nature, and of final ascent into union with the One."
-G.A. Gaskell, Egyptian Scriptures Interpreted Through the Language of Symbolism Present in All Inspired Writings

ASTON MARTIN

Aston Martin logo

Mini Cooper logo

On the left, *Jesus* is seen using the Holy wood to heal. On the right, Thoth is building energy with the rods and transferring that energy through the Ankh.

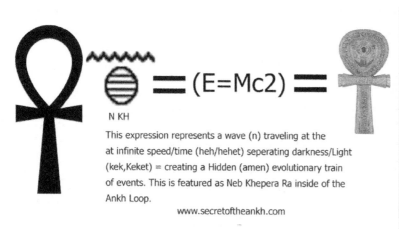

N KH

This expression represents a wave (n) traveling at the at infinite speed/time (heh/hehet) seperating darkness/Light (kek,Keket) = creating a Hidden (amen) evolutionary train of events. This is featured as Neb Khepera Ra inside of the Ankh Loop.

www.secretoftheankh.com

$$(E=Mc2)$$

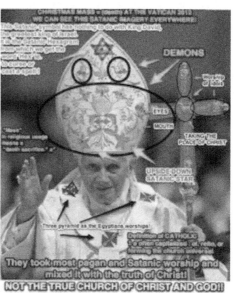

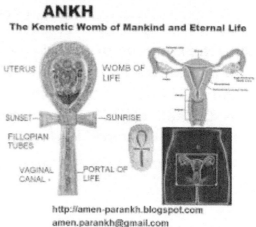

DIVINE LAWS OF MA'AT *Analysis*

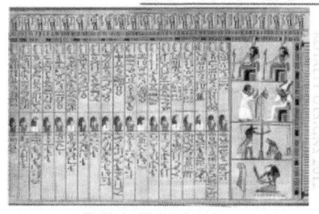

ORIGINAL
ANCIENT KMT/AFRIKAN/NUBIAN LAWS

PLAGIARIZED
ROMAN/CANAANITE COMMANDMENTS

From the Introduction: What passes as spontaneous "social change" is in fact an organized process of satanic possession. This development is not an isolated or recent phenomenon. Western society is based on a rebellion against God and the natural and moral order. The so-called "Enlightenment" refers to Lucifer as the "light giver." It was an assertion of the Illuminati's determination to reject Reality -- the Creator's Design – and construct an artificial reality more conducive to their interests and perversions. This is what the Cabalist bankers mean by "remaking the world" or "changing the world." There is no way to sugarcoat this. Satanist (Cabalist) Jews and Freemasons are waging a covert war against God and man and are close to achieving victory.

Many Jews and Freemasons have been a subversive force throughout history - the real reason for anti Semitism. Of course, the majority of Jews (and Christians) aren't aware of this process of satanic possession. We have all succumbed to it. Passing as "secularism" and "humanism," Satanism is the secret religion of the West.

Why would "jesus" had used these hand symbols like the baphomet. I don't think so. Paul speaks of another jesus they will come preaching.

241

What does this hand gesture mean in Icons?

The fingers spell out "IC XC", a widely used four letter abbreviation of the Greek for Jesus (**I**HCOY**C**) Christ (**X**PICTO**C**). It is by the name of Jesus that we are saved and receive blessings: *"At the name of Jesus every knee should bow, of things in heaven, and things in earth, and things under the earth;"* (Phil 2:10). **Symbolism of the Blessing**

The three fingers of Christ – as well as spelling out "I" and "X" – confess the Tri-unity of God: Father, Son and Holy Spirit. The touching finger and thumb of Jesus not only spell out "C", but attest to the Incarnation: to the joining of divine and human natures found in the body of Jesus Christ.

Please watch these two documentaries........NOW

The central claim of *Anonymous* is that the plays and poems of Shakespeare were actually written by Edward de Vere, seventeenth earl of Oxford, who was forced to keep his authorship secret and watch the drunken, illiterate actor William Shakespeare take credit. But in the movie's funhouse-mirror version of Elizabethan history, this conspiracy is just one part of a larger web of intrigue, in which **(SPOILER ALERT!)**

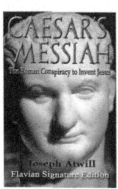

Caesar's Messiah reveals the key to a new and revolutionary understanding of the origin of Christianity. ... A cogent exegetical **review** of the evidence that the entire New Testament itself was a historically attentive but fictional.

Psalms 46 is not unknown to cipher enthusiasts. This is the famous Psalms where it has been written that Shakespeare wrote his name in cipher. You see, the 46th word from the beginning is "Shake", and the 46th word from the end (not counting the final "Selah") is "Speare". The theory goes that Shakespeare was 46 years old when the KJV was printed.

242

The legendary Thomas Cochrane, a British sea captain, gained fame fighting Napoleon's Navy. The movie, *Master and Commander: The Far Side of the World*, starring Russell Crowe, as hero, was based on his exploits. Here he is shown giving not only the Royal Arch Mason sign, but the "left triangle" as well. (Painting: National Maritime Museum, London)

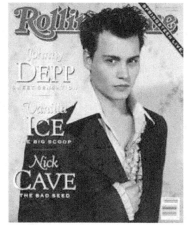

Karl **Marx** (b. 1818 – d. 1883) German - Jewish revolutionary and communist icon. Marx authored The Communist Manifesto in 1848

Has Hollywood waged a war on God?

This issue of the intriguing publication, Paranoia magazine, included a feature article examining the tragic life of popular young actor River Phoenix, who died of a drug overdose on Halloween in 1993. The article's writer, Al Hidell, told of Phoenix's upbringing in the sordid sex cult known as the Children of God, also called "The Family."

Freemason Symbols in Movies and Social Media Decoded

Masonry in a way acknowledges what it calls the Grand Architect of the Universe; but prefers to symbolize him by three persons, whom we now proceed to investigate.

" Signs and symbols rule the world , not words nor law "

Masonic lapel pin

First, the symbolic structure of Masonry is supported by three symbolic pillars; namely, wisdom, strength, and beauty. These three pillars are in Masonic terms, Solomon, representing in the Masonic trinity the pillar of wisdom. Hiram, King of Tyre, representing the pillar of strength, and Hiram Abiff, the widow's son, representing the pillar of beauty. Here we have the Masonic foundation.

Revelation 18:3 before our eyes:

"For all **nations** have drunk the wine of the passion of her sexual immorality,
and the **kings of the earth** have committed immorality with her,
and the **merchants of the earth** have grown rich from the power of her luxurious living."

"Our country like so many before us, and like so many after us, was in fact founded by Freemasons. Freemasonry, in one form or another, has played a role in almost every government that was founded in this world. It is powerful in operation today throughout the world.

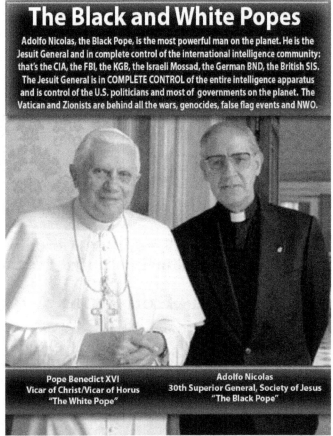

The Black and White Popes

Adolfo Nicolas, the Black Pope, is the most powerful man on the planet. He is the Jesuit General and in complete control of the international intelligence community: that's the CIA, the FBI, the KGB, the Israeli Mossad, the German BND, the British SIS. The Jesuit General is in COMPLETE CONTROL of the entire intelligence apparatus and is control of the U.S. politicians and most of governments on the planet. The Vatican and Zionists are behind all the wars, genocides, false flag events and NWO.

Pope Benedict XVI
Vicar of Christ/Vicar of Horus
"The White Pope"

Adolfo Nicolas
30th Superior General, Society of Jesus
"The Black Pope"

However, we do want to establish first that what we are not talking about is Blue Masonry, or the Masonic lodges in your home town. We are not talking about the Freemasons that live across the street from you. We're talking about a worldwide fraternal organization that is powerful enough, old enough, and wise enough to operate behind all governments in the world, behind fraternal institutions, and behind international monetary systems in the world. And, yes, they are, in fact, connected."
Jordan Maxwell

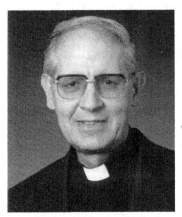

Superiors General are elected by the General Congregation of the Society, summoned upon the resignation, retirement or death of an incumbent. Superiors General are elected for life and almost all have served life terms, the exceptions being Father Pedro Arrupe (resigned for reasons of failing health) and his successor, Father Peter Hans Kolvenbach. Kolvenbach's resignation was announced in February 2006, which led to the convocation of the 35th General Congregation. That General Congregation elected the current Superior General of the Society, Father Adolfo Nicolás, who succeeded Kolvenbach.

https://warningilluminati.wordpress.com/the-most-powerful-man-in-the-world-the-black-pope/

Months of unclean spirits in the Vatican calendar

Month	Named after...		Origins of the demons
January	Janus		Roman god, presides over doors and beginnings
March	Mars		God of war, the most important Roman god after Jupiter
May	Maia		a goddess associated with Vulcan and Mercury worshiped on May 1 and May 15
June	Juno		wife of Jupiter, the most important goddess of the Roman state
July	Julius Caesar		100–44 bc, deified Roman general and statesman, dictator of the Roman Empire
August	Augustus Caesar		63 bc – ad 14, the first Roman emperor, self-proclaimed the 'son of God,' deified

https://sites.google.com/site/romethegreatwhoreofbabylon/home

Demons' days in the Gregorian calendar

Day	Named after...		Origins of the demons
Sunday	Sol Invictus		Sol Invictus, "Unconquered Sun" official sun god of Roman Empire
Monday	Luna		Roman divine embodiment of the Moon, the female complement of the Sun (Sol)
Tuesday	Tīw		Germanic god of Law, portrayed as a one-handed man
Wednesday	Odin		a major god in Norse mythology and the ruler of Asgard
Thursday	Jupiter		Roman king of the gods and the god of sky and thunder
Friday	Frigga		the wife of Odin goddess of married love and of the hearth
Saturday	Saturn		Roman god of agriculture; its feast the Saturnalia the predecessor of Christmas

Objects, actions or creatures that have a deeper significance and are so understood by those who see them or use them.

Symbolic objects

The rainbow: a symbol of God's covenant *See also* Ge 9:13; Eze 1:28; Rev 4:3
A stairway: a symbol of the way to God Ge 28:11-13; Jn 1:51
Thunder, lightning, cloud and smoke: symbols of God's majesty Ex 19:16-18; Ex 24:17; Ps 97:2,4; Rev 4:5; Rev 8:5; Rev 11:19
Thunder: a symbol of God's voice Ps 29:3; Ps 68:33
Trumpets: a symbol of God speaking Ex 19:19; Rev 8:6
The pillar of cloud and fire: a symbol of guidance Ex 13:21
A throne: a symbol of God's glory Isa 6:1; Eze 1:26; Rev 4:2; Rev 22:3
Dry bones: a symbol of spiritual death Eze 37:1-2,11
White hair: a symbol of wisdom Da 7:9; Rev 1:14
The wind: a symbol of the Holy Spirit Jn 3:8; Ac 2:2
Fire: a symbol of the Holy Spirit Ac 2:3
Stars and lampstands: symbols of God's ministers Rev 1:20
A signet ring: a symbol of authority Est 8:10; Hag 2:23
Arrows: symbols of God's judgments Ps 38:2; Ps 120:4
A sceptre: a symbol of God's rule Ps 2:9; Rev 2:27; Rev 19:15
The capstone: a symbol of pre-eminence Mt 21:42 pp Mk 12:10-11 pp Lk 20:17; Ps 118:22
A rock: a symbol of stability Ps 18:2; Ps 40:2
The human body: a symbol of interdependence 1Co 12:27
Grass: a symbol of human frailty Ps 90:5-6; 1Pe 1:24

Symbolic creatures

The serpent: a symbol of Satan's subtlety Ge 3:1; Rev 12:9; Rev 20:1-3
Locusts: a symbol of God's judgment Ex 10:12; Joel 1:4; Rev 9:3
Beasts: symbols of earthly kingdoms Da 7:2-7,17; Da 8:20-22
A dove: a symbol of the Holy Spirit Mt 3:16 pp Mk 1:10 pp Lk 3:22
A lamb: a symbol of Jesus Christ's sacrifice Rev 5:6

This is what these companies are all about, though most employed at them probably have no idea what they are working towards (the antichrist beast system). The pentagram image above reveals the truth. The logo for the Order of the Eastern Star (Masonic organization for women) also reveals this truth.

The newly updated Microsoft logo, and the newly updated Google logo both feature the same four colors. They are the four magickal elements, earth, air, fire and water. There is more going on here than meets the eye. These logos must be designed by people who are familiar with the demonic realm with the intention of capturing souls. The four elements combine to produce a fifth element, (demonic) spirit from the other side.

Symbolic actions

Breaking a jar: a symbol of the destruction of Jerusalem Jer 19:10-11

The cursing of a fig-tree: a symbol of judgment Mt 21:18-19 pp Mk 11:12-14

Washing hands: a symbol of innocence Mt 27:24

Being thirsty: a symbol of spiritual need Ps 63:1; Jn 7:37

Baptism: a symbol of salvation in Jesus Christ Ac 22:16; Ro 6:3-4; 1Pe 3:21

The Lord's Supper: a symbol of union with Christ Mt 26:26-29 pp Mk 14:22-24 pp Lk 22:19-20 pp 1Co 11:23-26

Anointing: a symbol of empowering by God's Spirit 1Sa 16:13; Lk 4:18; Isa 61:1

Harvesting: a symbol of judgment day Joel 3:12-13; Mt 13:29-30; Rev 14:15

Tearing garments: a symbol of anger and sorrow Ge 37:29,34; Jos 7:6

Spitting: a symbol of contempt Isa 50:6; Mt 26:67 pp Mk 14:65

Shaking off dust: a symbol of rejection Mt 10:14 pp Lk 9:5; Ac 13:51

Sitting in sackcloth and ashes: a symbol of repentance Ps 69:11; Isa 22:12; Jnh 3:5-6; Mt 11:21

Lifting of hands: a symbol of prayer Ps 63:4; 1Ti 2:8

Covering the head: a symbol of submission 1Co 11:3-10

Symbols expressing God's nature and character

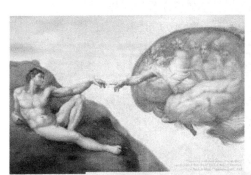

God's face: a symbol of his presence Nu 6:25-26; Ps 34:16

God's arm or hand: a symbol of his power Ps 21:8; Ps 89:13

God's eyes: a symbol of his awareness Pr 15:3; 1Pe 3:12

God's ear: a symbol of God listening Ps 31:2; Isa 59:1

Symbols of God

God the Father
Manus Dei (Hand of God)

God the Holy Spirit
Descending Dove

http://www.churchofsatan.com/faq-the-black-house.php

The Symbols of Wicca

The Goddess

The God

Spirit / Air / Fire / Earth / Water

Air

Fire

Earth

Water

Wheel of the Year

PROOF
Not for printing.
Copyright La Bohème – Laura Sea

Pentagram

Hexagram

1st Degree Wiccan

2nd Degree Wiccan

3rd Degree Wiccan

Celtic Knot

Triqueta

Triple Spiral

Triskel

WHY DO SATANISTS WORSHIP THE DEVIL?

DO SATANISTS PERFORM SACRIFICES?

I HEARD THAT SATANISM SUPPORTS SEX WITH CHILDREN AND OTHER WAYS TO HARM THEM—HOW DO YOU JUSTIFY THAT?

DO SATANISTS RITUALLY ABUSE PEOPLE?

WHAT IS "THEISTIC SATANISM"?

ISN'T LAVEY'S SATANISM JUST PLAGIARIZED FROM OTHER SOURCES?

1967 – a big year for the Church of Satan if ever there was one. LeVay's Satanism appeals to hedonist Hollywood attracting celebrity members, such as Sammy Davis Junior, Jayne Mansfield, and allegedly a young Marilyn Monroe.

In Ancient Greece, homosexuality wasn't frowned upon as it became later in history.

Don't believe the hype.

The Greeks weren't as hateful and certain "higher" classes (educated, land owning) didn't have a problem with soldiers having relations with each other or a slave-owner fucking his slaves. But men of any means were still expected to sire children because for all cultures in all nations everywhere on Earth until just recently, to not produce children was a massive, massive disgrace (limited exceptions for entering the priesthood or convents). "Homosexuality" was a very different concept back then and it was a bit more nuanced. You weren't gay unless you took a dick up the ass. If you just penetrated a lesser-born person, then you weren't homosexual. To be fucked up the ass was a huge disgrace for a man of any means or notoriety and could result in huge issues.

  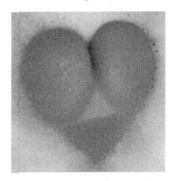

Below is an image of a Roman coin celebrating this sort of relationship with a younger "pais." Pederasty was so common in Roman culture, they literally put it on the money.

Goat Head The horned goat, goat of mendes, Baphomet, god of the witches, the scapegoat. It's a Satanists way of mocking Jesus as the "Lamb" who died for our sins.

"Her shapely rounded hemispheres were so appreciated by the Greeks that they built a special temple Aphrodite Kallipygos, which literally meant, Goddess with the Beautiful Buttocks.

Greek poet Anacreon with his lover.

<u>Spiral</u> Ancient Goddess symbol of universal pattern of growth in nature. A variation with three lines was used by some to represent the number of the beast.. 666

Target Corporation is the second largest discount retailer company in United States, with more than 351,000 employees and $2.21 billion of net income as of 2009. Founded in Minneapolis, Minnesota in 1902, Target Corporation has its headquarters on Nicollet Mall in Minneapolis.

DESIGN ELEMENTS OF TARGET LOGO

The Target logo is an ideal example of an ingenious, simple design. **Shape and Color of the Target Logo:** It was quite a difficult task for the designer to create a logo with obvious imagery. On the other hand, the homocentric circle-within-a-circle interpretation of a target is outstandingly simple and communicates universally. While designing this classic logo, the thickness of the negative space, which makes the third ring on the target, was determined very carefully and skillfully. The target logo utilizes the red and white palette which holds the simplicity from shape to color, and looks brilliant with the overall brand imagery. The red color represents purity and business responsibility of the company. **Font of the Target Logo:** The Target logo uses the Helvetica Neue Bold font

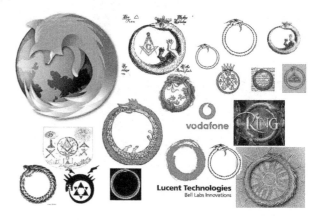

http://www.atlanteanconspiracy.com/2014/07/school-court-church-cult.html

SCHOOLS, CHURCHES, AND COURTS: THE CULT OF SATURN

First you pay out your "tuition" to get into "universe"-ity where they strip you of your Intuition and give you an Indoctrination. Then you receive a "Ma-Stars" Masonic "degree," while wearing a Masonic mortar board cap and Cult of Saturn black robes to become an Alumni/Illumini. Graduation means to increment or retard progress.

As Jordan Maxwell says, "*the true meaning of Graduation is gradual indoctrination.*" Indeed. Stick a bunch of 5 year-olds in a room full of 5-year olds for a year, then a bunch of 6-year olds with 6-year olds and so on for 20 years, until you're so indoctrinated they give you a doctorate.

Jews and Muslims alike worship a huge black cube/box called Kabba at Mecca. Their god YHWH is known as the "Tetra-gramaton" meaning their 4-letter (4-sided) God. The "Kabballah" of Jewish mysticism/Masonry comes from Kabba-Allah or "Cube-God" around which people gather and ceremonially walk in circles. Thus it can be said they are "circling the square." Masons are also constantly referring to "circling the square" and "squaring the circle." For instance, this is why a "box-ing" match is fought for "rounds" in the "ring" but it is actually a 4-sided square arena with corners. The Freemasonic G (Geometry/God) symbol within a compass and T-square symbolizes this as well. Just as people circle around their Cube-God Kabba, so the Masons use a compass/square around their "G" God/Geometry.

Acts 7:43

And you took up the tent of Molek, and the star of your mighty one Kiyyun, images which you made to bow before them. Therefore I shall remove you beyond Bab'el

In this segment of the article we will examine the "tent of Molek" and "Kiyyn" to acertain what Stephan was speaking of when he was before the high priest and council on the day of his death

http://www.yahuahreigns.com/saturn%20and%20the%20occult.html

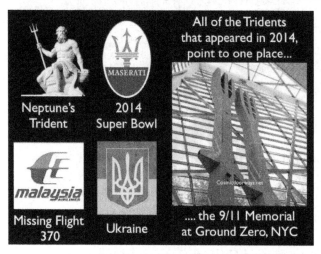

Neptune's Trident

MASERATI
2014 Super Bowl

malaysia AIRLINES
Missing Flight 370

Ukraine

All of the Tridents that appeared in 2014, point to one place...

.... the 9/11 Memorial at Ground Zero, NYC

Occult Symbolism : Saturn Worship

You might not know it, but the entire world has been worshiping Saturn for thousands of years. The cult has never stopped and its rites are still present to this day. Saturn, dubbed the "Lord of the Rings", is the reason why we exchange rings at weddings or put halos on the heads of godly people. This article exposes the attributes of the god Saturn and the perpetuation of his cult through pop culture.

Apple store on Fifth Avenue, NYC
*note: Most people believe the fruit eaten in the Garden of Eden was an apple. So what does it mean for a computer company to have a partially eaten apple as their logo?

The Macintosh computer was named after Apple, as you might expect.

Photograph: DPA/Press Association Images

The forbidden fruit grants wisdom, just like Apple computers do. Of course, the sin of partaking in the tree of knowledge is also the original sin that accounts for the fall of man. If you've ever seen the *Terminator* movies, you know that technology will *also* be the fall of man! How appropriate.

So, if the Bible doesn't specify the fruit as an apple, how did the apple become a primary symbol of this creation myth? The most likely reason comes from fine art.

https://www.theguardian.com/technology/2013/dec/23/apple-iphone-ipad-mac-steve-jobs-wozniak

The Tree of Knowledge is the science of sexuality, which in Hebrew is Da'ath, known in the east as Tantra, and hidden in the West as "Alchemy.

The Apple Logo is truth in plain sight. Apple offers us the forbidden fruit, just like in the garden, it is the serpent, satan. Genesis 3:5 For God doth know that in the day ye eat thereof, then your eyes shall be opened, and ye shall be as gods, knowing good and evil. The problem is, the "gods" are little g gods, actually the angels that fell with Lucifer, who are damned eternally. They would love for us to join them in their fall, but it doesn't have to be so, you must choose everlasting life or death. We are presented with the same choice as Adam and Eve in the garden, nothing has changed. Choose who you will serve in this life, but choose wisely.

the APPLE a symbol of ZEUS

1st Apple logo Sir Isaac Newton sitting under an apple tree waiting for the APPLE TO FALL
waiting for A POLE to FALL
waiting for the POLAR ICE CAPS
the fruit of eden

Mc or Mac = Son Of

*APPLE MAC
Son Of Zeus*

1976 to 1998
the Rainbow
apple logo
USED 12 YEARS

the rainbow
the promise
to NOAH
concerning
the FLOOD

computer AGE AYE EYE

1998 to present
the
monochrome
apple
USED 12 YEARS
IF USED TILL 2010
2010 WINTER OLYMPICS
@ VANCOUVER / WRESTLER - MOUNT OLYMPUS WASHINGTON

Not i, but Christ

Made for iPad
Made for iPhone
Made for iPod

Therefore shall they eat of the fruit of their own way, and be filled with their own devices. Proverbs 1:31

*http://
chemtrailsaredemonic.org/
demonicStargatePortals.php*

Occult & Illuminati holiday traditions

Occult & Illuminati holiday traditions

September 18, 2013 By IlluminatiWatcher 71 Comments

I'm going to attempt to convey the symbolism found in virtually all of the holidays and the occult importance they each have. When you take a step back and try to look at the purpose for the odd symbolism found in our holidays (e.g. why would a rabbit lay eggs??), you'll begin to understand the manipulation that happens on all levels around us. You'll see that the holidays each have their own part to play in the occult worship of the ancient pagan god Nimrod and goddess Semiramis. Most of the holidays and symbolism attached have ties to human sacrifice and magic as well. I'll try to make

MASONIC AND OCCULT SYMBOLS ILLUSTRATED

Includes 728 Illustrations
Dr. Cathy Burns

Discover the most fascinating and in-depth meanings behind the symbols used by the Masons, occultists, witches, New Agers, Satanists, and others. This book uncovers the hidden meanings behind the symbols that we see around us every day. In this well-documented book you will see hundreds of illustrations along with their explanations. You will find many organizational logos, hand signals, tarot cards, zodiac signs, talismans, amulets, and humanist symbols, as well as the meaning of the peace symbol, hexagram, pentagram, yin/yang, circle, all-seeing eye, caduceus, oroborus, ankh, triskele, and the triangle. Also revealed in this book are numerous Masonic and Eastern Star symbols such as the clasped hands, point within a circle, broken column, gavel, obelisk, pomegranate, and the cornucopia.

254

The BEST place to hide a LIE is between two TRUTHS!

THE SHOCKING TRUTH ABOUT JEHOVAH'S WITNESSES

Do you really know who is knocking at your door?
While they may seem polite, cheerful, and well-mannered, the real truth about
Jehovah's Witnesses and their beliefs may shock you. Consider the following:

PEDOPHILIA

✓ A child sex assault victim must produce a witness to their attack before their case is heard by elders.[1]

✓ Confessed pedophiles may be put in positions of authority over others, including children. They are also required to participate in door-to-door preaching.[1]

✓ Only in rare and extreme cases are parents warned that a pedophile is in their congregation, even if that person has authority over them and their children.[1]

RAPE

✓ Jehovah's Witnesses have blamed women for raising rapists, stating that they have "come short" in teaching their sons "respect for womankind."[2] Women have also been told to treat a rapist "respectfully" and "understandingly."[3]

✓ A woman is required to scream and fight during an attack, and if not, "she would be viewed as consenting to the violation" and may face disfellowshipping [excommunication] and subsequent shunning.[4]

✓ Elders are told to use "discernment" if a woman claims to have been raped, taking into account her "mental disposition," the circumstances leading up to the incident, and any "delay in reporting."[5] She may then be disfellowshipped and shunned based on their "discernment" of her claim.

SHUNNING

✓ Jehovah's Witnesses are told not to contact or communicate with a disfellowshipped [excommunicated] family member, not even through e-mail.[6]

✓ Even "young ones" may be shunned if they leave the religion.[7]

✓ Those who have left the religion have been referred to as "mentally diseased."[8]

JW VICTIMS .ORG — TO FIND OUT THE REAL TRUTH ABOUT JEHOVAH'S WITNESSES, INCLUDING THEIR MANY HURTFUL AND ABUSIVE POLICIES, PLEASE VISIT OUR WEBSITE.

While Jehovah's Witnesses often claim to be a religion based on love of family and love of neighbor, because of their belief that an accused or even confessed child molester has the right to confidentiality, they put children at risk by not alerting authorities in these cases.

Women are encouraged to stay with abusive men in the hopes of converting them, with little to no mention of the effects of that abuse on them or their children.

Jehovah's Witnesses do not allow blood transfusions even in emergency situations and even for their children, and at one time also did not allow organ transplants, calling these a form of cannibalism.

Higher education and independent research is strongly discouraged among members.

Additionally, the leaders of the religion ask those in even the poorest areas of the world to donate funds, while themselves earning billions of dollars in real estate transactions alone. The religion practices no official charitable works despite their profits.

1) October 1 2012 Letter to All Elders Worldwide, 2) March 8 1974 Awake, 3) February 22 1984 Awake, 4) January 15 1964 Watchtower, June 1 1968 Watchtower, February 22 1984 Awake, 5) "Shepherd the Flock of God in Your Care," Published in 2010, 6) January 15 2013 Watchtower, 7) 2013 Public Discourse delivered by Watchtower Representative Steven Bell, 8) July 15 2011 Watchtower

http://www.jesus-is-savior.com/False%20Religions/false_religions.htm#jw

It is hard for some people to accept there are Subliminal, demonic images in the Watchtower publications. We would like you to have an open mind and at least look. Remember it is not APOSTASY to expose what's wrong. Some web sites that claim to have evidence of Watchtower Subliminal art are nothing but decoys. They have been designed to discredit the genuine findings.

 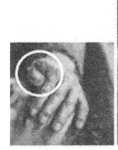  

FACE ON THE THUMB:

The following picture is on page 13 of "The Watchtower" magazine, issue August 15th, 2007:

Read the eye-opening, The Watchtower And The Masons (free online PDF book), by political prisoner and Christian, Fritz Springmeier.

They are the most militant arm of papal power to this day. Their goals were to reclaim those that had left Catholicism and to attack the reliability of the Textus Receptus. They would use ANY METHOD to regain control including confiscation, treachery, torture and assassination. Jesuits will stop at nothing to bring the whole world under subjection to the Vatican. The Jesuits ploy was to entice Protestants back to Rome. They knew they could not bring anyone back into the bondage of Catholicism as long as true believers clung to the pure text. So the Jesuits plotted to replace our Bible with pro-Catholic readings of Jerome's Vulgate. This would cause the Protestant scholars to believe our text was unreliable, unreadable and not scholarly. Once programmed, the scholars would attack the pure text, all the while, believing they were doing God's service.

Gal 4:16 asks "Am I therefore become your enemy, because I tell you the truth?" This blog is to warn fellow Christians and others, about what is happening in the churches, stand against the one world religion, and promote the truth of the Bible in standing up before a myriad of last days delusions.

The *Jehovah Witnesses* are a Satanic organization, based upon the occult of Freemasonry. Charles Taze Russell was a 33rd Degree Freemason; as was Joseph Smith, founder of the Mormon cult. Carefully notice the Masonic cross at the upper left corner of the photo below...

—False Religions—

"For false Christs and false prophets shall rise, and shall show signs and wonders, to seduce, if it were possible, even the elect." —Mark 13:22

"It is not a form of religious persecution to say and to show that another religion is false. For an informed person to expose publicly a certain religion on being false, thus allowing persons to see the difference between false religion and true religion." **(Watchtower 11/15/63, p. 688:)**

In his book The Watchtower & the Masons Fritz Springmeier says: "It has always been disconcerting that the Masons are so adept at smokescreens. The leader of the Anti-Masonic political party in the 1830-1840's turned out to be a Mason. Both C.T. Russell and J. Rutherford printed material that was less than favorable to Freemasonry. And yet I now know that C.T. Russell was a Freemason, a Knights Templar. I also know that Rutherford worked intimately with Freemasons who were his good friends."

The Masonic cross used by the Masonic Jehovah's Witnesses

A Masonic Temple

Charles T. Russell, founder of the "Jehovah's Witnesses", was a mason.

The pyramidal memorial for the Watchtower Society has the same cross and crown symbol found in Freemasonry and in masonic temples. This memorial is a masonic / occult pyramid.

9TH DEGREE
You're Not The Boss of Me
SeX Magic

You're Not The Boss of Me

Rulers of Darkness /Big brother
" For we wrestle not against flesh and blood, but against principalities, against powers, against the **rulers of the darkness** of this world, ...
What are "Principalities, Powers, World **Rulers** of **Darkness**, and Spiritual Wickedness in High Places"?

Introduction to sex magic and subliminal suggestion

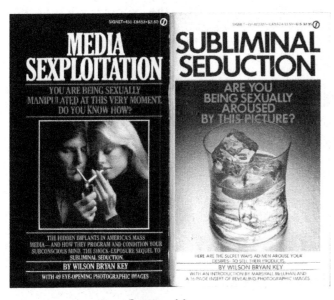

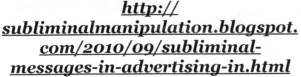

http://subliminalmanipulation.blogspot.com/2010/09/subliminal-messages-in-advertising-in.html

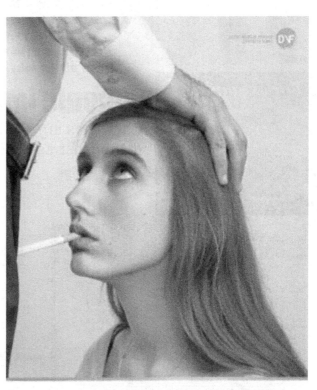

FUMER, C'EST ÊTRE L'ESCLAVE DU TABAC.

Subliminal Message. Inadequate to produce a sensation or a perception. 2 : existing or functioning below the threshold of consciousness

A **subliminal message** is a signal or **message** designed to pass below (sub) the normal limits of perception. For example it might be inaudible to the conscious mind (but audible to the unconscious or deeper mind) or might be an image transmitted briefly and unperceived consciously and yet perceived unconsciously.

Subliminal perception occurs whenever stimuli presented below the threshold or limen for awareness are found to influence thoughts, feelings, or actions. The term **subliminal perception** was originally used to describe situations in which weak stimuli were **perceived** without awareness.

Subliminal stimuli (/sʌbˈlɪmɪnəl/; literally "below threshold"), contrary to supraliminal stimuli or "above threshold", are any sensory stimuli below an individual's threshold for conscious perception.

Because of Crowley's sexual rituals, drug consumption and dabblings in Black Magick (he introduced the letter "k" at the end of "magic" to differentiate it from the entertainment kind) , Crowley was maligned and heavily criticized by the press during his lifetime. However, declassified documents have since revealed that the "Great Beast 666" led a double life: Crowley apparently maintained ties with the British Government and worked with the British intelligence and high-ranking members of the American Government. The O.T.O.–the secret society he popularized–held within its ranks some of the most influential people of the time, who in turn used their power to further the advancement of its main philosophy:

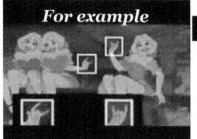

For example

Demonic images in children cartoons

Cartoons are being used to degrade her **children** ... from you is that mainstream entertainment is **satanic** and made to corrupt the masses.

The Book of the Law Found. —2 Kings 22 : 10, 11

Rocket to Uranus Anal Intercourse and the O.T.O.

The structure of the Ordo Templi Orientis (O.T.O.), like that of Freemasonry, is based on a staged series of initiations or degrees. The essence of the Order is in its higher degrees; strictly speaking only members of these degrees are considered to be members of the O.T.O. proper.

Aleister Crowley: *"Of the Eleventh Degree [of the Ordo Templi Orientis], its powers, privileges, and qualifications, nothing whatever is said in any grade. It has no relation to the general plan of the Order, is inscrutable, and dwells in its own palaces."* (Liber CXCIV, 1919)

Crowley: *"I am inclined to believe that the XIth degree is better than the IXth degree"*, diary entry 26 August 1916.

"Oh, how superior is the Eye of Horus to the Mouth of Isis!". Diary 1913 about a boy showered with *"foaming seed"*: *"While the other in his orgasm receives the waters." "Let it be no sin to us to have buggered the virle bum." "While the priest thrusts his thyrsus between boyish buttocks, All is accomplished; come Holy Dove!"* http://bluepyramid.tripod.com/index/id4.html. "The Equinox" IV;2, Maine 1998, 405. http://www.parareligion.ch/sunrise/xi.htm

260

"The Book of the Law", the Thelema and the Aeon of Horus

In 1904, Crowley and his new wife Rose visited Egypt for their honeymoon. It is during this trip that he wrote his most famous book *Liber Legis, The Book of the Law*, which would become the cornerstone of his life. According to his own account, Crowley's wife led him into a museum in Cairo where she showed him a seventh century BCE mortuary stele known as the Stele of Ankh-ef-en-Khonsu (which will be later revered as the Stele of Revealing). Crowley was astounded by the exhibit's number: 666, the number of the Beast in the Book of Revelation.

Later during their stay in Egypt, Crowley and Rose took part in a magical ritual during which he alleges to have received a message from an entity named Aiwass. As a result of this communication, Crowley wrote the first three chapters of the Book of the Law – a mystical text which, he believed, would revolutionize the future of mankind.

"It announced the advent of a new eon in which Crowley has become the priest-prince of a new religion, the Age of Horus. He was to formulate a link between humanity and the "solar-spiritual force, during which the god Horus would preside for the next two thousand years over the evolution of consciousness on this planet.

The message from Aiwaz, whom Crowley understood to be his own guardian angel, convinced him that his mission in life was to give the coup de grace to the Age of Osiris with its moribund appendage, the Christian faith, and build on the ruins a new religion based on the law of the Thelema – Greek for 'will'." [6. Peter Tompkins, The Magic of Obelisks]

The O.T.O's magical and initiatory system has among its innermost reaches a set of teachings on sex magick . One might even observe that the acronym of this order is rather phallic. Sex magick is the use of the sex act, or the energies, passions or arousals it evokes, as a point of which to focus the will or magical desire in the non-sexual world. It has been equated with the "life force" and the "kundalini". Through the ritualistic use of sexual techniques, inspired by Tantric schools of the East, the initiate can use the immense potency of sexual energy to reach higher realms of spirituality.

http://vigilantcitizen.com/hidden-knowledge/aleister-crowley-his-story-his-elite-ties-and-his-legacy/

261

SUBLIMINAL MANIPULATION

Subliminal perception is a deliberate process created by communication technicians, whereby you receive and respond to information and instructions without being aware of it. Messages in the form of printed words, pictures or voices presented either very rapidly or very obscurely bypass your conscious awareness. Anything consciously perceived can be evaluated, criticized, discussed, argued, and possibly rejected. Anything programmed subliminally to your subconsciousness meets no resistance. This subliminal information is stored in your brain and capable of influencing your judgment, behavior and attitudes.

The use of subliminal techniques in print communication media has been going on in the United States at least since the World War I period. For example, Norman Rockwell's first cover on The Saturday Evening Post during 1917 incorporated embedded SEXes. Whenever an embedded word or picture accidentally became consciously visible, the readers would pass it off as a joke, an accident, or a product of their imaginations.

http://subliminalmanipulation.blogspot.com

The phallic image of Pan is a celebration of the primal sexuality of Man in honor of his Animal self.

*Secret **Subliminal Manipulation**. Real Subliminal Influence & Persuasion Is Not Hidden. It Is All Around Us, hidden in plain site.*

The word SEX in print media is usually embedded into hair, creases in clothing, facial lines, or rough background surfaces. Often some noise added to disguise it, like in the House snapshot, or it can be spelled as "ssex" or "sexx", etc.

Letter-looking patterns can naturally occur in such mediums. An artist usually looks for these patterns and starts from there. For example in the following Jantzen ad the letter "X" is already formed by the stitches of the man's shirt. Then the shadow of his hand was modified a bit to look like an "E" and the letter "S"—purportedly a water ripple—was lightly painted in the gap under his arm.

The most common subliminal message is S E X.

Since almost all people have a strong affinity to sex, a sexual subliminal message would be the most effective one. Embedded on a product it's supposed to trigger viewer's attention, emotions and stir up affinity in him toward the product. Unfortunately, as you are going to see for yourself, this principle has been heavily misused, abused and misapplied. Blatant sexuality on the verge of pornography can be easily found in public advertising, family movies, cartoons and children products.

Skeleton Dance

263

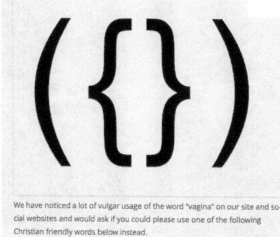

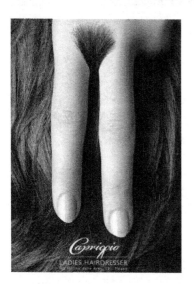

For decades a war has been raging between those who believe subliminal messages work and those who do not. This war has not just been confined to ordinary people

Ham? Really? Is that what it really looks like? Come on ad guys, you can't really think we are that blind to what it really looks like.

I love this one. Just underneath the banner you see two nuts, a thick pour and, let's face it, a chocolate vaginal opening.

https://thesocietypages.org/socimages/2012/01/11/subliminal-sex-in-the-media/

This is a REAL picture of Christina Aguillera at Disneyland with Donald Duck. Our research tells us this is real....even though you may find "edited" versions on the internet that cover this up and say it's a "photoshop". Our reasons why we disagree are from the other photos below. That even includes a lawsuit from a woman that says a Donald Duck employee molested her. Please do more of your own research on this

PROGRAMMING DECEPTIONS

In the programming, colors and directions are used. Be prepared to find out that sometime programmers use their creative imaginations such as using the color "octarine," or the direction "TURNWISE" or perhaps "WIDDERSHINS". During the most fundament programming which is done via LSD trips in sensory deprivation tank to lay in foundations of the Alpha, Beta, Delta, Ome and Theta programs, each programming memory will be given a code. Where one popular programming deception takes place that the programmer knows ahead of time h to sequence his memory codes so that instance, the fifth memory is coded as trip, and strenuous methods are used to up the memories of the first four trips. Victim's s mind will be told to forget the four trips. The memory codes are deceptively designed to fool the deprogrammer and the victim alike. Part of the reason the programmer does this, is that they know that IF a therapist should stumble onto these first memories, the backup programming to protect these memories is so severe that the therapist will shatter the victim's mind. Backup programs such as Atom bombs and vegetable programming are locked into place to protect the fundamental programs. *http://www.theforbiddenknowledge.com/hardtruth/the_disney_bloodlinept1.htm*

265

The "ice-cubes" which her index finger points to form an erect penis. These two cubes have been flesh colored and can easily be seen from a distance of several feet, once pointed out. Note how the penis angle is correct for proper virile erection. Since a penis in a glass is considered taboo, this image would be immediately repressed. People only see what they expect to see.

The woman's lips are in close proximity to this erect, flesh-toned penis. This idea of fellatio is reinforced by the satyr blowing on a flute or phallic-shaped object. Oral sex is a commonly desired quest and fantasy of males of all ages. By retouching and airbrushing in this symbolic sexual message we've elevated a mere glass of whiskey into a potent aphrodisiac.

Next to this erect penis is a red cherry. Red is a hot, loud and active color. On the right of this red cherry is a happy fornicating rabbit. This rabbit is an apt symbol for love and sex. It's common knowledge that the logo for *Playboy* magazine is the promiscuous rabbit. Male boastings of sexual prowess often include emphasis on the partners ability to "fuck like a rabbit".

Note that the ice-cube area surrounding the rabbit's engorged penis is creamy white. The ice-cube area above the cherry is also creamy white rather than a see-through clearness. In this ad's blatant sexual context, this creamy white color correlates with the creamy whiteness of sperm. Obviously ejaculation by fellatio will be successful, enhancing the virility appeal of this product. Below the fornicating rabbit is a happy smiling human face to symbolize a drink that tastes good and will make one happy. It also correlates with love for oral sex - licking her lips in anticipation.

Below this smiling face are several other penises in varying stages of sexual excitement. To the left of these aroused penises are several female shapes with large breasts. The large breasts help activate instinctual maternal sucking impulses associated with the pleasure principle. The female shapes visually stimulate any repressed sexual desires in the viewer.

The model's middle finger on her left hand is visually touching the genital area of the large breasted female shape. The middle finger is associated with sex and sexual gestures such as "Fuck you;" fuck being a sexual connotation implying intercourse. This touching of the genitals by her middle finger is subconsciously interpreted as being bisexual or impish (game for anything) in character. Since male fantasies often include acts of lesbianism, we took the liberty to airbrush this visual enticement into the sexual repertoire our impish hostis tempting the viewer with.

Earlier it was stated that the satyr and choker indicated the model's willingness to be sexually submissive to the viewer's own fantasies. To help aid in this submissive interpretation we instructed the model to look upward. This looking upward visually places her in a lower position than the viewer. In this context it would subconsciously be interpreted as being on her knees or at level convenient for oral sex. The large white areas of her eyes were retouched to match the exact hue of the white, creamy ice-cubes. Exhaustive research indicates the subconscious reads this as "she has eyes" for spurting sperm, she loves climatic pleasures, she's voyeuristic.

What does her mouth shape and her hand position communicate to you? What invisible shape is she holding in her hand and placing to her lips?

You mean a <u>woman</u> can open it?

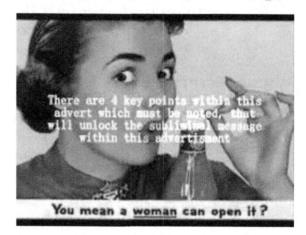

You mean a <u>woman</u> can open it?

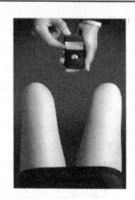

The advertisements mask the subliminal messages the advertisers send to consumers that are damaging and offensive.

DECEPTION DIMINISHES POWER

Knowledge is power, and lies diminish the knowledge of deceived dupes, and therefore diminishes the power of the deceived. Deception obscures the alternatives that people have. It also clouds up various objectives people would work toward. Some people give up certain objectives due to their misperceptions that the objective is undesirable or unattainable. *http://www.theforbiddenknowledge.com/hardtruth/the_disney_bloodlinept1.htm*

266

DISNEY, ILLUMINATI, SATANISM & SEX SYMBOLS EXPOSED!

Disneyland has underground tunnels and underground entrances that even most employees don't know about. One victim of total mind-control mentioned that a tunnel entrance was at Matterhorn mountain. (The Matterhorn was opened by Walt and his good-friend Richard Nixon, who rode in the first car down the mountain.) Disney productions has given the Illuminati the cover to bring together Illusionists, magicians, and special effects artists without anyone being suspicious.

Ape spanking the monkey in Disneyland:

A 4 frames sequence from Who Framed Roger Rabbit.

Astonishing video on the extravagant amount of satanic and sexual subliminal messages in Disney films. From the obvious to the absurd. Ridiculously inappropriate for children. Considering that Walt's grand niece, Abigail Disney, confirmed his staunch racist and sexist views, I can't say that this controversy is too surprising. -Amy Haben

267

WAS WALT DISNEY AN OCCULTIST AND A SECULAR HUMANIST? WAS HE A CHAIN SMOKER THAT SPENT WEEKS IN THE TUNNELS UNDER THE TRAGIC KINGDOM? DID THEY AIRBRUSH ALL OF HIS PHOTOS SANITIZING AND MAKING A SAINT OUT OF HIM? WHO DID HE SPEND HIS TIME WITH IN THE TUNNELS UNDER PLEASURE ISLAND AND OTHER TUNNELS ALL OVER DISNEYLAND? WHY DID HE DIE OF LUNG CANCER WHEN THERE ISN'T A PHOTO ON THE PLANET WITH A CIGARETTE IN HIS HANDS?

Only 32nd Degree Scottish Rite Masons (the highest degree attainable other than the honorary 33rd) or Knight Templars of the York Rite could join the Shriners. This means that uncle Stan is a high level Freemason. This would also mean he knows what's up with all of these symbols floating around.

Children are watching violence at a rate like NO OTHER GENERATION IN HISTORY. Violence has increased 720% since 1982.

Walt Disney Studios Chairman Joe Roth is in charge of Walt Disney as well as subsidiaries, Touchtone, Miramax, and Hollywood Pictures, which were all created to camouflage the Disney production of adult films. Disney operates in a clandestine manner regarding the promotion, distribution and rating of the films produced by their subsidiaries.

So sexy so soon: the new sexualized childhood, and what parents can do to protect their kids (with Diane E. Levin) ~Jean Kilbourne

This woman is just going for a ride and so is Donald.

The hidden truth behind Disney films the pixar theory

http://thefullertoninformer.com/disney666-2/

269

The problem with people who are spiritually blind is they think they can see. If you think we are the ones seeing things that aren't there after reading the below article and you are still skeptical after all the self evident facts and truths presented, let us direct you to this expose' so you can understand why we are able to see what's really happening and it's really you that can't: <u>WHY MOST PEOPLE CAN'T SEE THE TRUTH</u>

https://theconspiracyzone.podcastpeople.com/posts/32979

"The cultural values that (TV/Movies) are teaching: Nothing is off-limits: sex outside marriage, euthanasia, homosexuality, abortion, drugs, child abuse, alcohol consumption, rape, murder, and now cannibalism." I want to add one other set of values which TV is teaching our children, occultism. Our children are watching occultic meditations, seances, and rituals that would normally be observed only by a member of an occultic coven."

Taste the Rainbow: Doritos to Launch Pride Flag-Inspired Tortilla Chips

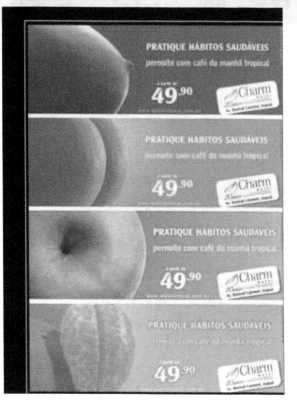

Apparently obscene language is effective in triggering viewers attention and emotions. So, in this Krispy Kreme commercial aired on NBC you can see the slogan "So good, you'll suck dick"... Their excuse was that the on-air graphics operator got this image from Google Images and used it without thorough examination. This is of course not true. They knew exactly what they were doing.

The Hidden Templar Symbology of the OREO Cookie

The OREO cookie is one of the most powerful, and secretive cookies in all the world. It could be called the Holy Grail of creme filling and cookie wholesomeness.

Almost 500 billion have been sold. In fact, if you were to stretch out all the OREOs ever sold, you could circle the globe with OREO cookies 341 times. But did any of these billions of people ever notice the hidden Knights Templar symbology etched into a Oreo cookie as they dipped their OREO's in milk; or licked off the white creamy filling from the Cross Pattee emblazoned cookies?

Let me tell you that I used to love OREO cookies when I was a little fat and ignorant kid growing up in Southern California during the 70's and 80's. However, I was never a creme licker who likes to lick all the creme off and then proceed to eat the cookie. I liked eating my OREO's all at once, and I used to love dipping them in my milk! Now back to the symbology....

The current design of the OREO was formulated in 1952 by some secret cookie designer, that must have been affiliated with the Templars, or he just loved their symbology. You can see right above, the circle with the word "OREO" has a cross with a two-bar cross; this is known as the Cross of Lorraine which was carried by the Knights Templar into the Crusades. The Cross of Lorraine is part of the heraldic arms of Lorraine in eastern France. Between 1871 and 1918 (and again between 1940 and 1944), the northern third of Lorraine was annexed to Germany, along with Alsace. (Wikipedia) There are also exactly 12 Templar Cross Pattees in a circle, with also 12 dots and 12 dashes. **http://gnosticwarrior.com/oreo.html**

National Biscuit Company (Nabisco), the food processing company was founded in New Jersey in 1898 and began marketing cookies and crackers. Oreo cookies hit the US market in 1912 and have been a bestseller ever since.

In 1985, R.J. Reynolds bought out Nabisco in a leveraged buyout (See Barbarians at the Gate) before being sold off to Kraft Foods. Freemasons refer to masonry as "the Craft".

Tobacco giant Philip Morris bought Kraft Foods in 2000 and spinned it off into a different company, Mondelēz International, in 2011.

The antenna-like logo was first used for the company's now discontinued Uneeda Biscuits. The IN-ER SEAL was a reference to the interfolded cardboard which kept the cookies fresh.
http://illuminatisymbols.info/nabisco-oreo-double-cross/

The god Sobek, which was depicted as a crocodile or a man with the head of a crocodile was a powerful and frightening deity; in some Egyptian creation myths, it was Sobek who first came out of the waters of chaos to create the world. As a creator god, he was occasionally linked with the sun god Ra. Curiously we even see soft drink companies such as Sobe' subliminally resurrecting the ancient Egyptian god to sell more energy boosting soft drinks by suggesting that you are in fact ingesting light. He was also shown with an ankh, representing his ability to undo evil and so cure ills. Once he had become Sebek-Ra, he was also shown with a sun-disc over his head, as Ra was a sun god.

http://labyrinthofthepsychonaut.blogspot.com/2008/08/pandoras-box-sobek-and-gateway-to.html

To the ordinary, without foreknowledge of psychology and how the mind perceives matter, sure it all merely fits the paranoid ramblings of an overtly suspicious group of people who make up a small (yet growing) percentage of consciousness, but that is fine. If you look through to the way the mind actually interprets subliminals and how genetic DNA and ancient worship is done then the only real difference between 'then and now' is that then, **people were aware** of it and now people are simply **too distracted** or high in their ego to be either interested, bothered by it, open minded, are engineered or don't have enough **free** time to ponder such possibilities.

http://leemonster.blogspot.com/2009/12/so-be-it-sobek-and-dna.html

272

13 bloodlines

"The Illuminati use what I call reverse symbolism. They place their symbols all around us but present them with the reverse of their true meaning. For example, the dove symbolizes peace to most people, but to the Illuminati bloodlines it represents their goddess, Queen Semiramis [Isis]. The lighted torch means freedom and liberty to the population, but to the Illuminati it is the very symbol of their agenda and control. The Nazis reversed the ancient symbol of the swastika to symbolize the negative and Satanists have reversed the pentagram to point downwards for the same reason. Everything is symbolism and ritual to the Illuminati, and always has been." -David Icke, "Alice in Wonderland and the World Trade Center"

Many people fear the number 13 this may be a reference to the 13 bloodlines of the Illuminati

A Concise Description of the Illuminati
by David Icke

The Illuminati, the clique that control the direction of the world, are genetic hybrids, the result of interbreeding between a reptilian extraterrestrial race and humanity many thousands of years ago. The center of power is not even in this dimension – it is in the lower fourth dimension, the lower astral as many people call it, the traditional home for the "demons" of folklore and myth. These fourth-dimensional reptilian entities work through these hybrid bloodlines because they have a vibrational compatibility with each other. This is why the European royal and aristocratic families have interbred so obsessively, as do the so-called Eastern Establishment families of the United States, which produce the leaders of America. Every presidential election since and including George Washington in 1789 has been won by the candidate with the most European royal genes. Of the 42 presidents to Bill Clinton, 33 have been genetically related to two people, Alfred the Great, King of England, and Charlemagne, the most famous monarch of what we now call France. It is the same wherever you look in the positions of power... they are the same tribe.

As well as an obsession with interbreeding with each other to preserve their genetic structure, the Illuminati are also obsessed with symbolism and ritual. Interestingly, conventional science has documented that the reptilian part of the human brain (the R-complex as they call it) is the source of the following behavior traits. An obsession with ritual, cold blooded behavior, territorialism "this belongs to me", and an obsession with top-down hierarchical structures. This sums up the Illuminati mentality perfectly, and it goes that if you have more of that R-complex, or that it is activated more than normal, you will manifest these traits far more profoundly.

But their ritual is not just for ceremonial purposes or gratuitous horror. The rituals are designed to re-wire the energy fields and grids of the planet and therefore to fundamentally affect human consciousness. The rituals these bloodlines performed in the ancient world are the same as they do now. See The Biggest Secret for the background. They have a detailed annual calendar of events on which they perform their sacrifice rituals in line with key lunar, solar, and planetary cycles to harness that energy for their sick agenda to take complete control of Planet Earth in the very near future.

The Illuminati love to hide their symbolism in plain sight as a way of communicating between the "initiated" that those who are not "enlightened" (in their eyes) cannot understand – and they love it so much they hide the symbols in the infrastructure they control and rule.

Our society is run by insane people for insane objectives. I think we're being run by maniacs for maniacal ends and I think I'm liable to be put away as insane for expressing that. That's what's insane about it. - *John Lennon*

273

MCDONALD'S NUMBER 13 AND DOUBLE ARCHES

McDonald's golden arches logo represents the number 13, the traditional number for a coven of witches. The Golden arches represent double rainbows, a reference to monarch mind control. They could also represent the two Masonic pillars according to other researchers.

M is the 13th letter of the alphabet.

McDonalds (shown repeatedly by Fritz Springmeier and others to be in the service of the Illuminati) uses the M and often underlines it in advertisements making a 13 on its side. Arby's and Westell also have similar 13s encoded in their logos.

Since M looks like a 3 on its side, Hershey's M+M's give us 33, another Illuminati number.

Other potentially relevant double M's include: Master Mason, Mother Mary, Mary Magdalene, Magic Mushroom, and MaxiM Magazine; possible MKUltra victims Marilyn Monroe, Marilyn Manson, Eminem (Marshall Mathers), and Marky Mark; creations of 33rd degree Mason Walt Disney, Mickey Mouse and Minnie Mouse; Masonic Warner Bros.

Robert H. Brown's astronomical rendition of the Royal Arch.

"The accompanying diagram of the Royal Arch is but a geometrical projection, and, therefore, gives nothing more than the relative positions of the various constellations and signs of the Royal Arch. The summer solstice is represented as the keystone of the arch, and has the astronomical sign of the sun inscribed upon it, showing that the 21st of June the sun is exalted to the summit of the arch."[3]

A more elaborate graphic (taken from Ovason's **Secret Architecture**) that was popular in the late 18th Century and renders the same idea can be seen at the left. Here, the progression of the signs is from left to right, and we see the sign of Cancer as the entire keystone. The reason that the signs appear to be going in the wrong direction is that we are looking into the "temple" from the outside. Notice that a cluster of 7 stars float below the keystone, which are symbolic of the Pleiades. Notice also the heraldric shield that depicts an ox, an eagle, a lion, and a man. These are direct references to the fixed signs of the zodiac, namely Taurus, Scorpio, Leo, and Aquarius.

The Sun and Moon hover above the arch, and above the two pillars that support the arch. These pillars are called *Jachin* and *Boaz*, are sometimes simply labeled as **J** and **B**, and are important elements in understanding the Royal Arch via operative Masonry.

It's much more evident in the Chicago White Sox logo:

French Connection UK

Somebody referred to what I do as subliminal activism, which I like. Edward Burtynsky Read more at: https://www.brainyquote.com/quotes/keywords/subliminal.html

Royal Arch Masonry (also known as "Capitular Masonry") is the first part of the York Rite system of Masonic degrees. **Royal Arch** Masons meet as a Chapter, and **the Royal Arch** Chapter confers four degrees: Mark Master Mason, Past Master, Most Excellent Master, and **Royal Arch** Mason.

The Starbucks logo that we know today is based on **15th Century artwork**, which includes a **topless Greek mermaid** with two tails. Of course, the original logo which had the breast visible is now covered by the mermaid's wavy hair. On the modern logo the two tails can be seen and the mermaids arms reaching to grab them.

275

Subliminal messages are there to do what they do best: influence people. They often are incorporated into ads to influence people to buy products,

Supraliminal Perception

- Perception of stimuli that are above the level of conscious awareness is called ***supraliminal perception*** which is generally known as ***perception***.

Subconscious vs. Subliminal

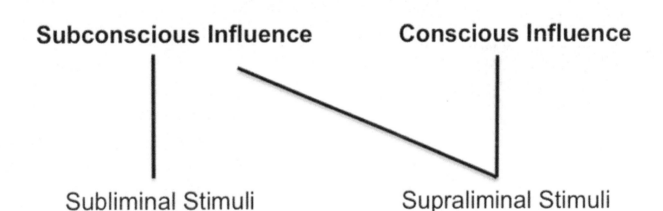

Subconscious Influence   Conscious Influence

Subliminal Stimuli   Supraliminal Stimuli

Advertisers have never shied away from using sex to sell their products because, as the old adage goes, sex sells. And over the last decade, some fast food chains have upped the ante with more sexual innuendo in their television and print advertisements.

There's an entire genre of racy fast food ads, like the Hardee's promotion that talks to consumers about "creamy balls" and "happy holes" for its biscuit holes campaign.

Subliminal messages are everywhere (even in Disney!) Many of them sexual!

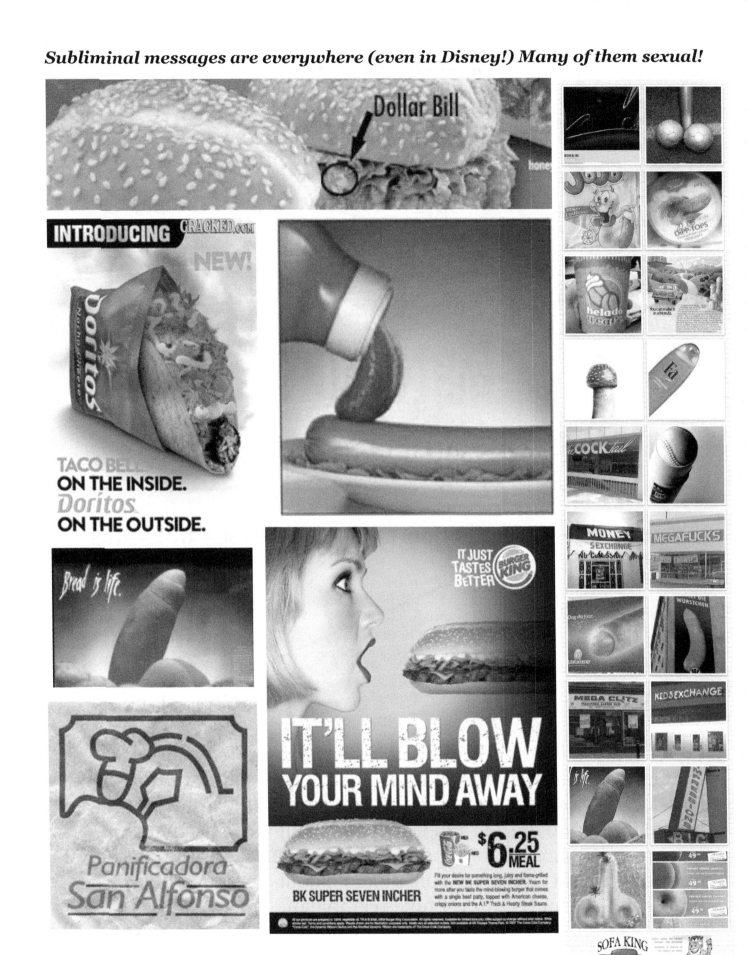

In an attempt to beautify its corporate logo, Procter and Gamble inserted an inverted 666 and two horns on its logo. It also included 13 stars. This caused many to boycott Colgate and other P&G products in the 80s!

Rumors died down but were revived in 1995 after top distributors for household product competitor Amway started telling customers that Proctor and Gamble financed satanic cults. P&G won a settlement of $19.25 million.

TACO BELL 666

Does the restaurant chain have the number of the beast hidden in its corporate logo? The bell's clapper forms the first six. The bell's inner mouth forms the second '6' while its outer lip forms the final '6'. Hola Taco Bell.

Our favourite example of 'people in the letters'. Tostitos manages to show off exactly what you're meant to do with their product within the logo. The two 'T's are shaped like people sharing a tortilla chip, while the 'i' handily holds the dipping salsa.

When our consciousness has become automatic, we are at the mercy of our emotions and past choices, fearing life itself. Conversely, when we seek the truth, and bravely face our fears, they melt away as the truth expands and infuses them. As such, if any idea, belief or concept causes a reaction of fear or disgust, it is the Universe's way of saying *you can transmute this*. Hence the mystery school adage that emotions are our *compass* for self mastery and evolution.

Why are you paying the Kosher "Tax"?

Check these products for yourself. If you have any of these products, carefully check the box for the following Kosher symbols. Included below are the corresponding Kosher-Certification agencies. Every single one of these products is Kosher and is priced accordingly.

 Union of Orthodox Jewish Congregations
(http://www.ou.org)

 Committee for the Furtherance of Torah Observance
(http://www.ok.org)

Rabbi Ralbag Kosher

Star-K Kosher
http://www.star-k.org

Beverly Hills Kosher
http://kosher.org

SUBLIMINAL MESSAGES IN LOGOS ILLUMINATI

The Burger King logo has the words 'Burger' and 'King' hidden inside of it. I have outlined it with black pen. The illuminati leader is known the 'The King of Burgers'

SAMSUNG ARE ACTUALLY THE ILLUMINATI!!!11 LOOK.

If you take the letter 'U' from the logo...

And then round it off...

And then put a triangle around it...

LOOK IT IS ILLUMINATI ALL SEEING EYE!!!

Take a look at the McDonalds logo.
It's actually in the shape of an 'M' (outlined in black) which happens to be the first letter of 'McDonalds' HOLY SHIT.

THE LETTER 'M' IS ALSO IN 'ILLUMINATI'

The KFC logo has a hidden face of the guy who founded it. Colonel Sanders. I have drawn a ring around it as it is very hard to spot and you need a keen eye in order to see it. ALSO... 'KFC' stands for Kentucky Fried Chicken which is the catchphrase the illuminati uses on Saturday mornings when they wake

 KFC

ALL TRUTHS

Look very carefully at the FedEx logo.
It stands for Federal Express. Mind = Blown.
The illuminati disguised it as 'FedEx' because it is disguised.

WARNING. THE ILLUMINATI ALSO CONTROL CHRISTMAS LIGHTS. YOU MAY HEAR PEOPLE SAY 'TIME FOR THE ILLUMINATIONS' ON THE STREET AROUND CHRISTMAS. THE HINT IS IN THE NAME. >>ILLUMINATI<<ONS. >>ON<<S. = ILLUMINATI ON. THEY ARE SWITCHING ON THE LIGHTS AS WELL AS YOUR BRAINS TO WORSHIP THEM.

Hike's over... Have a Pepsi

Good time to relax, be sociable . . . and enjoy
ice-cold Pepsi. Today's lighter Pepsi refreshes without filling.
Good idea to have plenty of Pepsi in your pack.
It's the up-to-date refreshment.

Be sociable... Have a Pepsi

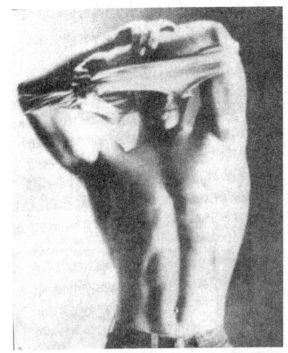

Besides the overt sexual message this image has
the word SEX written subliminally on the fella's
chest and a phallic form appears in the shadows of
his abnormal abs.

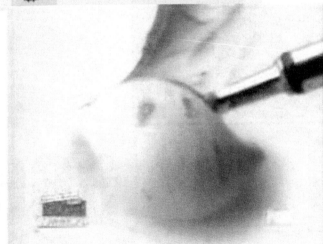

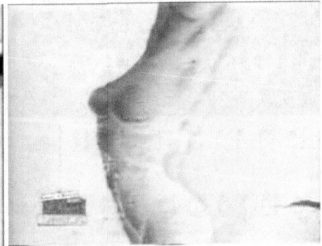

*In this ice-cream commercial you can see that the spoon trail in the ice-cream
has a shape of naked female torso:*

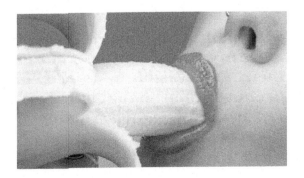

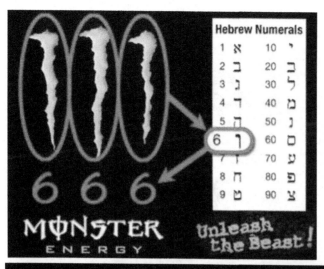

6
6
6

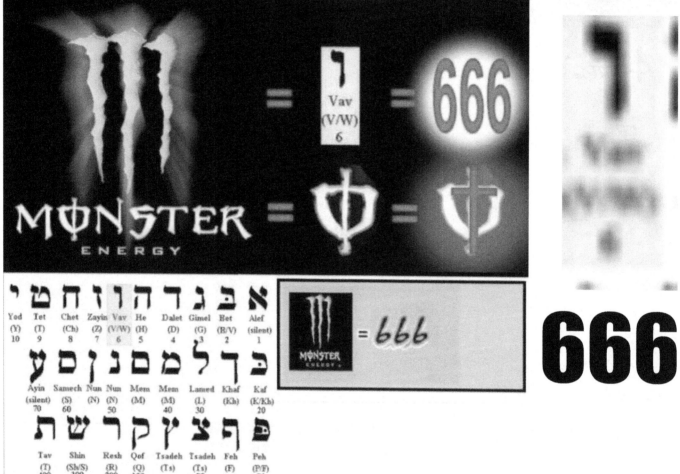

Yod	Tet	Chet	Zayin	Vav	He	Dalet	Gimel	Bet	Alef
(Y)	(T)	(Ch)	(Z)	(V/W)	(H)	(D)	(G)	(B/V)	(silent)
10	9	8	7	6	5	4	3	2	1
Ayin	Samech	Nun	Nun	Mem	Mem	Lamed	Khaf	Kaf	
(silent)	(S)	(N)	(N)	(M)	(M)	(L)	(Kh)	(K/Kh)	
70	60		50		40	30		20	
Tav	Shin	Resh	Qof	Tsadeh	Tsadeh	Feh	Peh		
(T)	(Sh/S)	(R)	(Q)	(Ts)	(Ts)	(F)	(P/F)		
400	300	200	100		90		80		

666

Our subliminal mental processes operate outside awareness because they arise in these portions of our mind that are inaccessible to our conscious self; their inaccessibility is due to the architecture of the brain rather than because they have been subject to Freudian motivational forces like repression. Leonard Mlodinow

Read more at:
https://www.brainyquote.com/quotes/keywords/subliminal.html

282

Sun-kiss or SIN kist

Solar Calendar
Pagan Witchcraft

365 days = 4 seasons
Spring > Summer > Fall > Winter

6 is the number of man
Elevation of man ~ Ascension of man

Produce or 6?
Eye of Horus or Mercury?
If O is 6, then 666?

The magic circle
The squared circle
The four elements

North - Green - Earth
East - Yellow - Air
South - Red - Fire
West - Blue - Water

leaf or fire?

By subliminal, I mean things that occur in our world that are below the threshold of consciousness but do have a psychological effect on us. Leonard Mlodinow

Read more at: https://www.brainyquote.com/quotes/keywords/subliminal.html

Advertising, music, atmospheres, subliminal messages and films can have an impact on our emotional life, and we cannot control it because we are not even conscious of it. Tariq Ramadan
Read more at:

Who or what is dead?

If you read it from left to right (mirror orientation)
it clearly says: "NO MOHAMMAD NO MEKKAH"
in arabic letters ➔ (لا محمد لا مكة)

Subliminal messages and images that were cloaked in print ads to appeal to our subconscious mind while our eyes glanced across the page.

Trigger words are a very important part of subliminal seduction. Trigger words are words that titillate, or outright arouse desire, on a conscious or subconscious level. Everyday words that are often associated with sex are great trigger words. Provocative banter is another way you can arouse desire in a person. Now arousing desire in people is rather easy for anyone who is articulate to any degree. Words are an extremely powerful means of arousing desire. The real trick to subliminally seducing someone through the use of trigger words and provocative banter, is to become the object of the desire that you are arousing. http://www.beyondblonde.com/MatureThemes/SubliminalSeduction/subliminal_seduction.html

285

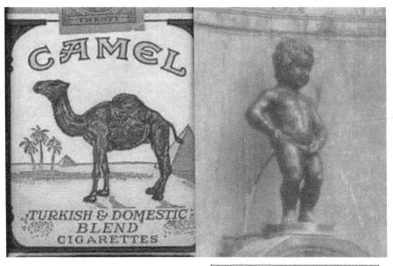

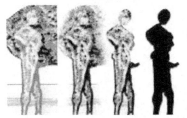

source: Psychology Today, May 1977

Dirty Bird restaurant's fried chicken logo not-so-subtly hides phallic symbol

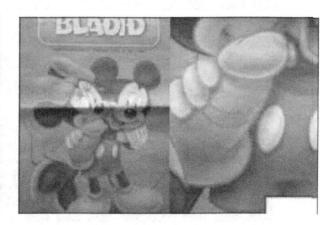

Of course, since then research has said that subliminal messages in advertising are not as effective as earlier claimed

Spider-Man: Peter Parker's Man Juice

Supraliminal Perception

- Perception of stimuli that are above the level of conscious awareness is called _supraliminal perception_ which is generally known as _perception_.

10TH DEGREE

Illuminati
vs
Illuminazi
WAR

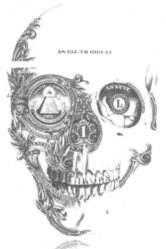

ILLUMINAZI VS ILLUMINATI

The Illuminati have left behind and still leave clues of their influence through a vast number of signs and symbols with special meaning, Symbols, Signs, Meanings & History Revealed Even though it had been in existence for long, The Illuminati love to hide their symbolism in plain sight as a way of ... By inverting a symbol, you ascribe an opposite meaning,

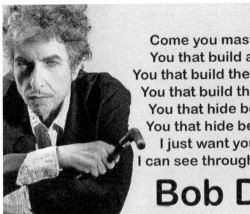

Come you masters of war
You that build all the guns
You that build the death planes
You that build the big bombs
You that hide behind walls
You that hide behind desks
I just want you to know
I can see through your masks

Bob Dylan

Father, father
We don't need to escalate
You see, war is not the answer
For only love can conquer hate
You know we've got to find a way
To bring some lovin' here today
~Marvin Gaye

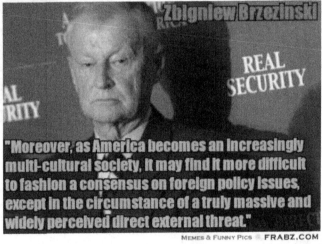

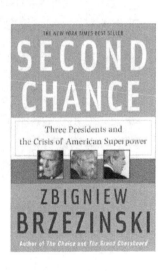

http://mynym.blogspot.com/2014/03/ukraine-on-grand-chessboard.html

Anyway, note Zbigniew's conclusion on the impact of the internet:
[The] major world powers, new and old, also face a novel reality: while the lethality of their military might is greater than ever, their capacity to impose control over the politically awakened masses of the world is at a historic low. To put it bluntly: in earlier times, it was easier to control one million people than to physically kill one million people; today, it is infinitely easier to kill one million people than to control one million people," said Brzezinski during a 2010 Council on Foreign Relations speech in Montreal.
Great, huh? Why is this guy advising American politicians, again?

289

ILLUMINATI

BANKING AND MONEY GROUP
- International Money Center Banks
- Central Banks
- International Monetary Fund
- World Bank
- International Bank of Settlements
- World Conservation Bank
- Multinational Corporations
- Foundations

SECRET SOCIETIES GROUP
- Freemasonry
- Skull & Bones
- Grand Orient Lodge
- Grand Alpina Lodge
- Knights Templar
- Royal Order of the Garter
- Priory de Sion
- Rosicrucians

POLITICAL GROUP
- National Government Leaders
- United Nations
- Bilderbergers
- Trilateral Commission
- Council on Foreign Relations
- Club of Rome
- Aspen Institute
- Bohemian Grove
- Regional Federations
  (NATO, EEC, etc.)
- International Labor Unions

INTELLIGENCE GROUP
- CIA
- KGB
- FBI
- British Intelligence
- Mafia/Organized Crime
- Drug Cartels
- Interpol
- Communist Party

RELIGIOUS GROUP
- World Council of Churches
- National Council of Churches
- World Parliament of Religions
- Vatican/SMOM
- New Age Cults/Groups
- Liberal Protestant
  Denominations
- Unity Church
- Unitarian/Universalist Church
- Baha'i
- Temple of Understanding

EDUCATION GROUP
- UNESCO
- World Peace Groups
- Planetary Congress
- World Federalist Association
- World Constitution and
  Parliamentary Assoc.
- Environmental Groups
- Lucis Trust
- World Goodwill
- World Union
- Esalen Institute
- Media Establishment

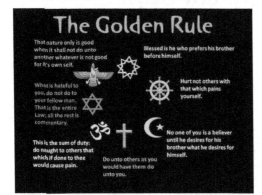

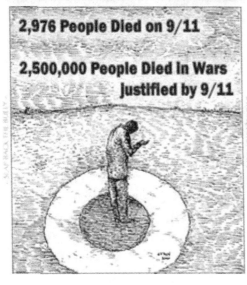

WORLD WAR III

The Third World War must be fomented by taking advantage of the differences caused by the "agentur" of the "Illuminati" between the political Zionists and the leaders of Islamic World. The war must be conducted in such a way that Islam (the Moslem Arabic World) and political Zionism (the State of Israel) mutually destroy each other. Meanwhile the other nations, once more divided on this issue will be constrained to fight to the point of complete physical, moral, spiritual and economical exhaustion...We shall unleash the Nihilists and the atheists, and we shall provoke a formidable social cataclysm which in all its horror will show clearly to the nations the effect of absolute atheism, origin of savagery and of the most bloody turmoil. Then everywhere, the citizens, obliged to defend themselves against the world minority of revolutionaries, will exterminate those destroyers of civilization, and the multitude, disillusioned with Christianity, whose deistic spirits will from that moment be without compass or direction, anxious for an ideal, but without knowing where to render its adoration, will receive the true light through the universal manifestation of the pure doctrine of Lucifer, brought finally out in the public view. This manifestation will result from the general reactionary movement which will follow the destruction of Christianity and atheism, both conquered and exterminated at the same time.

Albert Pike   Aug. 15, 1871

WAR AGAINST A FOREIGN COUNTRY ONLY HAPPENS WHEN THE MONEYED CLASSES THINK THEY ARE GOING TO PROFIT FROM IT.
GEORGE ORWELL

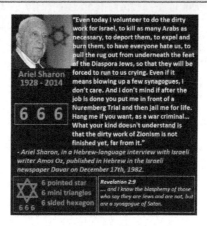

"Even today I volunteer to do the dirty work for Israel, to kill as many Arabs as necessary, to deport them, to expel and burn them, to have everyone hate us, to pull the rug out from underneath the feet of the Diaspora Jews, so that they will be forced to run to us crying. Even if it means blowing up a few synagogues, I don't care. And I don't mind if after the job is done you put me in front of a Nuremberg Trial and then jail me for life. Hang me if you want, as a war criminal... What your kind doesn't understand is that the dirty work of Zionism is not finished yet, far from it."
- Ariel Sharon, in a Hebrew-language interview with Israeli writer Amos Oz, published in Hebrew in the Israeli newspaper Davar on December 17th, 1982.

Ariel Sharon 1928 - 2014

6 6 6

6 pointed star
6 mini triangles
6 sided hexagon
6 6 6

Revelation 2:9
... and I know the blasphemy of those who say they are Jews and are not, but are a synagogue of Satan.

We killed over a million people, created the conditions that led to ISIS, funneled trillions of taxpayer dollars to military contractors, and destroyed the economy. But thanks for blaming the black guy.

Occupy Democrats

For America, the chief geopolitical prize is Eurasia. For half a millennium, world affairs were dominated by Eurasian powers and peoples who fought with one another for regional domination and reached out for global power. Now a non-Eurasian power is preeminent in Eurasia—and Americas global primacy is directly dependent on how long and how effectively its preponderance on the Eurasian continent is sustained. Obviously, that condition is temporary.
But its duration, and what follows it, is of critical importance not only to America's well-being but more generally to international peace.

ZBIGNIEW BRZEZINSKI
The Grand Chessboard

TIME TO WAKE UP PEOPLE...

MONARCH, ILLUMINATI & MAFIA

COUNCIL OF 13

FRONT GROUPS & CONTROL STRUCTURES (which are under co-option)

COMMITTEE OF 300

THE ROUND TABLE THINK TANKS

THE FREEMASON LODGES/SECRET SOCIETIES

WORLD FINANCIAL CONTROL

WORLD RESOURCE CONTROL

WORLD POPULATION CONTROL

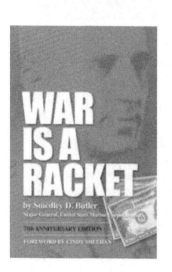

WAR IS A RACKET

by Smedley D. Butler
Major General, United States Marine Corps Retired

75th ANNIVERSARY EDITION
FOREWORD BY CINDY SHEEHAN

"War is a racket. It is the only one international in scope. It is the only one in which the profits are reckoned in dollars and the losses in lives."

"If only more of today's military personnel would realize that they are being used by the owning elite's as a publicly subsidized capitalist goon squad."

"I believe in adequate defense at the coastline and nothing else."

Author of "War is a Racket", Smedley Butler, US Marine Corps Major General. At the time of his death, he was the most decorated Marine in US history.

IF YOU DON'T COME TO DEMOCRACY

DEMOCRACY WILL COME TO YOU

"Our government has kept us in a perpetual state of fear - kept us in a continuous stampede of patriotic fervour - with the cry of grave national emergency. Always, there has been some terrible evil at home, or some monstrous foreign power that was going to gobble us up if we did not blindly rally behind it."
- General Douglas MacArthur

WHERE ARE YOU
IN THIS WORLD WIDE SCHEME?

CROWN COUNCIL OF 13
COMMITTEE OF 300
SUB-FAMILY ELITE
RICH & POWERFUL SUB-FAMILIES
GLOBAL THINK TANKS
WORLD FINANCIAL CONTROL
WORLD NATURAL RESOURCE CONTROL
PRIVATE CORPORATIONS
WORLD POPULATION CONTROL
GOVERNMENT   MEDIA   RELIGION   EDUCATION
HUMAN RESOURCE / LABOR UNIT CONTROL
IGNORANT DEBT SLAVES

FEEDTHEFIREFILMS

Lets be Honest!

The Revolutionary War - 1775-1783
The War of 1812 -1812-1814
The Mexican American War - 1836-1848
The American Civil War -1861-1865
The Spanish American War - 1897-1898
The Indian American Wars - 1775-1918
World War I -1914-1918
World War II - 1941-1945
Cold War 1945-1992
The Vietnam War - 1962-1973
The Invasion of Grenada - 1983-1984
The Invasion of Panama - 1989
Operation Desert Storm 1991-1992
Operation United Shield 1992-1995
Operation Determined Falcon 1998-1999
Operation Enduring Freedom 2001-2011
Operation Iraqi Freedom 2003-2011
Operation Freedom Falcon 2011-

We have been a country for 235 years.
&
WE HAVE BEEN AT WAR FOR

209 YEARS

FUGLY.COM

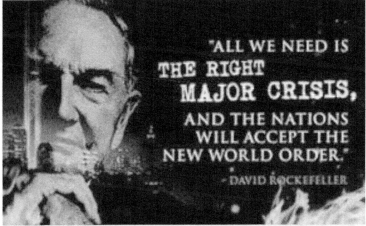

"ALL WE NEED IS **THE RIGHT MAJOR CRISIS,** AND THE NATIONS WILL ACCEPT THE NEW WORLD ORDER."
- DAVID ROCKEFELLER

THE TRUE STORY OF
GLOBAL DEPOPULATION

EUGENICS FLUORIDE VACCINES GMO WAR DRUGS ARMS

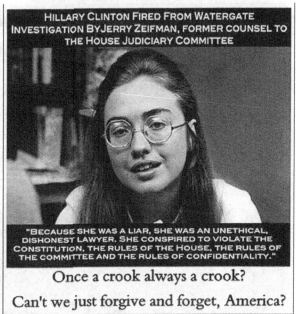

HILLARY CLINTON FIRED FROM WATERGATE INVESTIGATION BY JERRY ZEIFMAN, FORMER COUNSEL TO THE HOUSE JUDICIARY COMMITTEE

"BECAUSE SHE WAS A LIAR, SHE WAS AN UNETHICAL, DISHONEST LAWYER. SHE CONSPIRED TO VIOLATE THE CONSTITUTION, THE RULES OF THE HOUSE, THE RULES OF THE COMMITTEE AND THE RULES OF CONFIDENTIALITY."

Once a crook always a crook?

Can't we just forgive and forget, America?

NEO   CONNED

There should be absolutely no doubt about the true agenda of Hillary Clinton. As a dyed-in-the-wool globalist, she is the war candidate.

293

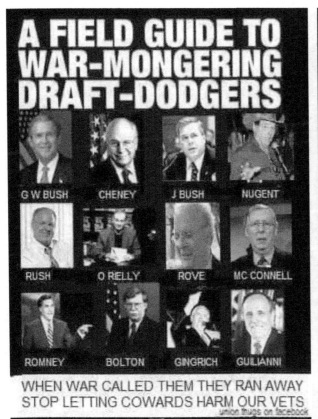

A FIELD GUIDE TO WAR-MONGERING DRAFT-DODGERS

G W BUSH · CHENEY · J BUSH · NUGENT
RUSH · O RIELLY · ROVE · MC CONNELL
ROMNEY · BOLTON · GINGRICH · GUILIANNI

WHEN WAR CALLED THEM THEY RAN AWAY
STOP LETTING COWARDS HARM OUR VETS
union thugs on facebook
www.unionthugs.org

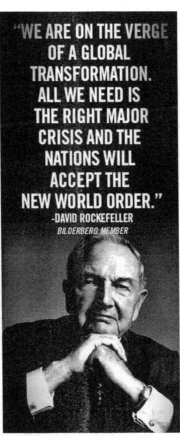

"WE ARE ON THE VERGE OF A GLOBAL TRANSFORMATION. ALL WE NEED IS THE RIGHT MAJOR CRISIS AND THE NATIONS WILL ACCEPT THE NEW WORLD ORDER."
-DAVID ROCKEFELLER
BILDERBERG MEMBER

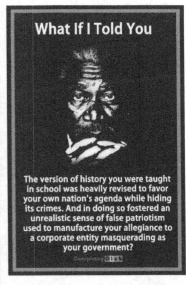

What If I Told You

The version of history you were taught in school was heavily revised to favor your own nation's agenda while hiding its crimes. And in doing so fostered an unrealistic sense of false patriotism used to manufacture your allegiance to a corporate entity masquerading as your government?

BEYOND TREASON

http://dangerousintersection.org/2012/08/10/the-cost-of-u-s-warmongering/

LIBYA & SYRIA · IRAQ & AFGHANISTAN
PANAMA, IRAQ, SOMOLIA · BEIRUT & GRENADA
VIETNAM · BOSNIA & KOSOVO

"WAR BECOMES PERPETUAL WHEN IT IS USED AS A RATIONALE FOR PEACE."
-NORMAN SOLOMON-

DID THESE BANKERS DESTROY TESLA TO STOP HIS GIFT OF FREE ENERGY FOR ALL?

MORGAN · WARBURG · ROCKEFELLER

JP Morgan and other bankers first pretended to back Tesla, but effectively they were only seeking to control him. When they found out he was planning to give the world FREE ENERGY as a gift, they silenced Tesla using the newspapers they controlled.

WHO IS THE WARMONGER?

WHICH COUNTRY HAS ATTACKED, BOMBED SABBOTAGED OR ATTEMPTED TO OVERTHROW OTHER GOVERNMENTS?

Syria & Iran

Yes, HILLARY, OBAMA, biden, Kerry, panetta, and ALL the so-called "liberal Democrats" TRAITORS - (much less the Rethuglican traitor thugs) JUST LOVE those

Please Share!

U.S.A.

China 1945-46	Argentina 1976
Syria 1949	Turkey 1980
Korea 1950-53	Poland 1980-81
China 1950-53	El Salvador 1981-92
Iran 1953	Nicaragua 1981-1990
Guatemala 1954	Cambodia 1980-95
Tibet 1955-70s	Angola 1980
Indonesia 1958	Lebanon 1982-84
Cuba 1959	Grenada 1983-84
Democratic Republic of the Congo 1960-65	Philippines 1986
	Libya 1986
Iraq 1960-63	Iran 1987-88
Dominican Republic 1961	Libya 1989
	Panama 1989-90
Vietnam 1961-73	Iraq 1991
Brazil 1964	Kuwait 1991
Belgian Congo 1964	Somalia 1992-94
Guatemala 1964	Iraq 1992-1996
Laos 1964-73	Bosnia 1995
Dominican Republic 1965-66	Iran 1998
	Sudan 1998
Peru 1965	Afghanistan 1998
Greece 1967	Yugoslavia - Serbia 1999
Guatemala 1967-69	Afghanistan 2001
Cambodia 1969-70	Iraq 2002-3
Chile 1970-73	Somalia 2006-2007
	Iran 2005-present
	Libya 2011

www.facebook.com/ConspiracyWatch

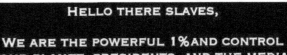

HELLO THERE SLAVES,

WE ARE THE POWERFUL 1% AND CONTROL YOUR PLANET, PRESIDENTS, AND THE MEDIA. WE OWN THE WORLD'S BANKING SYSTEM. WE ARE NEW WORLD ORDER AND PLAN TO ENSLAVE THE ENTIRE HUMAN POPULATION. KILLING 90% AND WE WILL DO IT LEGALLY THROUGH WARS, DESEASE, VACCINES AND MORE.

PLEASE SIT BACK AND WATCH US START WW3.

ROTHSCHILD · SOROS · KISSINGER · ROCKEFELLER

Rockefeller

"We are grateful to the Washington Post, the NY Times, Time Magazine and other great publications whose directors have attended our meetings and respected their promises of discretion for almost 40 years. It would have been impossible for us to develop our plan for the world if we had been subjected to the lights of publicity during those years. But now the world is more sophisticated and prepared to march towards a world government. The supra national sovereignty of an intellectual elite and world bankers is surely preferable to the national auto-determination practiced in past centuries."

– David Rockefeller
Private Banker
Council on Foreign Relations

conspiracycards.com © 2008

"Some even believe we are part of a secret cabal working against the best interests of the United States, characterizing my family and me as internationalists and of conspiring with others around the world to build a more integrated global political and economic structure; one world, if you will. **If that's the charge, I stand guilty, and I am proud of it."**

DAVID ROCKEFELLER

ISIS
Who's behind it?

Groups and individual donors within these nation states have vested interests in keeping the 'war on terror' alive and well for as long as possible, so as to further their agendas:

- FINANCIAL GAIN (ARMS SALES)
- CONTROL OF REGIONAL RESOURCES
- ENGINEERING OF POLITICAL AND RACIAL TENSION
- JUSTIFICATION FOR MASS SURVEILLANCE AND MONITORING OF THE GLOBAL POPULATION
- CENTRALISATION OF POWER

ISRAEL	
USA	
NATO	
QATAR	
SAUDI ARABIA	
TURKEY	

After the **terrorist** attacks of September 11, 2001, the Bush administration declared a worldwide "**war on terror**," involving open and covert military operations, new security legislation, efforts to block the financing of **terrorism**, and more.

THESE ARE 30 MEN AMONG 38 DEAD

MSNBC REPORTED THEY DIED IN A HELICOPTER CRASH BUT HAS SINCE CHANGED IT TO "SHOT DOWN"

OVER 20 OF THESE MEN WERE IN U.S. SEAL TEAM 6 THE SEAL TEAM THAT REPORTEDLY KILLED OSAMA BIN LADEN

FEEL SICK YET?

KNOW YOUR COMMUNIST ENEMY

"it can be inferred that NROL-39 is the third satellite in the NRO's current-generation radar reconnaissance fleet. It follows the NROL-41 mission, or USA-215, launched in September 2010, and NROL-25 (USA-234) which was launched by a Delta IV in April 2012.

The radar imaging program is believed to be a remnant of the NRO's Future Imagery Architecture (FIA) program, which was intended to produce new-generation optical and radar-imaging surveillance satellites, replacing the earlier KH-11 and Onyx radar imaging spacecraft."

"Know Your Communist Enemy" p.3 in Robert B. Watts (1977), "Our Freedom Documents", The Supreme Council, Washington

In 2003 Mays testified before the US Senate that the deregulation of the telecommunications industry had not hurt the public. However, in an interview that same year with Fortune Magazine, he remarked,
"We're not in the business of providing news and information. We're not in the business of providing well-researched music. We're simply in the business of selling our customers products."

http://vigilantcitizen.com/
latestnews/new-u-s-spy-satellite-
logo-octopus-engulfing-world-
words-nothing-beyond-reach-
underneath/

||

"In one of the most shocking articles that the New York Times has ever put out...

At least the CEO of Clear Channel Communications was honest:

Was the US National Reconnaissance Office serious when they designed their latest insignia, or was it some sort of twisted joke? When the US launched a spy satellite into space on December 6, its vulgar choice of insignia was more appropriate than its designers might have intended. Yet it was grotesquely fitting for the mission's purpose and scope. https:// rhetoricalinquisition.wordpress.com/tag/ empire/

'Nothing is beyond our reach,' National Reconnaissance Office's new logo claims

http://snippits-and-slappits.blogspot.com/
2012/07/the-new-york-times-admits-that.html

Esoteric And Illuminati Symbolism In Film

Symbolism of the esoteric variety, is willfully placed in works of entertainment and intended to be understood by a small group of individuals capable of recognizing and interpreting the hidden meaning or occult symbolism depicted. Various films, television programs, and even advertisements will feature interior or hidden elements such as: Easter Eggs, Metaphors & Allegories, and even Illuminati or Esoteric Symbolism.

In the aftermath of World War II, thousands of scientists and Nazi elites were brought to the United States and employed in the Office of Strategic Services (OSS) and later by the CIA. Many of these individuals remained sympathetic or loyal to the Nazi party and are believed to have even participated in human torture and trauma induced mind control programs of the OSS. The US created false employment and political biographies for the scientists in order to circumvent President Truman's anti-Nazi order (as well as the Allied Yalta & Potsdam agreements). Operation Paperclip was the clandestine title for this operation and it is shown in the film Captain America – The Winter Soldier. As part of Operation Paperclip, former Nazi's also held high-ranking positions at NASA and the US Air Force.

Shutter Island (2010) Nazi Documents Scene & CIA MK-Ultra Files (1953)

https://gematriacodes.wordpress.com/tag/the-crow/

Operation Paperclip Which Brought And Employed Nazis In The US – Black Ops MK Ultra Files & Nazi Eugenics

The Nazi's had developed a racially based plan of sterilization and elimination of undesirable persons known as 'Lebensunwertes Leben' – lives unworthy of life. These persons included those with physical or mental problems which the Nazi's viewed as unworthy of living – such as homosexuals and the schizophrenic. Allegedly more than 400,000 individuals were sterilized while another 300,000 were institutionalized and eventually killed under the Nazi Eugenics & euthanasia program. The Nazis believed in racial superiority thanks in large part to the Eurocentric Eugenics agenda that originated from Charles Darwin's theory of evolution and developed/exploited further upon by Darwin's cousin Francis Galton.

Through the 1900's Eugenics was an academic discipline at many colleges in the US and led many a Eurocentric to develop racist pursuits of cleansing the genetic pool of people deemed 'less fit' racially. In the 20th century many governments enacted policies such as birth control, water fluoridation, and abortion based upon the Nazi/Eurocentric secularist agenda for world population control.

The Peace Sign

The logo commonly recognized as the "peace sign" since the late '50s supposedly began as the logo for the Campaign for Nuclear Disarmament (CND). According to the CND, it was designed in 1958 by an English professional artist/designer named Gerald Holtom. Holtom presented his design to officials in the Peace News office in London and to the Direct Action Committee Against Nuclear War.

The symbol was brought to the U.S. by Bayard Rustin, a U.S. civil rights protester, who had participated in the Aldermaston march. The peace sign was first used in the United States later in the same year when a pacifist protestor, Albert Bigelow, sailed his small boat near a scheduled U.S. nuclear test site displaying the CND banner. It was later used on civil rights marches and appeared at anti-Vietnam War demonstrations.

"There will never be any peace until GOD is seated at the conference table"

http://www.christfirstministries.com/-31/January-17-2014-Satanic-Symbols-Are-Everywhere-4400

Cross of Nero - Or Peace sign is another sign that mocks the cross of Jesus. It is also know as "The Dead Man Rune." It appears on the tombstones of some of Hitler's SS troops.

In addition to depicting an upside down cross which mocks and dishonors Christ, his sacrifice and his death, the peace sign speaks of false peace. Turned upside down the peace sign is a Trident which is symbolic of Satan's fork.

Whatever the origin, meaning, and usage of the peace sign, this much is clear: it represents a false peace - **"They have healed also the hurt of the daughter of my people slightly, saying, Peace, peace; when there is no peace."** Jeremiah 6:14.

There can be no true peace unless: **Therefore being justified by faith, we have peace with God through our Lord Jesus Christ:** Romans 5:1.

Rather than looking for peace in a symbol, may we all turn our eyes to the only true source of peace. **The Prince of Peace - Jesus Christ.**

For unto us a child is born, unto us a son is given: and the government shall be upon his shoulder: and his name shall be called Wonderful, Counsellor, The mighty God, The everlasting Father, The Prince of Peace. Isaiah 9:6

Frontal view of bent cross. Compare the symbol to the image of the upside down peace sign below. It is the same symbol. The upside down peace sign is also a Trident. A Trident is a three prong fork which is symbolic of Satan.

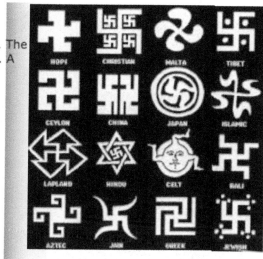

"War is Peace; Freedom is Slavery; Ignorance is Strength;" is one of the three slogans of the English Socialist Party ("INGSOC" for short) of Oceania.

The goal of the INGSOC is to achieve total control over the people and, more importantly, over their minds. And here lies the answer.

One of the main mind programs of The Party was the so called "double thinking", or *doublethink*, which "describes the act of simultaneously accepting two mutually contradictory beliefs as correct, often in distinct social contexts."

"War is peace" and "freedom is slavery" are good examples of double thinking. Though contradictory by definition, they are both accepted as correct, simultaneously, by the citizens of Oceania.

This means that even though Oceania is in a constant state of war, the people are acting like there is peace as well, hence they can easily switch from one emotion to the other, in accordance to what The Party asks of them.

"Freedom is slavery" also acts as a subconscious discouragement for anyone who might consider seeking freedom, whilst the last part of the slogan, "Ignorance is strength," encourages the people to accept as fact everything that The Party tells them, without using rational thinking. Believe and never question! http://humansarefree.com/2013/01/what-means-war-is-peace-freedom-is.html

Order Form

Symbology - The Psychological Covert War on Hip Hop - Book 2 - - - $25.00
The Psychological Covert War on Hip Hop - - - $25.00
Who Stole The Soul - - - $20.00
Analytixz - - - $20.00
Acapella Revolution - - - $20.00
Warrior's Tapestry - - - Out of Print

To place an order online through PayPal:
Symbology - - - sales@jmeonsultingbiz.com
PCW - - - PCWHipHop@gmail.com
Who Stole The Soul - - - 7thoctave@gmail.com
Analytixz - - - 7thoctave@gmail.com
Acapella Revolution - - - 7thoctave@gmail.com
Warrior's Tapestry - - - Out of Print

QTY	DESCRIPTION	UNIT PRICE	TOTAL
	Symbology	$25.00	
	The Psychological Covert War on Hip	$25.00	
	Who Stole The Soul	$20.00	
	Analytixz	$20.00	
	Acapella Revolution	$20.00	
	Warrior's Tapestry	Out of Print	

PAYABLE TO HEIRZ TO THE SHAH

SUBTOTAL		
SHIPPING & HANDLING		$5.75
TOTAL		

MAIL PAYMENTS TO:

KAVON SHAH
P.O. BOX 11902
ATLANTA, GA 30355

Please print clearly, so we may get the book to the correct address

Your Name: _____

Address: _____

City: _____ State: _____ Zip Code: _____

Please allow 2 weeks for domestic shipping and 3 weeks for international shipping.
To check on orders please call 678.557.2919 or email professorgriffpe@gmail.com

Made in the USA
Middletown, DE
24 April 2021